THE CAMBRIDGE COMPANION TO WILK

Wilkie Collins was one of the most popular writers of
He is best known for *The Woman in White*, which inau
novel in the 1860s, and *The Moonstone*, one of the first d   ᵤᵥₑₗₛ; but he
wrote more than twenty novels, plays and numerous short stories during
a career that spanned four decades. This Companion offers a fascinating
overview of Collins's writing. In a wide range of essays by leading scholars, it
traces the development of his career, his position as a writer and his complex
relation to contemporary cultural movements and debates. Collins's exploration
of the tensions that lay beneath Victorian society is analysed through a variety
of critical approaches. A chronology and guide to further reading are provided,
making this book an indispensable guide for all those interested in Wilkie
Collins and his work.

JENNY BOURNE TAYLOR is Professor of English at the University of Sussex.

THE CAMBRIDGE COMPANION TO
WILKIE COLLINS

EDITED BY
JENNY BOURNE TAYLOR

CAMBRIDGE
UNIVERSITY PRESS

1-25-2007
WW
$24.99

CAMBRIDGE UNIVERSITY PRESS
Cambridge, New York, Melbourne, Madrid, Cape Town, Singapore, São Paulo

Cambridge University Press
The Edinburgh Building, Cambridge CB2 2RU, UK

Published in the United States of America by Cambridge University Press, New York

www.cambridge.org
Information on this title: www.cambridge.org/9780521549660

First published 2006

Printed in the United Kingdom at the University Press, Cambridge

A catalogue record for this book is available from the British Library

ISBN-13 978-0-521-84038-5 hardback
ISBN-10 0-521-84038-4 hardback
ISBN-13 978-0-521-54966-0 paperback
ISBN-10 0-521-54966-3 paperback

CONTENTS

ILLUSTRATIONS

CONTRIBUTORS

JOHN BOWEN is Professor of Nineteenth-Century Literature at the University of York. He is the author of *Other Dickens: Pickwick to Chuzzlewit* (2000) and has edited *Barnaby Rudge* (2003) for Penguin and, with Robert L. Patten, *Palgrave Advances in Charles Dickens Studies* (2005). He is a member of faculty of the University of California Dickens Project and a Fellow of the English Association.

JIM DAVIS is Professor and Chair of Theatre Studies at the University of Warwick. Formerly he was Head of the School of Theatre, Film and Dance at the University of New South Wales. He has written extensively on nineteenth-century British theatre, is the author of books on the actor John Liston and on the Britannia theatre, and is the co-author (with Victor Emeljanow) of *Reflecting the Audience: London Theatregoing 1840–1880* (2001).

CAROLYN DEVER is Professor of English and Women's and Gender Studies and Associate Dean of the College of Arts and Science at Vanderbilt University, Tennessee. She is the author of *Death and the Mother from Dickens to Freud* (1998) and *Skeptical Feminism* (2004), and co-editor of *The Literary Channel: The Inter-National Invention of the Novel* (2001). She is currently working on a book entitled *Queer Domesticities: Art and Intimacy in Victorian Britain*.

TIM DOLIN is Research Fellow in the Australia Research Institute at Curtin University of Technology in Perth, Western Australia. He is the author of *George Eliot* (2005) in the Oxford 'Authors in Context' series and co-editor of *Thomas Hardy and Contemporary Literary Studies* (2004). He has written essays and chapters on the Victorian novel, and is currently working on an empirical study of fiction reading in Australia between 1888 and 1914.

KATE FLINT is Professor of English at Rutgers University, New Jersey. She is the author of *The Woman Reader 1837–1914* (1993) and *The Victorians and the Visual Imagination* (2000), as well as numerous articles on nineteenth- and twentieth-century literary and cultural history. She is currently completing *The Transatlantic Indian, 1776–1930*.

JOHN KUCICH is Professor of English at Rutgers University, New Jersey. He has written several books and many articles on Victorian literature and culture, including *Repression in Victorian Fiction: Charlotte Brontë, George Eliot, and Charles Dickens* (1987) and *The Power of Lies: Transgression in Victorian Fiction* (1994), and edited, with Dianne F. Sadoff, *Victorian Afterlife: Postmodern Culture Rewrites the Nineteenth Century* (2000). His forthcoming book is *Imperial Masochism: British Colonial Fiction, Social Class, and Omnipotent Fantasy* (2006).

GRAHAM LAW is Professor in Literary and Media History at the School of International Liberal Studies, Waseda University, Tokyo. In addition to a wide range of articles on nineteenth-century literary and publishing history, he is the author of *Serializing Fiction in the Victorian Press* (2000) and *Indexes to Fiction in the 'Illustrated London News' and the 'Graphic'* (2001). He has produced scholarly editions of many Victorian novels, including Collins's *The Evil Genius* (1994); he is also editor of the *The Public Face of Wilkie Collins: The Collected Letters* (2005) and co-editor of the *Wilkie Collins Society Journal*.

RACHEL MALIK teaches literary studies at Middlesex University. Her most recent publications are 'Fixing Meaning: Intertextuality, Inference and the Horizon of the Publishable', *Radical Philosophy* 124 (March/April 2004) and 'We are Too Menny: Literature's Proletariat', *New Left Review* 28 (July/August 2004). She is currently working on a book about the relations between publishing, reading and writing practices from the mid-Victorian period to the present.

LILLIAN NAYDER is Professor of English at Bates College, Maine, where she teaches courses on nineteenth-century British fiction. Her books include *Wilkie Collins* (1997) and *Unequal Partners: Charles Dickens, Wilkie Collins and Victorian Authorship* (2002). She is writing a biography of Catherine Dickens and co-edits the *Wilkie Collins Society Journal* with Graham Law.

LYN PYKETT is Professor of English and a Pro Vice-Chancellor at the University of Wales, Aberystwyth. She has published widely on nineteenth- and early twentieth-century literature and culture. Her books include *Emily Brontë* (1989), *The Improper Feminine: The Women's Sensation Novel and the New Woman Writing* (1992), *The Sensation Novel from 'The Woman in White' to 'The Moonstone'* (1994), *Engendering Fictions: The English Novel in the Early Twentieth Century* (1995), *Charles Dickens* (2000) and *Wilkie Collins* (2005) for the Oxford 'Authors in Context' series.

JENNY BOURNE TAYLOR is Professor of English at the University of Sussex. She has published a range of material on nineteenth-century literature and culture, including *In the Secret Theatre of Home: Wilkie Collins, Sensation Narrative and Nineteenth-Century Psychology* (1988); she has edited, with Sally Shuttleworth, *Embodied Selves: An Anthology of Psychological Texts 1830–1890* (1998), and with Martin Ryle, *George Gissing: Voices of the Unclassed* (2005). She has also edited Wilkie Collins's *The Law and the Lady* (1992) and Mary Elizabeth Braddon's *Lady Audley's Secret* (1998).

RONALD R. THOMAS is President of the University of Puget Sound in Tacoma, Washington, where he also has an appointment as Professor of English. The author of chapters in more than a dozen books on Victorian literature and culture, he has also written three books of his own, including *Dreams of Authority: Freud and the Fictions of the Unconscious* (1990) and *Detective Fiction and the Rise of Forensic Science* (1999). He is co-editor of and contributor to *Nineteenth-Century Geographies: The Transformation of Space from the Victorian Age to the American Century* (2002).

ANTHEA TRODD was Senior Lecturer in English, and is Honorary Research Fellow at Keele University. She is the author of *Domestic Crime in the Victorian Novel* (1989), and books and articles on Victorian and early twentieth-century writing. She is currently working with John Bowen on a study of the collaborative works of Dickens and Collins.

NOTE ON REFERENCES AND ABBREVIATIONS

Although *The Woman in White* and *The Moonstone* have remained in print since they were first published, until recently it has been difficult to obtain much of Collins's work (the AMS press 30-volume edition is not annotated and is hard to locate). However, many texts have come back into print in the past few years: in the Oxford World's Classics series, in the excellent Broadview editions and in the reprints by Alan Sutton Publishing. Yet there is still no authoritative edition of Collins's work and in general this *Companion* makes parenthetical references to chapter numbers (e.g., ch. 3) when quoting from texts. There are, however, some important exceptions. Collins characteristically breaks with the conventional chapter format in his major works, so when quoting from the following texts, page numbers will be used (e.g., p. 65) to refer to the following Oxford World's Classics editions:

> *Basil* ed. Dorothy Goldman (Oxford: Oxford University Press, 1990)
> This is a facsimile of the 1862 edition.
> *The Moonstone* ed. John Sutherland (Oxford: Oxford University Press, 1999).
> *No Name* ed. Virginia Blain (Oxford: Oxford University Press, 1986).
> *The Woman in White* ed. John Sutherland (Oxford: Oxford University Press, 1998).

The edition of the short stories used is Julian Thompson (ed.) *Wilkie Collins: The Complete Shorter Fiction* (London: Robinson, 1995).

The following short references will be used for frequently cited critical material and letters:

> *B&C*   William Baker and William M. Clarke (eds.), *The Letters of Wilkie Collins*, 2 vols., (Basingstoke: Macmillan, 1999).

BGL&L   William Baker, Andrew Gasson, Graham Law and Paul Lewis
        (eds.), *The Public Face of Wilkie Collins: The Collected Letters*
        (London: Pickering and Chatto 2005).
CH   Norman Page (ed.), *Wilkie Collins, The Critical Heritage*
        (London: Routledge and Kegan Paul, 1974).
Peters Catherine Peters, *The King of Inventors: A Life of Wilkie Collins*
        (Princeton: Princeton University Press, 1991).

CHRONOLOGY

1824   Born at 11 New Cavendish Street, St Marylebone, London, on 8 January, elder son of William Collins and Harriet Collins (*née* Geddes).

1826   The family moves to Pond Street, Hampstead.

1828   Brother, Charles Allston Collins, born.

1829   The family moves to Hampstead Square.

1830   The family moves to Porchester Terrace, Bayswater.

1835   Starts school at Maida Hill Academy.

1836–8   The family visits France and Italy.

1838–40   Attends Mr Cole's private boarding school in Highbury.

1840   The family moves to 85 Oxford Terrace, Bayswater.

1841   Apprenticed to Antrobus & Co., tea importers.

1843   First signed publication, 'The Last Stage Coachman', appears in the *Illuminated Magazine* in August.

1844   Travels to Paris with Charles Ward.
Writes first novel, 'Ioláni, or Tahiti as it was; a Romance'.

1845   'Ioláni' submitted to and rejected by Chapman and Hall.

1846   Enters Lincoln's Inn to study law.

1847   William Collins dies.

1848   The family moves to 38 Blandford Square, using drawing room for amateur theatricals.
            Memoirs of the Life of William Collins Esq., RA published by Longmans in November.

1849   Exhibits a painting, *The Smugglers' Retreat*, at the Royal Academy Summer Exhibition.

1850   *Antonina, or the Fall of Rome* published by Bentley in February.
            The family moves to 17 Hanover Terrace.
            Collins goes on a walking tour of Cornwall with artist Henry Brandling in July and August.

1851   *Rambles Beyond Railways* published by Bentley in January.
            Collins meets Charles Dickens for the first time in March, and acts with him in Edward Bulwer-Lytton's *Not So Bad As We Seem* in May.
            'The Twin Sisters', Collins's first contribution to *Bentley's Miscellanies*, published in March, and his first contribution to Edward Pigott's radical journal the *Leader* published in September.

1852   *Mr Wray's Cash-Box; or, The Mask and the Mystery* published by Bentley in January.
            'A Terribly Strange Bed', Collins's first contribution to *Household Words*, appears in April.
            Goes on tour with Dickens's company of amateur actors in May.
            Basil published by Bentley in November.

1853   Stays with Dickens in Boulogne from July to September; tours Switzerland and Italy with Dickens and Augustus Egg from October to December.

1854   *Hide and Seek* published by Bentley in June.
            Stays with Dickens in Boulogne in July and August.

1855   Collins's first play, *The Lighthouse*, performed by Dickens's theatrical company at Tavistock House in June.
Sails to Scilly Isles with Pigott in September.

1856   *After Dark*, a collection of short stories, published by Smith, Elder in February.
Visits Paris with Dickens from February to April.
A Rogue's Life serialised in *Household Words* in March.
Joins staff of *Household Words* in October.

1857   *The Frozen Deep* performed by Dickens's theatrical company at Tavistock House in January.
The Dead Secret serialised in *Household Words* from January to June and published in volume form by Bradbury & Evans.
The Lighthouse performed at the Olympic theatre in August.
The Lazy Tour of Two Idle Apprentices, based on Dickens's and Collins's walking tour in the north of England, serialised in *Household Words* in October.
Collaborates with Dickens on 'The Perils of Certain English Prisoners'.

1858   *The Red Vial* produced at the Olympic theatre in October.
Collaborates with Dickens on *A House To Let* for the Christmas number of *Household Words*.

1859   Starts to live with Caroline Graves and her daughter Harriet.
Lives at 124 Albany Street in January and February then moves to 2a Cavendish Street in April.
The Queen of Hearts (collection of short stories) published in three volumes by Hurst & Blackett in October.
The Woman in White serialised in *All the Year Round* from November to August 1860.
Moves to 12 Harley Street in December.

1860   *The Woman in White* published in volume form by Sampson Low in August.

1861   Visits Whitby in North Yorkshire with Caroline Graves.

1862	Resigns from staff of *All the Year Round* in January. *No Name* serialised in *All the Year Round* from March to January 1863 and published in volume form by Sampson Low in December. Begins to suffer seriously from rheumatic gout.
1863	*My Miscellanies*, a collection of journalism from *Household Words* and *All the Year Round*, published by Sampson Low in November. Visits German spas and Italy for his health with Caroline Graves.
1864	*Armadale* serialised in the *Cornhill Magazine* from November to June 1866. Moves to 9 Melcombe Place, Dorset Square, in December.
1866	*Armadale* published in volume form by Smith, Elder in May. *The Frozen Deep* produced at the Olympic theatre in October.
1867	Moves to 90 Gloucester Place, Portman Square, in September. *No Thoroughfare* published as the Christmas number of *All the Year Round*; the dramatised version opens at the Adelphi theatre on 26 December.
1868	*The Moonstone* serialised in *All the Year Round* from January to August; published in volume form by Tinsley in July. Harriet Collins dies. Forms liaison with Martha Rudd ('Mrs Dawson'), and attends the marriage of Caroline Graves and Joseph Clow.
1869	*Black and White* written in collaboration with Charles Fechter, and produced at the Adelphi theatre in March. Collins's and Martha Rudd's daughter, Marian Dawson, born.
1870	*Man and Wife* published in volume form by S. F. Ellis in June. Dickens dies.

1871   Collins's and Martha's second daughter Harriet Constance
Dawson born.
The Woman in White produced at the Olympic theatre in
October.
Poor Miss Finch serialised in *Cassell's Magazine* from October to March 1872.
Miss or Mrs? published in the Christmas number of the
Graphic.

1872   *Poor Miss Finch* published in volume form by Bentley.
The New Magdalen serialised in *Temple Bar* from October to
July 1873.

1873   *Miss or Mrs? and Other Stories in Outline* published by
Bentley in January.
Dramatic version of *Man and Wife* performed at the Prince of
Wales's theatre in February.
Charles Allston Collins dies.
Tours America and Canada, giving readings of his work, from
September to March 1874.
The New Magdalen published in volume form by Bentley and
the highly successful dramatic version is performed at the
Olympic theatre in May.

1874   *The Frozen Deep and Other Stories* published by Bentley in
November.
Collins's and Martha Rudd's son, William Charles Dawson,
born.
The Law and the Lady serialised in the *Graphic* from September
to March 1875.

1875   Copyright in most of Collins's work transferred to Chatto &
Windus.
The Law and the Lady published in volume form by Chatto &
Windus in February.

1876   *Miss Gwilt* performed at the Globe theatre in April.
The Two Destinies serialised in *Temple Bar* and published in
volume form in August.

1877   Dramatic version of *The Moonstone* performed at the Olympic theatre in September.

1878   *The Haunted Hotel* serialised in *Belgravia* from June to November.

1879   *The Haunted Hotel and My Lady's Money* published by Chatto & Windus in volume form.
           The Fallen Leaves serialised in *The World* and in *Canadian Monthly* and published in volume form by Chatto & Windus in July. The planned sequel to *The Fallen Leaves* never appeared, owing to the novel's poor reception.
           A Rogue's Life published by Bentley in April.

1880   *Jezebel's Daughter* published in volume form by Chatto & Windus in March following syndication by Tillotson & Son of Bolton.

1881   *The Black Robe* published in volume form by Chatto & Windus in April.
           Starts to employ A. P. Watt as his literary agent.

1883   *Heart and Science* serialised in *Belgravia* and provincial newspapers and published in volume form by Chatto & Windus in April.
           Collins's play *Rank and Riches* produced at the Adelphi theatre in June – a disaster.

1884   'I Say No' published in volume form by Chatto & Windus in October, following serialisation in *London Society*.
           Becomes Vice-President of Society of Authors, founded by Walter Besant.

1886   *The Evil Genius* published in volume form by Chatto & Windus in September, following serial syndication by Tillotson & Son.
           The Guilty River published in *Arrowsmith's Christmas Annual*.

1887   *Little Novels* published by Chatto & Windus.

1888   *The Legacy of Cain* published in volume form by Chatto & Windus in November, following serial syndication by Tillotson & Son.
Moves to 82 Wimpole Street, Marylebone.

1889   Collins dies at 82 Wimpole Street on 23 September, following a paralytic stroke. He is buried in Kensal Green Cemetery.

1890   The final third of Collins's last novel, *Blind Love*, completed by Walter Besant following Collins's detailed scenario, and the novel is published in volume form by Chatto & Windus in January.

1895   Caroline Graves dies and is buried with Collins.

1919   Martha Rudd dies.

JENNY BOURNE TAYLOR

Introduction

Wilkie Collins was a popular and prolific novelist whose career spanned most of the second half of the nineteenth century. It began in 1850, when Charles Dickens, William Makepeace Thackeray and Charlotte Brontë were at the height of their powers and George Eliot was still to publish a work of fiction, and ended in 1890, as the Victorian novel itself was drawing to a close, in the era of Thomas Hardy, H. G. Wells, Rudyard Kipling and George Gissing. Collins published more than twenty novels, numerous short stories and perceptive and witty pieces of journalism. He collaborated closely with Dickens during the 1850s and 1860s and was involved with Dickens in dramatic productions as well as adapting his own work for the stage. He was a busy and hard-working professional writer who negotiated a rapidly changing literary marketplace and was able to make use of new forms of publication and distribution of fiction at both national and global levels.

Collins's popularity as a compelling storyteller, a 'master of suspense' who inaugurated the sensation novel and played a key role in shaping detective fiction has remained undiminished. Andrew Lloyd Webber's musical version of *The Woman in White* played to packed audiences in London's West End during 2005, and Sarah Waters's novel *Fingersmith*, which reworks Collins's signature themes of deception and substitution, was shortlisted for both the Man Booker and the Orange prizes in 2003. Meanwhile, in contemporary criticism Collins's reputation has moved from the margins to the mainstream. Although T. S. Eliot praised the intellectual sophistication of Collins's work in the *Times Literary Supplement* in 1927, for much of the twentieth century he was seen as Dickens's rather lightweight protégé and dubious companion – an interesting figure in the development of genre fiction, but not really worth sustained academic study. That view started to shift in the 1970s with the publication of William Marshall's *Wilkie Collins* in the Twayne Authors series in 1970 and Norman Page's *The Critical Heritage* volume in 1974, together with several articles exploring the complexity of sensation narrative and stressing the radical and subversive elements of Collins's work. The shifts in modern criticism towards popular narrative forms; the growing interest in exploring the relationship between 'high' and 'popular' culture, and the renewed attention to how literary forms interact with the social and intellectual processes that surround and shape them, have all been kind to Collins. During the past twenty-five years, there has been a veritable explosion of interest – not only in monographs and articles devoted both to his work and to sensation fiction, but also in general studies of Victorian literature and culture, where Collins is regarded as a serious writer as much as a popular novelist – as he always hoped he would be.

Indeed, the distinctive features of Collins's work – his exploration of how social identities and relationships are enacted and maintained, his fascination with the unstable boundary between the normal and the deviant, his reworking of Gothic conventions to explore the power relations at work in the Victorian family – have all made it a particularly fruitful subject for many of the key theoretical and critical concerns of the 1980s and 1990s, and these debates continue.[1] Critics have discussed how Collins's multi-voiced, self-reflexive narratives, with their use of testimony, letters and buried writing, their preoccupation with secrecy, illegitimacy, doubling and disguise, themselves dramatise covert or explicit power struggles within Victorian culture. These discussions have formed part of a debate over Collins's ideological significance. The question of whether his writing offers a radical critique of Victorian orthodoxy or reinforces it preoccupied many critics during the 1980s and 1990s, and this debate, too, continues.

However, much of the most fruitful critical work has refused to pin down the novels to a fixed set of meanings, preferring to remain as unsettled as the texts themselves in exploring how Collins's work enacts a complex interplay of subversion and containment, critique and compromise. Collins portrays marriage, for example, as the site of conflict, confusion and intrigue as well as the means of resolution, at a moment in the 1850s and 1860s when marriage was being reassessed as a legal contract, with profound social implications. He represents disturbingly cross-gendered androgynous male and female figures alongside models of conventional masculinity and femininity. His representation of race, and the role that imperialism plays within English society, first discussed in John R. Reed's seminal essay 'English Imperialism and the Unacknowledged Crime of *The Moonstone*' in 1973, has been much debated in relation to contemporary imperialist ideology and concepts of racial difference. Collins also demonstrates how the boundary between sanity and madness is slippery and unstable, and critics have both drawn on psychoanalytic theories to explore his representation of double and fractured subjectivities and investigated his use of mid-nineteenth-century debates on asylum reform and contemporary theories of consciousness to dramatise how strangeness exists at the heart of the self.

The essays in *The Cambridge Companion to Wilkie Collins* take up many of these questions and develop other areas of interest. Both the popular image of Collins as a writer and the majority of critics have, until recently, focused on the 'sensation decade' of the 1860s – on *The Woman in White* and *The Moonstone*, and to a lesser extent *No Name* and *Armadale*. In the past few years, however, there has been growing interest in the full span of Collins's writing, reflected in and generated by the increasing availability of his lesser-known work. The somewhat simplistic image of Collins as a 'Victorian rebel', too, has been revised and complicated by what has become the definitive biography, Catherine Peters's *The King of Inventors: A Life of WilkieCollins* (1991), which both investigates Collins's complicated personal life and traces his intricate web of literary, artistic and theatrical friendships. Collins's letters have also been published over the last few years, in a two-volume edition in 1999 and a fuller and closely annotated four-volume series in 2005; these provide detailed insights into Collins's life as a professional writer. The essays here grow out of this widening appeal, and place discussion of the better-known work in a range of historical and critical contexts.

Collins's shifting identity as a professional writer is investigated by Tim Dolin, Anthea Trodd, Jim Davis and Graham Law, who each take up specific aspects of his multifaceted cultural position. Focusing on the early part of Collins's career, Tim Dolin places his early work in the setting of the artistic circles in which he grew up and spent much of his twenties. Dolin reads the narrative style that would peak in the 1860s as an interplay of opposition to and assimilation of very different groups and artistic generations. On the one hand, there was that of his father William Collins and his father's friend and fellow-artist Sir David Wilkie; on the other, the two groups of younger contemporaries, with contrasting views of modern life, that met in the Collins household – the Pre-Raphaelite Brotherhood and the group of painters known as 'The Clique'. Anthea Trodd surveys Collins's early writing – journalism and shorter pieces as well as the novels – as experiments in genre, identifying the specific elements of narrative voice and point of view that formed the basis of his more complex narratives, particularly his interest in the intensity of perspective created by marginality and social exclusion. She also discusses Collins's changing relationship with Dickens during the 1850s, and touches on their collaborative theatrical productions – a topic taken up in Jim Davis's essay on Collins and the theatre. Exploring an area of Collins's work that is attracting growing interest, Davis assesses Collins's plays – both successes and failures – and places Collins's own dramatic views and values in the context of the nineteenth-century stage. Collins lived through profound changes in the production and reception of the novel, and in a wide-ranging survey Graham Law analyses his position as a professional writer. From the beginning of his career, Collins aimed to participate in and exploit new trends in publishing and attract new groups of readers, and the ways in which he negotiated the changing forms of the novel through the different stages of his career makes him a fascinating case study in the sociology of literature during the second half of the nineteenth century.

The chapters by John Bowen, Lyn Pykett and Ronald R. Thomas focus on Collins's shaping of the short story, sensation fiction and the detective novel respectively – though all stress how unstable these categories are, and I, too, highlight the disturbing generic uncertainty that pervades Collins's fiction after 1870. Bowen's essay on the shorter fictions dovetails with Trodd's overview, and picks up her point that Collins's early writing is suffused with anxieties over influence and plagiarism. Collins wrote a wide variety of short stories throughout his writing life, and Bowen shows that it is the very marginality of the form itself – with its different narrative voices, its focus on secrecy and detection, and the ambiguous nature of evidence and identity as performance – that makes it a crucible for the sensation novel as much as the detective genre.

Pykett, Thomas and I all place Collins's narrative methods within contemporary social, scientific and psychological contexts, reading them as aspects of his elaborate response to, and treatment of, modern subjectivity and forms of knowledge as much as experiments in genre. Pykett opens her discussion of the sensation novel of the 1860s by highlighting how this hybrid, and implicitly gendered, form was held together by contemporary anxieties about the breaching of cultural and social boundaries. The sensation novel was widely regarded as a morbid symptom of modernity – 'Preaching to the nerves' in one critic's evocative phrase – and Pykett analyses the ways in which *The Woman in White* and *No Name* explore the modern nervous subject, above all in their representation of gender identity. *The Moonstone* 'dramatises a sustained effort of recovering a lost incident' through an intricate process of historical detection and reconstruction, and Thomas analyses the ways in which it becomes the prototypical detective novel by exploiting the emergent field of criminology, setting the novel within the development of forensic science in the mid-nineteenth century. Collins's fiction after the 1870s contains some of his most bizarre and socially explicit writing, and I explore how it also engages with contemporary theories of the mind to amplify Collins's preoccupation with mistaken identity, multiple selves, inheritance and the workings of memory. Collins becomes increasingly sceptical towards the ambitions of modern science, but he also continues to use it, and I survey how much of the later fiction exploits the methods and theories it seems to be rejecting.

The chapters by Carolyn Dever, John Kucich, Lillian Nayder and Kate Flint approach Collins's work in the light of current critical approaches to sexuality, gender, race and disability. Both Dever and Kucich draw on modern psychoanalytic theory in their respective discussions of Collins's treatment of the marriage plot and male melancholia, and develop the growing critical interest in Collins's intriguing representation of same-sex bonds and masculinity. Collins's domesticated Gothic is put to its most devastating use in his critique of the position of women within marriage, and Dever argues that his critique goes deeper than attacking legal abuses – that in addressing the various meanings of 'marriage' itself, Collins unsettles the presumption that it must be based on a heterosexual union. While the novel form demands marriage as a means of narrative closure, the conventional couple is offset by a third figure whose relationship to the hero or heroine constitutes the primary bond, Dever argues in her discussion of *The Woman in White*, *Armadale* and *Man and Wife*. Collins's same-sex couples, she suggests, 'walk a fine line between affective convention and erotic transgression'. The other side of Collins's much discussed dissection of femininity is his depiction of the identity crisis facing Victorian men, and in his discussion of melancholia and masculinity in *Basil*, *The Woman in White*, *Armadale* and *The Moonstone* Kucich explores how the split in Collins's fiction between melancholic and self-aggrandising masculinity expresses wider social transformations and cultural shifts in gender norms.

Nayder and Flint discuss the ways in which Collins questions the seemingly natural boundaries of race and physical ability. Nayder examines Collins's ambiguous depiction of racial difference in the light of the political events and controversies that affected British imperial policy in the mid-nineteenth century. She looks at how Collins sets the domestic against the colonised and yet also challenges this opposition, both in *The Moonstone* – Collins's most explicit depiction of colonial expropriation – and in early novels such as *Antonina*, and the play *Black and White*. Nayder concludes by noting the arbitrariness of skin colour as the marker of identity in *Poor Miss Finch*, Collins's most sustained depiction of blindness, which Flint examines in her discussion of difference and disability. Stressing how Collins used various forms of sensory deprivation to encourage his readers to reflect on knowledge based on 'the evidence of the senses', Flint investigates the ways in which Collins both undercuts the boundaries of 'normality' while always refracting physical disability through the prism of social and gender identities.

These essays illustrate the extraordinary range of approaches that can be brought to bear on Collins's work. His influence on twentieth-century culture is too diffuse to be easily pinned down, and in the final chapter Rachel Malik stresses the continuities between mid-nineteenth- and twentieth-century cultural forms in her survey of the reworking of Collins's plots in early film, twentieth-century television, the pastiches of Victorian fiction by James Wilson and Sarah Waters, and the recent musical version of *The Woman in White*. Malik notes the ways in which Collins's preoccupation with substitution and secret lives can be rewritten in the light of our own anxieties and preoccupations, and as these essays show, it is in dramatising the concerns and anxieties of his own time that Wilkie Collins speaks so closely to our own.

NOTE

1. For a detailed overview of Collins criticism, see Lillian Nayder 'Wilkie Collins Studies: 1983–1999', *Dickens Studies Annual* 28 (1999), 257–329.

I

TIM DOLIN

Collins's career and the visual arts

When *Basil: A Story of Modern Life* was published in November 1852, the name of its author, W. Wilkie Collins, was familiar to a handful of readers and reviewers of his only two other works: a biography of his father, the late distinguished painter and Fellow of the Royal Academy, William Collins (1848); and a historical romance, *Antonina* (1850), which showed, among other signs of promise, that the RA's son had inherited 'a painter's eye for description'.[1] Understandably, then, when reviewers were faced with the unenviable job of reviewing *Basil* alongside William Makepeace Thackeray's great historical novel, *The History of Henry Esmond* (published in the same month), many of them seized on what they knew about Collins's family background to draw an analogy between fiction and the fine arts. As *Bentley's Miscellany* put it at the end of 1852:

> There is the same difference between them as between a picture by Hogarth and a picture by Fuseli. We had well nigh named in the place of [Collins] one of the great painters, whose names are borne by the author of *Basil* [Collins was named after his godfather, the renowned genre painter, Sir David Wilkie]. But in truth the writer of that work ought to have been called Mr. Salvator Fuseli. There is nothing either of Wilkie or Collins about it.   (*CH*, p. 45)

This reviewer was impressed by *Basil*, but could not subdue a note of alarm at the faintly republican, or at any rate foreign, undertones in its 'intensity': its 'passionate love and deep vindictive hatred' (*CH*, p. 46). 'It is of the Godwin school of fiction,' he remarked meaningfully, wondering, too, at Collins's audacious relocation of the 'violent spasmodic action' of cheap lower-class magazine fiction to the ordinary everyday middle-class neighbourhoods of a society in 'an advanced stage of civilization' (*CH*, p. 46). There is 'something artist-like', the reviewer concluded, keeping up the analogy, even in *Basil*'s 'apparent want of art'. But not *English* artist-like: if Thackeray embodied in literature the vigour and true feeling of the English school – the tradition of anecdotal and sentimental moral subject painting descended from Hogarth – Collins's first venture into a story of modern-day England was too wildly Romantic and weirdly surrealistic, too much like Salvator Rosa and Henry Fuseli, to be the work of the father's son – or the godfather's godson.

The argument for the un-Englishness of Collins's art would not prove prophetic. The 1860s sensation novel, of which *Basil* was the most significant precursor, succeeded precisely because it was *so* English, trading in the secrets lying in wait behind the façade of respectable English reserve and propriety. In a long 'Letter of Dedication' to *Basil*, moreover (and again ten years later in the Preface to *No Name* in 1862), Collins went out of his way to explain and justify what he was trying to do in language that might almost have been used to debate Sir Joshua Reynolds's *Discourses on Art* (1769–90), still the bible of academic English art practice in 1852. Only by being true to the Actual, Collins contended, echoing John Ruskin's *Modern Painters* (1843–60), would 'the genuineness and value of the Ideal [be] sure to spring out of it'. Few critics of *Basil* agreed. 'Mr. Collins, as the son of an eminent painter, should know that the proper office of Art is to elevate and purify in pleasing', the *Athenaeum* retorted.[2] 'It matters not whether the artist hold the pencil or the pen,' intoned the *Westminster Review* in October 1853 (under the anonymous editorship of Marian Evans (George Eliot)):

> the same great rules apply to both. He may simply copy nature as he sees it, and then the spectator has the pleasure proportioned to the beauty of the scene copied. He may give a noble, spirit-stirring scene . . . He may take the higher moral ground . . ., or, like Hogarth, read a lesson to the idle and the dissipated. He may also paint scenes of cruelty and sensuality so gross that his picture will be turned to the wall. (*CH*, pp. 52–3)

Collins's appeal to the visual arts in his 'Letter of Dedication' was calculated to raise these very questions of morality and 'truth to nature'. His aim was to defend the novel's extreme 'realism' – founded in the aesthetics of popular working-class radicalism and likely to be found thoroughly debased – in language (the *Westminster Review* noted) of 'no small pretension' (*CH*, p. 53). On the face of it, Collins seems to be borrowing the cultural authority of the artistic establishment, where such questions were central to definitions of high art. But there is more to it than that. The 'Letter' was, rather, an opportunity to declare his seriousness of purpose by associating himself not with advances in the novel (there was no authoritative aesthetics of fiction to which he could appeal: the novel was attacked and defended in terms generally borrowed from the moralised aesthetics of high culture) but with the most advanced thinking in London art circles. Collins's model was not only Ruskin, but the reformist young painters who rejected the rigid orthodoxies of the Academy. These painters fell into two groups. One was a group of older artists, led by William Powell Frith and Augustus Egg, and known as 'The Clique'. They had formed in the early 1840s to set up a venue for young artists in opposition to the Academy. Emphatically populist and democratic – they believed their work should be judged by nonartists, for example – they were committed to elevating the status of genre painting over history painting: that is, anecdotal narrative pictures of everyday-life subjects (in the tradition of Wilkie or Collins) over paintings of grand historical scenes, or incidents from the Bible or classical mythology. These mild heretics were soon overshadowed by a second, more controversial, clique, the Pre-Raphaelite Brotherhood, led by William Holman Hunt, Dante Gabriel Rossetti, and the prodigy of the Academy Schools, John Everett Millais, with their creed of 'truth to Nature' and their adherence to the aesthetic values of the early Renaissance. Both groups were implacably opposed to each other's principles and practices, yet in the late 1840s and early 1850s they all met together at 38 Blandford Square, where Collins lived with his mother, Harriet, and his brother, Charles Allston Collins (Charley), a close associate of the Pre-Raphaelites. Over the next few years, as each group pursued its different aims, they both began to think seriously about 'the aesthetic problem for the age': the problem, identified by Martin Meisel, of having to reconcile the new glamour of a booming modern society with the old glamour of high art. Meisel continues:

> the Victorian artist, working for a comprehensive audience, had a double injunction laid upon him. He found himself between an appetite for reality and a requirement for signification. Specification, individuation, autonomy of detail, and the look and feel of the thing itself pulled one way; while placement in a larger meaningful pattern, appealing to the moral sense and the understanding, pulled another.[3]

This was the very problem that Collins faced with *Basil*: how to find a 'larger meaningful pattern' for the representation of modern life beyond the prevailing mode of sentimental moral realism linking the mainstream middle-class novel before 1850 to the tradition of popular everyday-life subject painting still dominant under Sir Edwin Landseer and the descendants of William Hogarth. Collins was not alone in rejecting that particular strain of Wilkie and Collins that runs through Charles Dickens, Edward Bulwer-Lytton and Thackeray. But he was unique among the generation of novelists coming to prominence in the dramatically changed and changing social and economic conditions of the 1850s and 1860s – Elizabeth Gaskell, Anthony Trollope, Charles Kingsley, George Eliot and George Meredith. He had an unusual degree of mobility between what were, in practice, relatively distinct cultural networks – the London art world, the Dickens circle and its overlapping journalistic and literary circles, and the London theatrical scene – as well as an unusual degree of mobility between generally remote social classes. This multiple mobility allowed Collins to draw upon a much wider range of experiences of, and responses to, modernity than many of his English contemporaries.

Collins's life fell into three distinct phases which reflect that mobility: the years from his birth until 1851 when he lived 'very much in the society of artists' (B&C I, 53); his triumphant middle years as a journalist and novelist (between 1851, when he met Dickens, and 1870, the year of Dickens's death); and the last two decades of his life, in which he strove to make a name for himself in the theatre. Most short accounts of Collins's life lay the stress on the middle period, because, even now, when his critical reputation is higher than ever before, he is chiefly remembered for the work of a single decade: the 1860s, when he wrote *The Woman in White*, *No Name*, *Armadale* and *The Moonstone*. But Collins's early years in the art world were vital in laying the foundations for his successes – and failures – in the literary, journalistic and theatrical worlds. Because this phase is often passed over quickly, therefore, and because more detailed accounts of Collins's relationship with Dickens and experience in the theatre are given elsewhere in this volume, the following pages offer an interpretation of his working life framed, so to speak, by his early life among painters struggling to find an adequate expressive form for the experience of modernity.

William Wilkie Collins was born on 8 January 1824 into a relatively comfortable and happy family life. His father had struggled early in his career to establish himself as a painter. But through a combination of hard work, the tireless cultivation of rich and powerful patrons, and careful management of money, William Collins had reached a position of relative eminence by the 1830s and 1840s. He was elected a Fellow of the Royal Academy, and left an estate of £11,000 when he died of heart disease at the age of only 58 in 1847. The young Wilkie grew up surrounded by many of the leading figures in late Romantic literary and art circles. His mother was a cousin of the Scottish painter Alexander Geddes, and his aunt, Margaret Carpenter, was a well-known portrait painter. John Constable, Samuel Taylor Coleridge, Charles Lamb, Ruskin, and many others visited the family in a succession of houses in and around Marylebone and Hampstead. Collins attended day and boarding schools, where he never felt at ease, doubtless in part because he hated sports, was clumsy and, most of all, was an unusual-looking person. Even as an adult he was short (five foot three in his top-boots), with noticeably small, delicate hands and feet; and top-heavy – he had a large triangular head with an imposing bulge on his forehead

Figure 1 Photograph of Wilkie Collins 1864 by Cundall Downes & Co.
Reproduced with the permission of Paul Lewis.

above his right eye. In the 1850s he took advantage of the mid-Victorian fashion for long beards in an attempt to hide the striking disproportion of his upper and lower body (see fig. 1).

Yet although he was extremely self-conscious about his physical defects, and suffered from lifelong anxiety and restlessness (he was afflicted with 'strange tics and fidgets' (Peters, p. 100)), Collins seems to have been liberated as well as oppressed by them. His deformity, however slight, licensed the eccentricity which was a lifelong cover for his unconventionality. Rebellious as a youth, particularly against the evangelicalism and snobbery of his father, he developed a kind of strategic passive resistance to stifling middle-class social codes and customs. For a long time, doubtless freed by his father's early death, he simply refused to ascend to conventional

Victorian bourgeois manhood and independence. He chose instead to live on indefinitely with his mother, who had, like her son, been released by William Collins's death, in her case into a lively and unconventional widowhood. Collins stayed with his mother until he was thirty-two years old, and did not even have a bank account of his own until 1860, when *The Woman in White* became a hit. He hated formality. He dressed as he liked (never wearing evening dress for dinner, and instructing his guests in the same), said what he liked, ate and drank as much as he liked, and answered only to 'Wilkie' among friends, never to 'Collins' or 'Mr Collins'. He was a settled bachelor, untidy and awkward, who fled the stuffiness of London for Paris at any opportunity, and steadfastly resisted marriage to either of his two lower-class mistresses. Caroline Graves lived with him openly after 1859, however, along with her daughter Harriet, who became his amanuensis. He met Martha Rudd, the daughter of a shepherd, in 1864, and installed her as 'Mrs Dawson' in lodgings near his house. She bore him three children.[4]

Collins's domestic arrangements do not, however, imply actual bohemianism. Many of his contemporaries, including Charles Reade, the staid Frith and Egg, Mary Elizabeth Braddon and Marian Evans, lived with partners without being formally married (though with Braddon and Evans this was because their companions had wives still living). Similarly, Collins was also an opium eater, a sure sign, one might conclude, of a bohemian personality – a reputation he earned partly because the more hidebound Dickens allowed himself to be led astray in his younger protégé's company, visiting music halls and bordellos on the Continent, and venturing into seedier parts of London. But the truth is more complicated. Collins suffered increasingly poor health after 1853 for which he was prescribed laudanum sometime in the late 1850s. The cause was a debilitating rheumatic illness, apparently inherited from his father, which was agonisingly painful and ultimately bent him almost double (he later also contracted angina). Although he tried more than once to cure the addiction (resorting on one occasion to morphine), he never succeeded. Collins was no Coleridge or Thomas De Quincey, therefore, Setting aside the character of Ezra Jennings in *The Moonstone* (1868), his creative life does not appear, consciously at least, to have been greatly influenced by opium. His steeply declining health, too, was as likely to have been caused by a combination of his habits of excessive eating and drinking and that other endemic Victorian condition – overwork.

Although Collins was markedly at odds with mid-Victorian middle-class morality, therefore, and sympathetic to the vulnerability of social outsiders and the oppressiveness of social norms (most explicitly in his last phase, when he openly challenges a range of inequities), he was in other respects typical of his time. He declined, mildly and without show, to play the part of either the respectable Victorian or the pattern bohemian, but his career nevertheless followed the trajectory of someone imbued early in his life with the mid-Victorian work ethic. There was perhaps more of his father in him, then, than we might at first suspect. When he convinced William Collins that he was serious about literature by publishing a short story in a magazine, completing a full-length romance set in Tahiti, and undertaking research into a historical novel (*Antonina*, in 1845), his father agreed to remove him from the offices of Antrobus & Co., the tea merchants in the Strand where he had been employed as a clerk with a view to a career in the trade. Collins entered Lincoln's Inn to study for the legal profession, and was to a degree inculcated in the professional ethos. 'No barrister or physician ever worked harder at his profession,' his friend Edmund Yates later wrote, or 'devoted more time, or thought, or trouble to it, was prouder of it, or pursued it with more zeal or earnestness than Mr. Collins has done with regard to literature.'[5]

Collins's meticulous work habits were also a typical manifestation of the commercial evangelicalism underpinning the professionalisation of cultural practices during this period. He was in this regard much like his painter friend Frith (of whom more below): 'content to regard art as a profession like every other, and to clear [his mind] of any mysterious and sacramental ideas in connexion with it'.[6] And although he does not quite put it in the same terms, these were the values for which he praised his father in the two-volume *Memoirs of the Life of William Collins, Esq., RA* (1848). William Collins lived and worked, as G. M. Young would have it, in the 'dark and narrow framework of Evangelical and economic truth'.[7] A curious amalgam of devout low churchman and bigoted Tory, his success depended on the patronage of rich landowners and statesmen – not the manufacturers and capitalists who would come to dominate the art world – and was secured at the price of originality and, in the end, an enduring reputation. Collins was 'a painter of the coast and cottage life and scenery of England', whose scenes of rustic simplicity and 'quiet pathos' were a characteristic product of the Royal Academy of the period.[8] Like Charles Leslie, William Mulready, William Etty, Wilkie and many others of his generation, he painted children and families, 'realistic' in their social contexts and ragged clothes (working on the shore, for instance, or playing around their cottages) but idealised in conception: sentimentalised, prettified, cleaned up, and generalised by Academic precepts of proportion, harmony of colour, balance, finish and taste.

In the *Memoirs* Collins judiciously avoided any explicit evaluation of his father's work, claiming 'the difficulty and delicacy' of being called upon to write impartially about a man it had 'hitherto been his only ambition to respect' (I, ch. 1). Instead, he reframed the life of William Collins as an exemplary antibohemian fable of material success won from hard work and heroic persistence.[9] But when the *Memoirs* appeared, nearly two years after his death and at the end of the year of revolutions, 1848, William Collins was already like a ghostly figure from a simpler world. While the son was writing the father's life, sporadic violence and unrest was breaking out across London, and troops were being brought in to safeguard the Houses of Parliament. This was a time of momentous change, and Collins feared that it would, almost inevitably, hasten the annihilation of his father's reputation: he had been, after all, a producer of outmoded art in the pay of the old landed ruling classes. Would this man's life attract any attention, his son concluded doubtfully, 'in these times of fierce political contention, and absorbing political anxiety' (II, ch. 4)?

It was a good question because the moral worth of genre painting – the mainstay of the English school – was coming to be doubted in those confused days, when other cultural forms such as the novel were boldly taking up social themes and grappling more honestly with the conditions of contemporary life, and when the Pre-Raphaelites were arming themselves against a moribund art establishment. Could anyone still believe, as Richard Redgrave did, that 'some touching incident, some tender episode, or some sweet expression' really put the viewers of these paintings in touch with 'our higher humanity'?[10] Collins tried to head off that question in the Conclusion to the *Memoirs* by reclaiming his father as 'a painter for all classes' whose work would continue to 'appeal . . . to the uneducated, as well as to the informed, in Art' (II, ch. 4). It is difficult to imagine William Collins's best-known picture, *Rustic Civility* – which shows an idealised peasant child tugging his forelock to the shadow of the squire approaching his estate on horseback – appealing to Chartists.[11] Yet Collins here puts his finger on the very quality that would transform genre painting in the next few years; and the quality that would characterise his own literary art.

As the political climate cooled in the early 1850s, many of the leading genre painters began to reject the idealised rural home scenes of Wilkie, Collins and Mulready, turning their attention to images of everyday urban contemporary life. At the same time, the Pre-Raphaelites were intent on pushing their critique of petrified Academic aesthetics beyond history painting by appropriating and modernising the conventional materials of the English genre tradition. Working in parallel – and, in reality, the two camps had a good deal to do with each other in their day-to-day working lives – the Pre-Raphaelites and Frith and his friends together took the picture of modern life in the city in two distinct directions. The first was towards the condition-of-England picture – the problem picture, concerned with what Ruskin called the stern facts of modern life. These were characteristically intimate dramas of private (and usually sexual) morality set in urban or suburban domestic interiors; or, later, forms of social realism focused on working-class hardship. They are epitomised, respectively, by Holman Hunt's *The Awakening Conscience* (1854), Egg's *Past and Present* (1862) and Luke Fildes's *Houseless and Hungry* (1869). The other dominant form of contemporary picture was the so-called 'panoramic epitome' of English life and character.[12] Set outdoors in the vast public spaces of modernity such as parks, railway stations, post offices, city streets and race courses, these pictures represented class relations through minutely detailed and ordered anatomies of the mid-Victorian crowd. The best-known Pre-Raphaelite example is Ford Madox Brown's *Work* (1852–65); equally well known are Frith's crowd-pleasing 'hat and trousers pictures', of which *Derby Day* (1858) is the best known.[13]

Through the 1850s and into the 1860s, the Pre-Raphaelites dispersed and the Academy went on exhibiting mediocre anecdotal literary and historical subject pictures in the same old manner. Millais returned to the art establishment and became the leading Academic genre painter of his generation (and, in time, President of the Royal Academy), Rossetti was joined by the younger generation of medievalists, William Morris and Edward Burne-Jones, and Holman Hunt was left to recast himself as the authentic Pre-Raphaelite. Frith, for his part, also kept up conventional historical subjects. But the painting of modern life caught on and endured as a new popular art form. Aided by the rapid progress of photography, the improvement of commercial engraving technologies, the rise of the social cartoonists (such as John Leech and George du Maurier), and the advent of pictorial news magazines such as the *Illustrated London News* and the *Graphic*, a generation of Academy-trained genre painters encountered new ways of seeing and representing contemporary social subjects.[14] Because modern-life pictures flouted one of the first principles of the Royal Academy – Reynolds's dictum that contemporaneity was the enemy of universality – they were, at first, puzzling and confronting to Academy visitors, for whom high art meant mythical, allegorical or historical subjects.[15] In the first half of the 1850s, a picture such as Holman Hunt's portrayal of the remorse of a kept mistress, *The Awakening Conscience*, attracted huge public controversy, played out in letters to *The Times*.[16] In the same exhibition the first of Frith's gigantic panoramas, *Ramsgate Sands* (1854), was also dismissed as 'a piece of vulgar Cockney business unworthy of being represented even in an illustrated paper'.[17] But only four years later his follow-up *Derby Day* was so popular that it had 'to have a railing and a policeman placed in front of it to protect it from the throng of admirers' – the first picture to be so honoured since Wilkie's *Chelsea Pensioners* of 1822.[18] 'Some people go so far as to say "It is the picture of the age,"' Frith noted in his diary with satisfaction.[19] Ruskin was not among them. He described it scornfully as 'a kind of cross between John Leech and Wilkie, with a dash of daguerreotype here and there, and some pretty seasoning with Dickens's sentiment'.[20] That combination of the photographic, the journalistic, the novelistic and the Hogarthian proved spectacularly popular with the rapidly growing and increasingly diverse new markets for culture, however. The Victorians paid handsomely to marvel at a collective likeness of themselves in a work of art.

Like Frith, Collins recognised the vital necessity (and great challenge) of getting through to these 'greatly enlarged and heterogeneous . . . publics' – the educated and semi-educated readers, theatregoers, and buyers of pictures and engravings.[21] He was never able to reach the lucrative literary underclass that he dubbed (in 1858) the 'unknown public' – the millions of semi-literate lower-class readers of penny dreadfuls – but he did manage to tap into the large and miscellaneous market that emerged at the time of the Great Exhibition of 1851. The Crystal Palace extravaganza, which ran for five months over that summer, linked the arts to industrial progress, proclaimed a new faith in common social aims, and encouraged a new cultural populism. Hundreds of thousands of people attended from widely divergent regional and social backgrounds ranging upwards from the higher levels of the working class. The spectacle of them all mingling together has become a more enduring image of the period than any of the exhibits – partly because it fascinated the Victorians themselves, and, through the cartoons of Leech and others, laid the groundwork for Frith's pageants of social consent. What underpinned that consent was a sense of optimism and chauvinism that would be characteristic of the cultural nationalism of the next two decades.

Greatly increased demand from this growing sector precipitated new systems of cultural production in the 1850s and 1860s. These included the spectacular boom in fiction, painting (the system of patronage gave way to the picture dealer and commercial engraver at the same time) and theatre.[22] Dickens, unfailingly alert to social and cultural trends, successfully capitalised on this miscellaneous market in his twopenny weeklies, *Household Words* (1850–9) and *All the Year Round* (1859–93): they made him one of the most successful entrepreneurs of the cultural boom. But arguably it was Collins, not Dickens, who gave voice to the urban and (increasingly) suburban lives of this public. He recognised that in England in the 1850s and 1860s, modernity was experienced not as Dickens had imagined it in the more restive 1830s and 1840s, as a tumult of productive and destructive energy and change, but rather as an insidious, compulsory ordinariness.

To offer a definition of modernity – 'the social and cultural upheavals caused by rapid capitalist economic development and corresponding new modes of perception and experience of time and space as transitory, fleeting, fortuitous or arbitrary' – is to miss the subtle and crucial differences between the decades of *Oliver Twist* (1838) to *Dombey and Son* (1846–8) and that of *The Woman in White* (1859–60).[23] Those novels all express what Raymond Williams called a crisis of unprecedented experience: 'rapid and inescapable social change' that 'brought in new feelings, people, relationships; rhythms newly known, discovered, articulated', and produced 'a new kind of novel', a 'fiction uniquely capable of realising a new kind of reality'.[24] But in Collins the experience of modernity itself does not misshape the entire novelistic world as it does Dickens's world. So different are those worlds, in fact, that Henry James might just as well have said that 'the terrors of the cheerful country-house and the busy London lodgings' in Collins are far more terrifying than the terrors of *Oliver Twist*.[25] For what is Dickens's London to us, or we to it? After the 1860s, everything in Dickens, even the 'bran new' Veneerings (in *Our Mutual Friend*, 1864–5), feels older, *different*.

And the difference is this. Modernity in Dickens is externalised and melodramatised as a visible force: a reality that was, T. S. Eliot declared, 'almost supernatural'.[26] This is immediately apparent if we compare the work of Dickens's major illustrators, Cruikshank and Hablot Browne ('Phiz') – in Manichaean black and white – with the more naturalistic and mundane realism of Fildes, who was employed (at Millais's suggestion) to illustrate *Edwin Drood* (1870) after Collins's brother Charley (who was married to Dickens's daughter) was forced to withdraw owing to ill-health in 1869. George Cruikshank's 'vividly terrible images', James remembered, introduced something 'more subtly sinister, or more suggestively queer, than the frank badnesses and horrors' of *Oliver Twist*.[27] But Fildes's sober, realistic illustrations to *Edwin Drood*, an equally sinister and queer novel, and deeply influenced in many ways by Collins, show how dramatically the Dickens world had by then absorbed the visual codes of the new modern-life aesthetic as it was refracted through the sensation novel.

In Collins, on the other hand, what is visible on the surface is an eerily incomplete and sometimes apparently motionless landscape, where signs of change are omnipresent but the *processes* of change are subterranean and mysterious. The modern world looks unfinished – especially the houses and streets – and unused: in a permanently suspended state of transition from the old to the new. But that cataclysmic social change has been internalised and made secret: in the entanglements of the law, the silent movements of money, the violence of marriage, and the shattering of the nerves. The deceptive blandness of its stove-top hats, crinolines and check trousers hides a violent suppression of difference, an effect of commodification, rationalisation, and standardisation in capitalism, consent in politics and class relations, Puritanism in religion, and respectability in everyday life. The evacuation of meaning from character to plot in the sensation novel implies that protagonists are rarely able to act openly or freely, except where they are extraordinary or unusually diabolical or powerful figures. Only villains and aliens are fully and vividly realised, genuinely alive. Ordinary English men and women, on the other hand (typically, young people born into prosperity and serenity) are scarily passive, and turn out to be shell-shocked victims, mysteriously preyed upon and thrust into a world of fringe-dwellers: servants, the insane, half-castes, opium eaters, fanatics, criminals.

In doing so, Collins ushered a whole class of social outsiders to the centre of the English novel on the pretext of implicating them in the crisis of modern civilisation. Was this the achievement of a social radical and artistic innovator posing as a mere purveyor of popular entertainment? There is no simple answer to that question. Collins was an unconventional person who lived unconventionally, and who could, in his journalism at least, 'be sweepingly and unnecessarily offensive to the middle class'.[28] But he was not an intellectual, and there is little surviving evidence to show what he thought about any of the most important social and political issues of the day (perhaps his letters to Dickens, which the latter destroyed, revealed something of his opinions). In his youth he had clearly felt himself to be a political radical. In the early 1850s he became close to Edward Pigott, a longstanding friend whom he met at Lincoln's Inn; and between 1852 and 1855 he wrote reviews for Pigott's ultra-radical newspaper, The Leader, which had been set up in 1850 by G. H. Lewes and Thornton Hunt. Lewes and Hunt were freethinkers who espoused socialism, open marriage, atheism and other progressive causes, but they had fallen out when Hunt, true to his principles, took up with Lewes's wife (Lewes eloped with Marian Evans in 1855). Pigott took over the newspaper at that time.

From the tenor of Collins's letters to him, the former enthusiastically involved himself in the running of the Leader, though there is little to show that he was anything like as radical as his colleagues. His remarks on socialism in one letter, for example, are neutral and betray no political convictions. When the subject of religion came up, moreover, Collins, who was not conventionally religious, took issue with the radical tactics of the paper. 'Our Saviour's name' is 'something too sacred for introduction into articles on the political squabbles and difficulties of the day', he protested to

Pigott in April 1852, and thereafter he refused to have his contributions signed. It may have been that Collins was writing *Basil* and did not wish to harm its chances by having its authorship linked to the *Leader*.[29] Or, what is more likely, his unconventionality was not aggressive or confrontational. As he wrote to Pigott, 'I hate controversies on paper, almost more than I hate controversies in talk.'[30]

The same abhorrence of open controversy informed Collins's otherwise puzzling reaction to Pre-Raphaelitism in the early 1850s. Under cover of anonymity, he reviewed the 1851 Royal Academy Summer Exhibition where, alongside Millais's *Mariana* and Holman Hunt's *Valentine Rescuing Sylvia*, his brother Charley showed *Convent Thoughts*, his major contribution to the PRB (who would never fully admit him as a Brother). This was the painting that led Ruskin to a spirited defence of the Pre-Raphaelites in a letter to *The Times*, where he praised its minute botanical truthfulness: a crucial turning point in Pre-Raphaelite aesthetics, as Tim Barringer points out, leading the group away from 'the distortions and abstractions of the early, medievalising works' and towards a new resolve to paint truthfully from nature.[31] Wilkie Collins was not so sure. His own idea of art had been shaped precisely by Raphaelitism – he had been deeply impressed by a long stay in Italy with his family as a boy, and later letters home to his mother from Europe indicate his preference for historical painting. He had also exhibited a picture himself at the Royal Academy annual summer show two years earlier in 1849. It has never been described, so it is not known whether it was a conventional genre picture with figures, but its title, *The Smuggler's Retreat*, indicates that even if it were a landscape Collins wanted it to be read through the anecdotal tradition of the English school. Moreover, in 1851 the Royal Academy was open to 'the vast congregation of foreigners assembling in London' for the Great Exhibition. Just as the supremacy of British industry and institutions was on show at the Crystal Palace, here was an opportunity, Collins wrote, for visitors to 'learn for the first time what the English School of Painting really is – . . . [and] what our English artists really can do'.[32] In this context, Collins is intent on repatriating the Pre-Raphaelites to the English school. He summarises their style as 'an almost painful minuteness of finish and detail [and] a disregard of the ordinary rules of composition and colour' and notes disapprovingly their 'evident intention of not appealing to any popular predilections on the subject of grace or beauty'.[33] He concludes that these angry young men will soon grow out of their rebelliousness:

> they are as yet only emerging from the darkness to the true light; . . . they are
> at the critical turning point of their career; and . . ., on the course they are now

to take, on their renunciation of certain false principles in their present practice, depends our chance of gladly welcoming them, one day, as masters of their art – as worthy successors of the greatest among their predecessors in the English school.[34]

For all his close personal friendships with the Pre-Raphaelites, and for all his own unconventionality, Collins simply could not understand their perversely oppositional attitude, their refusal to concede *something* to public taste. Of Millais's *The Woodman's Daughter* he objects:

Why should not Mr. Millais have sought, as a model for his 'Woodman's Daughter,' a child with some of the bloom, the freshness, the roundness of childhood, instead of the sharp-featured little workhouse-drudge whom we see on his canvas? Would his colour have been less forcible, his drawing less true, if he had conceded thus much to public taste?[35]

Collins's own ambition was to be a writer for all classes (which is how he characterised his father's achievement as an artist). His professionalism bred a sense of duty to his paying public, and his first-hand knowledge of the financial insecurity to which artists were always vulnerable committed him to an uncontroversial popular art. Collins's great achievement was to show that a low, popular art form was capable of extraordinary subtlety and power. He discovered that it was by giving the reading public exactly what it wanted – 'violent and thrilling action, astonishing coincidences, stereotypic heroes, heroines, and villains, much sentimentality, and virtue rewarded and vice apparently punished at the end' – that you could tell it what it did not want to hear.[36] For that reason, sensation fiction runs counter to the dominant narrative of the genesis of literary modernism: its motto was not *épatez les bourgeois!* but *captivez les bourgeois!* By feeding the 'diseased appetite' of the reading public for 'excitement alone',[37] Collins opened fiction to a degree of moral ambiguity that was unavailable to other representations of modern life in the visual arts and on the stage; and that, in turn, opened it to new artistic possibilities. It was only in the last phase of his career that didacticism got the better of him, prompting Algernon Swinburne's famous posthumous dig: 'What brought good Wilkie's genius nigh perdition?/ Some demon whispered – "Wilkie! have a mission."'[38] In his own mind, though, perhaps Collins just saw himself as *The Woman in White*'s Count Fosco: 'I say what other people only think; and when all the rest of the world is in a conspiracy to accept the mask for the true face, mine is the rash hand that tears off the plump pasteboard, and shows the bare bones beneath.' Nothing of David Wilkie or William Collins about that.

NOTES

1. *Spectator*, 11 March 1850; *CH*, p. 40.
2. *Athenaeum*, 4 December 1852; *CH*, p. 47.
3. Martin Meisel, *Realizations: Narrative, Pictorial and Theatrical Arts in Nine-teenth-Century England* (Princeton: Princeton University Press, 1983), pp. 8, 12.
4. For detailed accounts of Collins's relationships with Caroline Graves and Martha Rudd, see Peters, and William M. Clarke, *The Secret Life of Wilkie Collins* (1988) (Stroud: Sutton Publishing, 2004).
5. 'W. Wilkie Collins', *Train*, June 1857; *CH*, p. 67.
6. *The Times* obituary, 3 November 1909, quoted in Paula Gillett, *The Victorian Painter's World* (Stroud: Sutton Publishing, 1990), p. 72.
7. G. M. Young, *Portrait of an Age: Victorian England* (London: Oxford University Press, 1977), p. 66.
8. W. Wilkie Collins, *Memoirs of the Life of William Collins, Esq., RA: With Selections from His Journals and Correspondence*, 2 vols. (Wakefield: EP Publishing, 1978), II, ch. 4. Further quotations will be cited parenthetically in the text.
9. The 'great truth which the career of Mr. Collins illustrates, – that the powers of the mind, however brilliant, are never too elevated to be aided by the moral virtues of the character' (*Memoirs* II, ch. 2).
10. Richard Redgrave, *The Sheepshanks Gallery* (London, 1870), p. 4. Redgrave was a leading figure in the promulgation of the English school and was himself an important forerunner of the modern-life painters.
11. Despite the fact that, as Lionel Lambourne argues in *Victorian Painting* (London: Phaidon, 1999), p. 173, this picture raises 'social issues that are both complex and thought-provoking'.
12. *Athenaeum*, 1 May 1858, p. 565. Quoted in Meisel, *Realizations*, p. 379.
13. W. P. Frith, *My Autobiography and Reminiscences*, 2 vols. (London: Richard Bentley and Son, 1887), I, p. 185.
14. See Meisel, *Realizations*, and Lynda Nead, *Victorian Babylon: People, Streets and Images in Nineteenth-Century London* (New Haven and London: Yale University Press, 2000), p. 57.
15. Gillett, *Victorian Painter's World*, p. 82.
16. See Tim Dolin and Lucy Dougan, 'Fatal Newness: *Basil*, Art, and the Origins of Sensation Fiction', in Maria K. Bachman and Don Richard Cox (eds.), *Reality's Dark Light: The Sensational Wilkie Collins* (Knoxville: University of Tennessee Press, 2003), pp. 1–33.
17. Frith, *Autobiography*, I, p. 173.
18. Julian Treuherz, *Victorian Painting* (London: Thames and Hudson, 1993), p. 106.
19. Frith, *Autobiography*, I, p. 285.
20. 'Notes on . . . the Royal Academy' (1858), in Edward T. Cook and Alexander Wedderburn (eds.), *The Works of John Ruskin*, 39 vols. (London: George Allen, 1904), XIV, pp. 161–2.
21. Gillett, *Victorian Painter's World*, p. 8.
22. In the 1860s and early 1870s, '[f]abulously high prices were paid for pictures, periodicals exclusively devoted to art were founded, and England's major

exhibition of contemporary art, that of the Royal Academy, caused tremendous interest and excitement each year' (Gillett, *Victorian Painter's World*, p. 13).

23. Alan Swingewood, *Cultural Theory and the Problem of Modernity* (Basingstoke: Macmillan, 1998), p. 144.

24. Raymond Williams, *The English Novel from Dickens to Lawrence* (London: Paladin, 1970), pp. 11, 28.

25. Henry James, 'Miss Braddon', *Nation*, 9 November 1865; *CH*, p. 123.

26. T. S. Eliot, 'Wilkie Collins and Dickens', in Ian Watt (ed.), *The Victorian Novel: Modern Essays in Criticism* (New York: Oxford University Press, 1971), p. 135.

27. Henry James, *A Small Boy and Others* (New York: Charles Scribner's Sons, 1913), p. 20.

28. Madeline House, Graham Storey and Kathleen Tillotson (eds.), *The Letters of Charles Dickens*, 12 vols. (Oxford: Clarendon Press, 1965–2001), VIII, p. 669.

29. See Kirk Beetz, 'Wilkie Collins and the *Leader*', *Victorian Periodicals Review* 15:1 (Spring 1982), 20–9, and Carolyn de la Oulton, *Literature and Religion in Mid-Victorian England: From Dickens to Eliot* (Basingstoke: Palgrave, 2003).

30. Quoted in Peters, p. 108.

31. Tim Barringer, *The Pre-Raphaelites: Reading the Image* (London: Weidenfeld and Nicolson, 1998), p. 61.

32. Wilkie Collins, 'The Exhibition of the Royal Academy', *Bentley's Miscellany* 29:174 (1851), 617.

33. Ibid., 623.

34. Ibid., 625.

35. Ibid., 624.

36. Patrick Brantlinger, 'What Is Sensational About the Sensation Novel?', in Lyn Pykett (ed.), *Wilkie Collins, Contemporary Critical Essays* (Basingstoke: Macmillan, 1998), p. 33.

37. *Quarterly Review* 113 (April 1863), 357.

38. *Fortnightly Review*, November 1889; *CH*, p. 262.

2

ANTHEA TRODD

The early writing

In the early spring of 1856, Wilkie Collins completed the novella *A Rogue's Life* in a pavilion in the grounds of a house in the Champs Elysées in Paris rented by Charles Dickens. At thirty-two he could look back on twelve years of writing which demonstrated an extraordinary range in genre, including four novels (one unpublished), many short fictions, some just republished in his first story collection, *After Dark* (1856), a drama, a biography, a travel book and assorted journalism. *A Rogue's Life*, a satirical narrative, written on a sickbed, parodies his own search for a secure niche in the literary world. The Rogue, son of a fashionable doctor, quits medical studies to become 'one of the young buccaneers of British Caricature; cruising about here, there and everywhere, at all my intervals of spare time, for any prize in the shape of a subject which it was possible to pick up' (ch. 2). Confined to a debtors' prison, he produces prints of prison life. Released, he becomes an unsuccessful fashionable portrait painter, until an experienced friend introduces him to the market for forging Old Masters, where demand exceeds supply, and the recent demise of the Rembrandt specialist has left a gap in the market. Evading the legal consequences of his foray into forging Rembrandts, he is briefly the secretary to a provincial literary institution, before descending, again under the guidance of a senior partner, to the forging of currency. Transported to Australia, he finally reinvents himself as a wealthy ex-convict landowner.

In this novella, which appeared in *Household Words* throughout March, Collins was both commenting on the diversity of his work, and assessing a career which had so far produced no widely recognised success. Like the Rogue, he was acutely aware of the difficulties of positioning himself in the market, and of the need to understand one's audience and be ready to adapt to their newly perceived needs. He had experimented widely, and produced a body of work which was consistently lively, innovative and sceptical of established values. He was committed to directing his fiction 'towards the light of Reality wherever I could find it', as he stressed in the

'Letter of Dedication' to *Basil* (1852). He was recognised as a promising writer by some discriminating critics, including Dickens, and the French critic Emile Forgues, who had written a long assessment of his career in the *Revue des Deux Mondes*.[1] Yet he worried about the necessity and dangers of patronage, imitation and collaboration, and was intermittently haunted by the figure of the forger. Much of his early writing meditates on the difficulties of finding a niche, on the disadvantages of paternal example, and on the dangers of plagiarism and forgery. His work had alluded to the manner of several literary Old Masters, notably Edward Bulwer-Lytton and Dickens, and he had just begun collaborating with Dickens, on the play *The Frozen Deep*. Like Dickens, he worried about the ever-present threat of imitators, but he also realised that collaborating with an established name might enhance his own reputation.

Biography, history, travel: the first four books

Collins began his writing career with two historical novels, but his first published work was a biography of his father, a respected painter of rural and maritime genre pieces. In the dutiful and well-received *Memoirs of the Life of William Collins, Esq., R.A.* (1848), Collins constructs his father's life as the exemplary story of a man who found his niche and cultivated it relentlessly. Collins Senior's particular speciality was 'bright places and happy objects', children playing, cottages, fishing scenes – the *Memoirs* give sympathetic, detailed descriptions of many of these. Collins later treated his father's work in the story 'A Passage in the Life of Perugino Potts' (1852), and in the figure of the mediocre painter Valentine Blyth in *Hide and Seek* (1854). His own novels, however, were to find the dark in the 'bright places', to disclose 'all that was coarse, violent, revolting, fearful', that, he explains, his father rejected. But William Collins's combination of commercial acumen and 'inflexible adherence to Nature and truth' had also provided his son with a potent example of the road to success.[2]

Collins laid aside his historical novel *Antonina, or The Fall of Rome* (1850) to write the *Memoirs* – a well-calculated move, Collins's most recent biographer, Catherine Peters, suggests, that allowed Collins to make his debut in the unexceptionable role of devoted son (Peters, pp. 75–7). Like its then unpublished predecessor, the 'romance' *Ioláni, or Tahiti as it was*, *Antonina* was an ambitious vision of a society disintegrating, while those figures who offer hope of social renewal wander the margins.[3] Collins wrote *Ioláni*, his first novel, which drew heavily on William Ellis's *Polynesian Researches* (1831) and other South Pacific literature, in 1844–5, while working for the tea merchants Antrobus & Co. A novel of Polynesian life might have seemed a promising idea in 1845; 1846 saw two Polynesian-based works, Harriet Martineau's *Dawn Island* and Herman Melville's *Typee*. Moreover, in Collins's Tahiti, a society where women and marginal figures resist entrenched oppression, the index to social malaise is the cultural practice of infanticide for poor and illegitimate children, and infanticide was a topic of widespread contemporary concern for 1840s Britain.[4] Despite this, however, two major publishers, Longman's, and Chapman and Hall, rejected the manuscript.

Collins embarked on *Antonina* while pursuing desultory law studies at Lincoln's Inn. In the aftermath of the 1848 siege of Rome, he had emphasised the topicality of a novel set during the ancient siege of the city in a letter to his publisher Richard Bentley (30 August 1849; *B&C* I, 56), and several passages invited comparison with Bulwer-Lytton's much-admired model of Roman historical romance, *The Last Days of Pompeii* (1834). *Antonina* resumes the themes of *Ioláni*: refugees and outcasts wander the wilderness, while in the declining centre patriarchs and priests exercise power despotically. In both novels a gentle oppressed heroine personifies domestic values that we are repeatedly reminded have not yet been established. Both novels, too, reach an impasse. The heroines find temporary refuge and the repressive patriarchs are overthrown, but so are the young rebel leaders, who find military and domestic virtues incompatible. Tamar Heller, in the fullest account of *Antonina*, links the 'patently fragile domesticity' of this ending to Collins's failure to 'tell the narrative of 1848'.[5] Collins can imagine the fall of the patriarchs, but not a society which could replace them. Nor had he yet discovered a voice of his own to replace the florid Bulwerian rhetoric that he often mimicked.

That voice began to emerge in Collins's next experiment with genre. *Rambles Beyond Railways* (1851), an account of a walking tour of Cornwall in the summer of 1850, is easily the most readable of his first four books. This landscape on the edge of modern life, still beyond the spread of the railways, allowed Collins to construct a new voice, which was relaxed, insouciant, curious, and combative. He moves between social commentary, comedy and landscape description, but at the book's centre are the accounts of marginal people who have drifted to this landscape, a cave-dwelling stone-cutter with a passion for mathematics, the ghost of a murderess, the nuns in a remote convent. In the chapter 'Legends of the North Coast', Collins passes rapidly by myth-laden Tintagel to tell instead the story of two gentlewomen who lived together in an isolated cottage, their lives and successive deaths observed by baffled eavesdroppers. He returns to the unexplained, incommunicable mystery of such lives in his next novel. *Basil* is partly set in Cornwall, and refers to 'solitary, secret people who had lived, years and years ago, in certain parts of the county – coming, none knew whence; existing, none knew by what means; dying and disappearing, none knew when', as Basil writes in the Journal that forms a section of the narrative (p. 313). The novel provides the back story for one of the 'secret people'.

Stories of modern life: *Basil* and *Hide and Seek*

Basil, Collins's second published novel, was his most important before *The Woman in White* (1860), and one of his most powerful works. Subtitled *A Story of Modern Life*, it moves decisively away from *Antonina*; Basil's naivety is signalled by the fact that he is writing a historical novel. In an acute study of early Collins, Walter de la Mare commented on the importance of the Prefaces from *Basil* on, noting how they 'reveal his sustained interest in fiction as an art, his eagerness in experimentation, his moral independence (within certain limits), and the endless thought and care he bestowed on story and characterisation'.[6] In the 'Letter of Dedication' to *Basil*, Collins announced himself as a serious realist novelist of contemporary urban life. He insists that he is not interested in 'the conventionalities of sentimental fiction', that the story will incorporate 'the most ordinary street-sounds that could be heard, and the most ordinary street-events that could occur', and that 'Scenes of misery and crime' are necessary to the treatment of contemporary life.[7] *Basil* is an innovative mingling of several genres – Gothic thriller, confessional narrative and domestic realism. Collins would not again use the single first person confessional narrator for the full duration of a novel, and in the multiple narrative methods of later novels he offered forms of order, distance and respite to the reader. There is no relief from Basil's dark journey into garish suburban villas, squalid railway hotels and public hospital wards, into hallucinations of a phantom city dissolving in a swamp, and to the delirium of his unfaithful wife. 'Scarlet roses! scarlet roses! throw them into the coffin by hundreds; smother me up in them; bury me down deep' (p. 295). A novel of extraordinary innovative power, *Basil* is the most unrelievedly dark of Collins's novels.

As Basil begins his confessional narrative, he contemplates a sunlit beach scene of children playing, and fishermen spreading nets. 'All objects are brilliant to look on, all sounds are pleasant to hear' (p. 2). Collins is looking, it would seem, at one of his father's paintings; but the narrative turns from the bright places which were William Collins's stock in trade to describe the guilt of a son renounced by his father. Basil moves from the historical novel he hoped to write to telling his own story. It is a dangerous departure: his enemy, Mannion, his wife's seducer and son of a hanged forger, once attempted to write a modern, realist novel. 'I called things by their right names; and no publisher would treat with me' (p. 231). His failure consigned him to becoming a hack author, plagiarising from foreign authors and the dead. His threat to Basil, 'Remember what my career has been; and know that I will make your career like it' (p. 250), partly succeeds. In his Cornish retreat Basil composes the kind of realist contemporary narrative that Mannion wished to produce. It is a strange, fragmented narrative, lacking any obvious overall authority, which includes dreams, hallucinations and letters, together with Mannion's long confession, and disintegrates into fragmentary diary entries, supplemented by letters from other people.

Basil had a mixed reception, as Collins's Preface foresaw. One sympathetic reader was Dickens, whom Collins first met in 1851, when he acted with him, as his valet, in Bulwer-Lytton's play, *Not So Bad As We Seem*. It was an interesting conjunction, as Bulwer-Lytton's historical novels had provided the model for Collins's work in that genre, and now Collins moved into Dickens's orbit. Between *Basil* and *The Woman in White* (1860), the story of Collins's career is one of increasing involvement with Dickens, as contributor to and then staff member on *Household Words*, and finally as collaborator. In this period Collins developed the distinctive narrative characteristics of the great 1860s novels: the plotting skills, the multiple narrative method and the subversive, bourgeois-baiting, authorial persona. Dickens's patronage had great advantages for Collins, but it also exacerbated anxieties about maintaining a distinct identity, and tellingly early in the relationship, Collins wrote two fictions, widely recognised as Dickensian, both treating the topic of the mediocre artist. For the Christmas market of 1851, Collins produced *Mr Wray's Cash-Box* (discussed by John Bowen elsewhere in this volume), a novella which uses a Dickensian framework to discuss the ethics of copying, and celebrates mediocre and imitative art as a benign activity which disseminates enthusiasm for great art to a wider public.

In Collins's third published novel, *Hide and Seek*, dedicated to Dickens, another mediocre and unoriginal artist, Valentine Blyth, indulges dreams of high art, but supports his crippled wife and mute adopted daughter through the production of 'small marketable commodities'. *Hide and Seek* experiments with heterogeneous materials. The mute heroine, an early example of Collins's interest in the effects of physical impairment, is rescued from a circus, in a narrative much darker than Dickens's simultaneous treatment of the circus in *Hard Times*. An American backwoodsman, adrift in England, pursues a mystery through letters and records recovered from an attic. That mystery revolves between two patriarchal households; in one the bohemian but responsible Valentine works at his mediocre art; in the other a self-righteous businessman oppresses his family, and guards his dark secret of seduction and betrayal. With that division of patriarchal attitudes, the heavy father, hitherto so prominent in Collins's work, made his last significant appearance in the novels. The mystery concerns hidden origins, the identity of an illegitimate child and a woman betrayed by a respectable suitor and cast off by her respectable family.[8] It is detected by a man whose scalped head and tracking skills mark him as a complete outsider, and who moves indifferently across the social boundaries that appear insurmountable to others. Although it lacks *Basil*'s drive and passion, *Hide and Seek* extended Collins's sense of his possibilities in narrative, most notably in comedy. Dickens, defending the novel to Georgina Hogarth against charges of imitation of himself, said, 'I think it far away the cleverest novel I have ever seen written by a new hand . . . Nor do I really recognise much imitation of myself.'[9] Where *Hide and Seek* does show the influence of Dickens is in the introduction of comedy, conspicuously absent from Collins's three previous novels. Throughout their association the most insistent note in Dickens's advice to Collins was on the necessity always to relieve the darkness with comedy, and in its domestic suburban scenes and satire of the artistic world, *Hide and Seek* is the first novel where Collins made use of comic relief.

Household Words

By the time Collins wrote *A Rogue's Life* in 1856, he had also written one drama, *The Lighthouse*, in 1855, in which Dickens played the central part when it was performed in Tavistock House in June that year, and was committed to another, *The Frozen Deep*, for Christmas 1856. Meanwhile, a bout of sickness during a stay in Paris in the spring had provided material for two contributions to *Household Words*, 'Laid Up in Lodgings', and 'The Diary of Anne Rodway'. In these two short works, which both describe underclass characters sympathetically, and experiment with the effects of restricted point of view, he discovered new possibilities. 'Laid Up in Lodgings' recounts Collins's successive sickbed experiences in lodging houses in Paris and London. In his life of his father, Collins describes how William Collins, on his deathbed, persisted in sketching the foot of his bed, and a tray laid there. Collins experiments with the narrative effects of a point of view almost as limited. He describes the limitations of mobility and vision, solitude, boredom alleviated by observation of minute detail, and his dependence on slight visual and aural clues to the world outside. In this exploration of a landscape of deprivation, 'in which my own sensations as a sick man now fill up the weary blank of my daily existence', he discovers how to accumulate suspense.[10] The article attempts to understand the significance of the obscure and undervalued people who enter his field of vision in his lodgings: the portress who sustains herself with a new looking-glass and its attendant flowerpots; the consumptive nursemaid; the exhausted police agent, snatching a rest before his window; the oppressed, inarticulate maids of all work:

> Life means dirty work, small wages, hard words, no holidays, no social station, no future, according to her experience of it. No human being was ever created for this . . . These thoughts rise in me often when I ring the bell, and the maid of all work answers it wearily. I cannot communicate them to her; I can only encourage her to talk to me now and then on something like equal terms.   (p. 121)

In the impoverished needlewoman narrator of 'The Diary of Anne Rodway', Collins created a voice for the marginalised and unnoticed figures whom he had observed in 'Laid Up in Lodgings'. Both works suggest how closely allied were Collins's interests in such figures, and in the process of detection. The story explores the significance of the obscure, and of the slight traces and clues that illuminate hidden meanings. When Anne sets out to discover the truth of a death that the police have dismissed as a commonplace accident, she patiently pursues her one, apparently insignificant, clue through the humble shops and back streets of London. Her diary, kept as a matter of regular habit, proves an essential record, in which she notes events and comments which, seemingly unimportant at first, accumulate to expose the mystery. Through Anne, Collins discovers how to give a voice to the unnoticed, and to find significance in the pursuit of the meaning of obscure clues.

'The Diary of Anne Rodway' was an important development in Collins's exploration of the detective mode. It also convinced Dickens that Collins was the writer closest to his own values. To his co-editor, W. H. Wills, he praised the story's pathos and humanity, and instructed him to invite Collins to join the regular staff of *Household Words*. Since 1851 Collins had been a regular contributor to the *Leader*, edited by his yachting friend Edward Pigott, but joining Dickens's staff proved a difficult decision.[11] Wills reported back to Dickens that Collins was afraid that he would be submerging his distinct identity as a writer in the journal's collective personality in which all articles appeared unsigned under Dickens's editorship. These were fears shared by other contributors – George Augustus Sala, in his autobiography, recalled his frustrations. 'When an attractive article appeared in *Household Words*, which might have been the work either of one of my colleagues or myself, people used to say that "Dickens was at his best this week." I materially suffered from the systematic suppression of my name.'[12]

Dickens pooh-poohed Collins's fears to Wills; 'such a confusion of author-ship (which I don't believe to obtain in half a dozen minds out of half a hundred) would be a far greater service than dis-service to him'.[13] He did, however, make an unusual concession: Collins's new serial novel, *The Dead Secret*, due to run in *Household Words* in early 1857, could appear under his name. Collins had managed to secure a significant departure from the journal's usual policy of anonymity. It was a mark of Dickens's respect for his work.

The Dead Secret, serialised in *Household Words* between January and June 1857, continued the sympathetic interest in the obscure of 'Laid Up in Lodgings' and 'The Diary of Anne Rodway'. Collins admitted in the Preface to the 1861 edition that the interest of the novel does not lie in the secret, but on how the secret preys on the mind of a nervous maidservant, 'the influence of a heavy responsibility on a naturally timid woman'. He deliber-ately defuses suspense to centre interest on a psychological case study of Sarah Leeson, a woman almost overwhelmed by excessive guilt. Again the secret is one of hidden origins, the detective this time a young heiress, who makes her way towards the document hidden in a Cornish mansion that will reveal her illegitimacy and the working-class identity of her real mother. The power lies not in the plotting, but in Sarah's fears, the heiress Rosamund's loss of identity, and the reaction of each to their relationship. As in *Hide and Seek*, class barriers are demolished. A conspiracy of mistress and maid establishes Rosamund's fortune; when adult, she is reconciled to her nameless identity and low birth.[14]

The Dead Secret was Collins's only full-length serial for *Household Words*. Elsewhere in the journal, from September 1856 until its demise in March 1859, he operated as its agent provocateur. His relationship with his editor is well illustrated by the article 'Highly Proper!' in October 1858. Dickens's injunction to Wills – 'not to leave anything in it that may be sweepingly and unnecessarily offensive to the middle class. He has always a tendency to overdo that' – is often quoted. However, it was Dickens himself who had given Collins the assignment, outraged when a private school expelled the son of his friend Alfred Wigan, simply for being an actor's son, and who urged the younger writer to be 'infinitely contemptuous' of middle-class mores.[15] Collins, it seems, was deputed to explore the limits of provocation, Wills to tone him down if necessary. This arrangement, with Collins acting as resident bohemian and kite-flyer, suited Dickens's editorial policy, while allowing Collins to develop further the subversive authorial persona of his novels. During this period Collins wrote a number of attacks on cultural pomposity. 'To Think or Be Thought For' (September 1856) continued the attacks of *A Rogue's Life* on fashion-driven gullibility about

Old Masters. 'Dramatic Grub Street' (March 1858) and 'A Breach of British Privilege' (March 1859) attacked acceptance of low standards in, respectively, writing and production at British theatres. 'A Clause for the New Reform Bill' (October 1858) derided the waste and pomposity of civic celebrations. Dickens arranged revision of other articles, including 'Burns Viewed As A Hat-Peg' (February 1859) which attacked the cant of Burns Night celebrations, and 'Dr Dulcamara M. P.' (December 1858). The latter was a scathing attack on Charlotte Yonge's *The Heir of Redclyffe* (1853), together with its admirers in high places, and its comic effects centre on the serial paroxysms of weeping in which Yonge's fans are said to indulge.

Collaboration with Dickens

Meanwhile, in November 1856 Dickens had raised the stakes for his new staff member, and proposed that they collaborate on that year's Christmas number for *Household Words*, *The Wreck of the Golden Mary*. Collins, under Dickens's close supervision, was to take the persona of the loyal mate, John Steadiman, who takes over the narrative from Dickens's overworked, stricken captain, and brings the wrecked ship's lifeboats to safety. Dickens later reported Collins's evident anxieties to Angela Burdett-Coutts: 'He was so desperately afraid of the job that I began to mistrust him. However, we went down to Gad's Hill, and walked through Cobham Woods to talk it over, and he then went at it cheerfully and came out as you see.'[16] We can guess at Collins's worries. As a collaborator, he stood even less chance of retaining his distinctive character than as a staff member. He might even come to be regarded as a kind of research assistant, as in the currently notorious example of Auguste Maquet, Alexandre Dumas's collaborator on *The Three Musketeers* and *The Count of Monte Cristo*. By the autumn of 1857, when the two men wrote *The Lazy Tour of Two Idle Apprentices*, Dickens had developed the idea of a seamless collaboration. He told John Forster that 'you would find it very difficult to say where I leave off and he comes in'.[17] The prospect of being engaged in a seamless collaboration with someone who habitually signed himself 'the Inimitable' was likely to exacerbate Collins's existing worries about the ethics of copying. Collaboration, like imitation, copying and forgery, is about erasing identity and difference. Partnership with Dickens offered access to a large readership, but perhaps at the cost of his individual reputation.

It was, however, in the collaborations that the Collins of the 1860s novels developed. Learning to move from frame narrator to interpolated story narrator, and to link to Dickens's narratives, produced his distinctive multiple narrative method. The two collaborative works to which Collins made the most significant contribution were *The Lazy Tour of Two Idle Apprentices* and *A House To Let* (1858). The *Lazy Tour* series, which ran for five episodes throughout October 1857 in *Household Words*, was based on the two writers' September excursion in northern England. The idea for the tour and the series was Dickens's, but the narrative model was Collins's, taken from his article 'A Journey in Search of Nothing', which appeared in *Household Words* as they were travelling. Here a fatigued metropolitan seeks peace in the country and at the seaside, only to discover that the diversions available, such as eating shrimps very slowly, or counting the fishing boats visible, are more exhausting than urban life. Again Collins explored how descriptions of boredom could generate narrative suspense. The boat-counting he was to reuse to sinister effect in *No Name* (1862).

Lazy Tour expands this theme. Two metropolitan *flâneurs*, accustomed to an overabundance of material objects and visual and aural sensations, find themselves in a succession of North Country towns, coping with the sudden absence of abundance. A dripping pump, a derelict outhouse, a wayward donkey all focus an attention used to perceiving such objects only as part of a crowded scene. The story is organised round opposing temperaments, and vacillates between distinctive modes of vision. Dickens's persona, Francis Goodchild, seeks obsessively for traces of the abundance to which he is accustomed. Collins's persona, Thomas Idle, accepts its absence. Idle's contributions resume the theme of the perceptions available to restricted mobility and point of view already explored in 'Laid Up in Lodgings'. On the ascent of Carrick Fell, night, fog and rain reduce observation to almost nothing. Idle's range of sensory experience is reduced still further on the descent, when, like Collins on the real climb, he sprains his ankle. Thereafter his view is confined to a succession of scantily furnished hotel rooms; he usually declines the window through which Goodchild restlessly seeks the restoration of metropolitan abundance. Idle's situation is treated comically, but Collins's interpolated story, later titled 'The Dead Hand', intensifies the same situation to sinister effect. A pleasure-seeking young man, in overcrowded Doncaster, accepts the only accommodation available, a hotel room where on the other bed a corpse is awaiting the undertaker. As in the ascent of Carrick Fell, the limited possibilities for observation are gradually reduced. The room is sparsely furnished, the only diversion a grubby riddle-book, and these resources are illumined by a single candle. The young man's experience of boredom slowly intensifies to fear as he imagines the moment when the candle will expire.

Lazy Tour was Collins's fullest exploration yet of his distinctive modes of perception. Dickens satirised in his persona his own need for metropolitan

abundance; Collins discovered that deprivation was his distinctive landscape. He explored the suspense inherent in restricted or obstructed vision
and mobility, the significance that ordinary objects assume in landscapes so
constrained, and the imaginative possibilities present in the experience of
boredom. In this series, organised around the opposition of the different
modes of perception of Idle and Goodchild, he developed his ideas of the
kind of writer he was, and the resources he possessed. Walter Benjamin
would later write of boredom as the essential context from which storytelling emerges. 'Boredom is the dream bird that hatches the egg of experience.
A rustling in the leaves drives him away. His nesting places – the activities
that are intimately associated with boredom – are already extinct in the
cities and are declining in the country as well.'[18] Collins's storytelling often
recreates the context of boredom within the story, boredom induced by
restriction of mobility, vision, or possibilities for diversion, which slowly
builds, through intense attentiveness to a limited range of objects, into fear
and suspense. From the crowded, tumultuous scenes of his early novels,
Ioláni and *Antonina,* he moved to a narrative mode based on lack.

A House To Let, the 1858 Christmas number for *Household Words*,
resumed the preoccupations of Collins's most important article. In 'The
Unknown Public' (August 1858), he discovered the penny journals, and
through them 'the enormous outlawed majority – of the lost literary tribes –
of the prodigious, the overwhelming three millions'.[19] Dickens was not as
fascinated by the idea of a vast hinterland of unliterary readers as Collins
was, nor as ready to credit the availability for novelists of the three millions.
For Collins, however, this discovery profoundly influenced his development
as a novelist. He began to formulate ideas about how this lost readership
might be brought within the pale of mainstream fiction. The unknown
public needed figures with whom they could identify, in particular narrators
who found literary matters perplexing or difficult. In *A House To Let* he
provided such a narrator.

The story was the only collaboration with Dickens in which Collins
played the dominant role. At some point early in the process of composition, Dickens's original idea for the number – that it should be a story of
a bitter recluse in a derelict house – disappeared, and the detection of a
mystery became the central interest. Dickens was on a reading tour for
much of the autumn of 1858, and the *Household Words* Office Book assigns
most of the number to Collins. In *A House To Let* a genial, elderly spinster,
convalescing at the window of a newly rented London house, becomes
obsessed by the mystery of the semi-derelict house opposite, which domin-
ates her restricted view. The detective is her old manservant, Trottle, and the
mystery is again one of hidden origins. Trottle discovers a child, apparently

illegitimate, in the attic of the house opposite, and follows a trail of forged records, which have erased the child's real identity. In Trottle Collins develops a narrative method based on eyewitness testimony, which claims an authenticity made persuasive by the narrator's evident suspicion of literary narrative. Trottle claims that his testimony depends on direct observation, and the detailed recounting of the exact nature of his experiences. *A House To Let* resumed the emphases of Collins's earlier detective work of autumn 1858; 'The Poisoned Meal' was a detailed reconstruction of a French court case of the 1780s, in which a bourgeois family framed their maidservant for their own crime. In both narratives the clear reconstruction of documentary and factual evidence is shown to rescue a voiceless victim from obscurity and injustice.

In the autumn of 1858, Collins turned to detective topics and a distinctive narrative method in a move which finally established his identity as a novelist. He had not worked on a novel since *The Dead Secret* finished in June 1857. In October he suffered a severe setback to his theatrical ambitions when his grim melodrama, *The Red Vial*, later rewritten as the novel *Jezebel's Daughter* (1880), was received with hilarity by the first-night audience at the Olympic Theatre. 'Mr Wilkie Collins has experimented in a drama without one break in the chain of crime and terror, and the audience therefore makes breaks for itself at very inconvenient moments,' his fellow staff-member on *Household Words*, Henry Morley, pointed out in the *Examiner*.[20] This conspicuous failure in the theatre was a bitter disappointment to Collins; indeed, its proximity to an intensified interest in detective fiction suggests that the noisy reception of *The Red Vial* may have had a role in redirecting and refocusing Collins's narrative interests. It may even have been a transforming experience comparable to Henry James's more famous debacle with his play *Guy Domville* (1895).

There was one other significant publication in the autumn of 1858 – the story 'A Paradoxical Experience', retitled 'Fauntleroy' in the collection *The Queen of Hearts* (1859). This piece returns to the topic of forgery in a sympathetic vignette of Henry Fauntleroy, one of the last men hanged for forgery; it depicts him acting benevolently when he knows he is on the brink of ruin. The historical Fauntleroy's defence lay in his role as junior partner and dogsbody in the firm; he had spent a decade forging the signatures of his senior partners, who escaped unscathed, in order to keep the firm solvent. The story is characteristic of Collins's readiness to sympathise with the outcast, but is also perhaps a kind of allegory of his own worries after two years of collaboration with a very eminent senior partner. By the end of 1858, however, Collins had reached the end of a long process of seeking his niche. His social and thematic preoccupations were already evident as early as *Ioláni*. Now, after years of experiment, which included working with and around the greatest writer of the day, he had evolved a distinctive narrative method. It was a method that used multiple narration, by narrators who included members of the 'Unknown Public', and which addressed itself to an extended popular audience, utilising the resources of boredom and of limited perception, pursuing slight traces uncertainly revealed, towards 'the light of Reality wherever I could find it', as he put it in the preface to *Basil*. His next novel, *The Woman in White*, would finally establish him as a leading novelist.

NOTES

1. Emile Forgues, 'William Wilkie Collins', *Revue des Deux Mondes* 12 (1855), 15–48.
2. W. Wilkie Collins, *Memoirs of the Life of William Collins, Esq., RA: With Selections from His Journals and Correspondence*, 2 vols. (Wakefield: EP Publishing, 1978), II, ch. 4.
3. *Ioláni, or Tahiti as it was* was first published by Princeton University Press in 1999, edited by Ira Nadel. For further background to the novel, see Nadel's introduction and Lillian Nayder's chapter in this volume.
4. See Josephine McDonagh, *Child Murder and British Culture 1750–1900* (Cambridge: Cambridge University Press, 2003) on the infanticide debate in the 1840s.
5. Tamar Heller, *Dead Secrets: Wilkie Collins and the Female Gothic* (New Haven: Yale University Press, 1992), p. 56.
6. Walter de la Mare, 'The Early Novels of Wilkie Collins', in John Drinkwater (ed.), *The Eighteen-Sixties* (Cambridge: Cambridge University Press, 1932), pp. 51–101.
7. On Collins's adherence to realism, see also the Introduction to Maria K. Bachman and Don Richard Cox (eds.), *Reality's Dark Light: The Sensational Wilkie Collins* (Knoxville: University of Tennessee Press, 2003), pp. xi–xxviii.
8. On the relationship between class and gender relations in the novel, see Lillian Nayder, *Wilkie Collins* (New York: Twayne, 1997), pp. 42–52.
9. Madeline House, Graham Storey and Kathleen Tillotson (eds.), *The Letters of Charles Dickens*, 12 vols. (Oxford: Clarendon Press, 1965–2001), VII, p. 376.
10. 'Laid Up in Lodgings' was reprinted in *My Miscellanies* (London: Sampson Low, 1863), a collection of twenty-four articles including 'Dramatic Grub Street', 'A Journey in Search of Nothing', 'The Poisoned Meal', 'To Think or Be Thought For' and 'The Unknown Public'. 'The Diary of Anne Rodway' and 'The Dead Hand' were collected in *The Queen of Hearts* (1859) and are reprinted in Julian Thompson (ed.), *Wilkie Collins: The Complete Shorter Fiction* (London: Robinson, 1995), and in Norman Page (ed.), *Mad Monkton and Other Stories* (Oxford: Oxford University Press, 1994).
11. Dickens, *Letters*, VIII, p. 189. See Kirk Beetz, 'Wilkie Collins and the *Leader*', *Victorian Periodicals Review* 15:1 (spring 1982), 20–9.

12. George Augustus Sala, *Things I Have Seen and People I Have Known*, 2 vols. (London, Cassell, 1894), I, p. 179.
13. Dickens, *Letters*, VIII, p. 189.
14. See Heller, *Dead Secrets*, pp. 1–12; Nayder, *Wilkie Collins*, pp. 52–9.
15. Dickens, *Letters*, VIII, pp. 669, 649.
16. Ibid., p. 234. *The Wreck of the Golden Mary* and *A House To Let* are collected in Charles Dickens, *Christmas Stories*, ed. Ruth Glancy (London: Dent, 1996). See also Lillian Nayder, *Unequal Partners: Charles Dickens, Wilkie Collins and Victorian Authorship* (Ithaca: Cornell University Press, 2002), and Anthea Trodd, 'Collaborating in Open Boats: Dickens, Collins, Franklin and Bligh', *Victorian Studies* 42:2 (Winter 1999–2000), 201–25.
17. Dickens, *Letters*, VIII, p. 462.
18. Walter Benjamin, 'The Storyteller', in Benjamin, *Illuminations*, ed. Hannah Arendt, trans. Harry Zohn (London: Fontana, 1973), p. 91.
19. Collins, *My Miscellanies*, p. 161. See also Patrick Brantlinger, *The Reading Lesson: The Threat of Mass Literacy in Nineteenth-Century British Fiction* (Bloomington: Indiana University Press, 1998).
20. Henry Morley, *The Journal of a London Playgoer 1851–66*, ed. Michael Booth (Leicester: Leicester University Press, 1974), pp. 190–91.

3

JOHN BOWEN

Collins's shorter fiction

Wilkie Collins was adept at exploiting the narrative possibilities that the growth of magazine and periodical publishing in the nineteenth century created, and this is evident as much in the shocking, surprising and uncanny effects of his shorter works as it is in the complex plotting, suspense and multiple narrators of his major novels. Characteristically concerned with the disjunctive, inconclusive and oblique, the short story is in many ways a marginal form, which often takes marginal or outlaw figures as its central concern. It troubles itself, and thus its readers, with remarkable or strange events, with the inexplicable, disorderly and queer. Collins's stories share many qualities with his novels – an interest in detection, documentary evidence and the instability of identity, in particular – but they are also significant and distinctive texts in their own right. The flexibility and openness of the short story suited Collins and let him experiment through-out his career, as the relative brevity of the form allows him to explore his interests in erotic rivalry and compulsion, transgressions of the law, and the maskings and doubling of the self. But it is the variety of his shorter fiction that is most striking. In a career spanning nearly half a century, Collins produced not only the detective fiction for which he is best known, but also novellas (*Miss or Mrs?*, 1873, and *The Haunted Hotel*, 1879); sentimental Christmas stories (*Mr Wray's Cash-Box*, 1852); comic stories ('The Fatal Cradle', 1861); 'antighost stories' such as 'The Dead Hand' (1857) and 'John Jago's Ghost' (1873–4), and humorous detective fiction ('The Biter Bit', 1858). In the process he created the first British detective story ('A Stolen Letter', 1854), the first appearance of a police officer ('A Terribly Strange Bed', 1852) and the first woman detective ('The Diary of Anne Rodway', 1856). In 'My Lady's Money' (1877), he even wrote a story featuring a detective dog, another first.[1]

Critically, however, these works have been almost entirely ignored. The dominance of the novel in contemporary critical accounts of Victorian prose has had many casualties, including the work of important essayists and humorists, but the common bypassing of shorter fiction is a particular loss. The major works of Collins scholarship concentrate for the most part on the handful of best-known novels, but even the recent extension of interest to the full span of his career rarely stretches as far as the shorter works. Historians and critics of the short story form also underplay Collins's significance and often present the emergence of the genre in England as a phenomenon of the last few decades of the nineteenth century. This neglect may not be surprising, as his shorter fiction deals with disturbing or uncanny material that cannot easily be assimilated or found a home, but it can lead to serious misrecognitions of the shapes of Collins's oeuvre and that of prose fiction in the nineteenth century more generally. There may be, for example, a peculiarly close relationship between the form of the short story and some key aspects of sensation fiction. Sensation and emotional impact are as central to the power of Collins's short stories as to his novels, taking as they do powerful psychic reflexes as their subject matter and seeking to produce equally strong responses in their readers. In the spaces it creates around the narrator and characters, in its economy and speed, the short story can resist explanation and lead to shocking, inexplicable and uncanny effects. One of Collins's most gripping tales, 'Blow up with the Brig!' (1859), is written from the point of view of a man who is strapped to explosives in the hold of a ship captured by pirates, rapidly dementing as the fuse and his life burn steadily away. At their best, his stories have an equally explosive force.

Gothic and uncanny

The two best-known quotations about Collins both stress the importance of the domestic to his work. In 1865 in the *Nation*, Henry James gave him 'the credit of having introduced those most mysterious of mysteries, the mysteries that are at our own doors' to fiction.[2] In his 1852 novel *Basil*, Collins himself spoke of 'those ghastly heart-tragedies . . . which are acted and re-acted, scene by scene, year by year, in the secret theatre of home' (pp. 75–7). This was a taste that began early in his life; an early letter tells of how much he enjoyed reciting 'the most terrible parts of the Monk and Frankenstein' (the Gothic fiction of an earlier generation), giving his relations 'a hash of diablerie, demonology, & massacre with their Souchong and bread and butter' (*B&C* I, 14). His short fiction similarly links everyday life with Gothic terror, but domesticity for Collins is more usually an *uncanny* rather than strictly Gothic matter. For Sigmund Freud, the uncanny was that class of sensation in which the seemingly unfamiliar turned out to be strangely familiar, and in which distinctions such as those between the living and the dead and the animate and inanimate are made uncertain or suddenly reversed.[3] The most celebrated of all uncanny texts, E. T. A. Hoffmann's 'The Sandman' (1816), is a short story and, like several of Collins's early stories, such as 'Mad Monkton' (1855), concerns a young man on the threshold of marriage who is frustrated in his progress to erotic consummation by strange and apparently supernatural forces.[4] Collins's use of uncanny material is much wider than this, however, exploiting to the full the disruptive power of compulsive repetition and the confounding of boundaries between the human and nonhuman within fiction. His stories, with such paradoxical titles as 'A Sane Madman' and 'The Dead Alive' (the original titles of 'A Mad Marriage' (1874) and 'John Jago's Ghost', respectively) constantly lead to contradictory knowledge and states of mind, in which the distinctions between life and death, sane and insane, self and other, tremble and melt. It is a world full of danger and mystery, populated with uncanny figures and forces: doubles, addicts and masks; poisoned meals, fatal cradles and deadly beds.

Collins is intrigued by the disruptive, terrifying and surprising, but he is equally interested in what can control and order such forces. One of the signs of this is the often noticed 'flatness' of his narration. He is sometimes criticised for an inability to make his characters sound different from one another, to give them distinct *voices*. A reviewer of his 1859 collection of stories, *The Queen of Hearts,* complained in the *Saturday Review* that 'Everybody, whatever may be his or her sex, age, or education, uses precisely the same language and entertains precisely the same views of right and wrong, of what is expedient, customary, and practical.'[5] Or, as another unsigned notice in the same journal brutally put it in August the following year, 'Like the women in Pope, most of Wilkie Collins's characters have no character at all.'[6] What such criticism fails to register is how a concern with the uncertainty of identity and fragility of voice is often precisely at the centre of the novels and stories themselves, at minimum one of their main themes. 'The Lady of Glenwith Grange' (1856), for example, tells a story of identity-substitution in which a criminal successfully impersonates, marries as, and lives for many years as an aristocrat, the Baron Franval, before his unmasking. The identity of name, voice, body and personhood is rarely taken for granted by Collins, either in his subject matter or in his narration. Neither Collins's voice and identity as an author nor the voices and identities of his characters are necessarily stable, readily identifiable or different from those that surround them.

Narration in Collins's shorter fiction is thus often centrally concerned with questions of evidence and documentation. Walter Benjamin made a famous contrast between the novel and the story: the novel, unlike the story, he argued, 'neither comes from oral tradition nor goes into it'.[7] Collins's stories are sometimes uncertainly poised between the oral and the written: many are narrated by a 'speaker', but this narration is often punctuated, mediated or usurped by the use of documents, such as wills, letters, confessions or diaries. 'The Diary of Anne Rodway' consists of a diary, 'The Biter Bit' of an exchange of letters, and the plot of 'John Jago's Ghost' is forwarded by two false confessions, a newspaper advertisement and a will. Many of the stories' narrators share a desire to document. The narrator of 'A Stolen Letter' says, on being asked to tell a tale, 'No, I absolutely decline to tell you a story. But, though I won't tell a story, I am ready to make a statement. A statement is a matter of fact; therefore the exact opposite of a story, which is a matter of fiction.'[8] The narrator of 'Mad Monkton' is equally precise about the status of his discourse: 'Thus far I have spoken from hearsay evidence mostly. What I have next to tell will be the result of my own personal experience' (p. 39). The narrator of 'The Dead Hand' (1857) is determined to distinguish certain knowledge from '[r]eport and scandal' (p. 258). Although these distinctions seem to operate in the interest of certainty and of a clear difference between truth and its others – report, scandal, hearsay and fiction – their effect in Collins's fiction is often very different, the making of a radically unassuageable doubt in the reader about any or all truth-claims.

Collins's narrators tend to identify, as does the English legal system, true testimony with the personally seen and known, but his stories are equally fascinated by states of mind and consciousness (such as drunkenness, madness, addiction, fainting, 'nerves', memory lapses and temporary insanity) that make such evidence doubtful. As narrators try to act like witnesses in a courtroom, there is often in consequence an emptying-out of character, as the emotional and affective are apparently stripped from what they say, only to return later, in more disturbing form. In one way, the reasonableness of the narration works to legitimate the story, convincing us of the credibility of the strange things that are being narrated. But in its lack of individual 'voice' it can also intensify that strangeness, by giving the reader the sense that somehow all narrators are interchangeable, or not fully individual, at risk, perhaps, of blending into or being confused with each other. Collins is fascinated by both literal and metaphorical masks – both *Mr Wray's Cash-Box* and 'The Yellow Mask' (1855) deal with this explicitly – and at times it seems as if all his characters are masked in one way or another. Identity becomes a kind of performance, behind which lies a secret, often a sexual one, that cannot be revealed. Just as his characters often find themselves trapped or imprisoned, so, too, their narration is a form of constraint, a controlled space within which the persistent, unaccountable strangeness of their witnessing can appear. Collins is very interested in the authority of experience, but at the same time he empties out that authority through multiple and competing frames of reference. His best stories do not seek to resolve or unify the events they narrate into the overarching order and temporal unity that are customary in novels. We do not know at the end of 'The Dead Hand', for example, whether the mysterious Mr Lorn is really the figure encountered as a corpse in an inn bedroom many years before, if he is really the illegitimate son that the narrator suspects him to be, or why the two brothers of the story should so uncannily have been drawn to the same woman.

A puzzling and entertaining example of this double pressure both to resolve and to leave unexplained can be found in one of Collins's last stories, 'The Devil's Spectacles' (1879). The opening frames a tale that begins in the frozen Arctic wastes where two men, having abandoned their shipmates, are starving to death. With many parallels to Collins's play (and later story) *The Frozen Deep* (1857; 1874), it sites itself on the terrain of what Eve Kosofsky Sedgwick has called the 'paranoid Gothic', 'in which a male hero is in a close, usually murderous relation to another man, in some respects his "double" to whom he seems to be mentally transparent'.[9] On the death of one of the men, the other, Septimus Notman, begins to eat his corpse, whereupon he is visited by what appears to be the Devil, who offers him a pair of spectacles that enable him to read the mind of anyone he encounters. At his death he bequeaths these spectacles to the narrator of the story, an affluent young man who is trying to decide whom to marry. Through the spectacles the young man, Alfred, is able to understand the real motives and thoughts underlying the actions of his mother and his potential brides. It is a characteristic Collins story in its use and transfer of some key Gothic tropes into and across a contemporary story set in a realistic world. The supernatural of an earlier Gothic tradition is both maintained and mutates into an exploration of a kind of knowledge that is abnormal, disturbing and/or telepathic. The interest in sexuality and sexual difference, in complex motivation that cannot be admitted within the conventions of normal bourgeois behaviour, and in the relation of an exotic world to 'respectable' English life, are typical of much of Collins's work. The story also contains within it an idea or dream of a privileged knowledge and power, which would stem from the ability to know for sure what the thoughts of other people are. It appears in a cannibalistic, transgressive, desperate and fatal scene between two men; it promises to reveal the truth about female desire, which is radically unknowable without supernatural power. But such a longing, even if successful, may be also a kind of madness. This is one of Collins's most persistent fantasies: a desire, at times paranoid in intensity and compulsive force, for knowledge, often of a sexual nature (secrets of passion, illegitimacy, sexual transgression), that is barely distinguished from insanity. To read his fiction may be to be infected with such a desire.

The narration of 'The Devil's Spectacles' is full of the kinds of undecidability that are at the heart of 'uncanny' effects in fiction, and its ending is particularly striking. Two unnamed voices (of 'the Reader and the Editor') speak:

> Are we to have no satisfactory explanation of the supernatural element in the story? How did it come into the Editor's hands? Was there neither name nor address on the manuscript?
>
> There was an address, if you must know. But I decline to mention it.
>
> Suppose I guess that the address was at a lunatic asylum? What would you say to that?
>
> I should say that I suspected you of being a critic, and I should have the honour of wishing you good morning. (p. 719)

The first voice (which may be yours, or mine) looks for closure and an identifiable conclusion, explanation, name and address that would resolve our doubts about the host of possibilities – of supernatural power, desire, lunacy – that the mysterious manuscript has raised. But it is not satisfied. Both the origin and the destiny of the document remain uncertain and divided. What we have instead is a repetition in miniature of the matter of the story itself: a dialogue of two speakers, each trying to understand what the other is thinking or motivated by. But the address of the manuscript is not given, and the critic is politely turned away.

Precursors, plagiarism and the law

One of the more interesting and troubling elements of Collins's shorter work is the matter of plagiarism. His novels are deeply interested in the fragility and vulnerability of human identity; in *The Woman in White* (1860), for example, Laura cannot establish her identity to her uncle, even when she is in his presence. But that instability of identity is also true of Collins's own narration, which at times appears to have an unusually close and derivative relationship to the work of his precursors, in particular that of Charles Dickens and Edgar Allan Poe. Anthea Trodd has discussed elsewhere in this volume Collins's complex working relationship with Dickens, and the question of how far he could be judged merely an imitator of him; this issue ran through early reviews of his work, both positively and negatively, and more recently Julian Symons has described Collins's 'The Stolen Letter' (1854) as 'almost a crib' of Poe's celebrated story 'A Purloined

Letter' (1845).[10] Is Collins simply a derivative author, then, or is his relation to his precursors a more complex one?

It is clear that Collins's very first story, published when he was only nineteen, owes a lot to Dickens. 'The Last Stage Coachman' (1843) recounts a vision, set in a deserted coaching inn, in which the narrator encounters the Last Stage Coachman mourning the coming of the railway and the consequent loss of his livelihood. It resembles both 'The Last Cab Driver, and the First Omnibus Cad' in Dickens's *Sketches by Boz* (1836) and 'The Story of the Bagman's Uncle' in *The Pickwick Papers* (1836–7); the coachman himself is a close relative of Tony Weller in the same novel. Collins's sketch shares a concern with its precursors in its portrayal of the loss of a wild and romantic life of the past, as the old gives place violently to the new. Plagiarised or pastiched as it seems to be from Dickens's 'originals', Collins's career seems to begin either in dutiful apprenticeship or abject dependence. But even this early in his career, Collins transforms the material he takes, and the story ends in a most un-Dickensian way, with the surreal vision of the arrival of a ghostly stage coach 'with a railway director strapped fast to each wheel, and a stoker between the teeth of each of the horses', driven by a man 'clothed in a coat of engineer's skin, with gloves of the hide of railway police' (p. 5), carrying passengers who include Julius Caesar and the eighteenth-century murderer Elizabeth Brownrigg. The relationship of past and present in the story suddenly becomes a powerfully vengeful one, full of violence and Gothic excess. The coach and its coachman, which appeared to have been superannuated, come back, powerful, undead and clothed in human skin, violently avenging themselves on their presumptuous successors. It is a story that both borrows from what comes before and fears its uncanny and murderous return.

The complexity of inheritance and the threat of vengeance in 'The Last Stage Coachman' is played out more fully in one of Collins's most substantial early tales, the 1851 Christmas story, *Mr Wray's Cash-Box; or, The Mask and the Mystery,* which tells the story of the itinerant and elderly Mr Wray, a former minor actor at Drury Lane, and his granddaughter Annie. Wray is a teacher of elocution and acting, whose life is dedicated to the memory of John Philip Kemble, the actor with whom he worked, and to Shakespeare, whose plays he loves. In a fit of excited author-worship, Wray makes a plaster cast of Shakespeare's bust in Stratford-upon-Avon without permission and then feels profoundly guilty about this object, which he carries around in a cash-box. There is then an attempted robbery on his house, during which the mask is broken, whereupon Wray loses his mind; it is only restored when his daughter's fiancé goes to Stratford to make a copy of the bust. When Wray sees it 'whole as ever! white, and smooth and beautiful' (ch. 9), he seems to die but then is restored to life like a newborn child. A benevolent squire (who is, coincidentally, also an unsuccessful play-wright) then consults a lawyer, who declares that Wray has committed no crime in making the cast and can indeed make as many copies of the bust as he wants. In conclusion, the squire then joins Wray and his daughter for Christmas dinner and rewards them beneficently in various ways, while Wray gets a steady income from the production of a potentially endless series of identical, equally original, Shakespeare masks.

John Ruskin described this story as a 'gross imitation of Dickens . . . not merely imitated – but stolen', and at first this seems to be a fair judgement.[11] *Mr Wray's Cash-Box* is a Christmas book (a form which Dickens himself had invented with *A Christmas Carol* in 1844), and is written in a 'Dick-ensian' style, particularly in its familiar, buttonholing, self-conscious narra-tor: 'The question is superfluous. Let us get on at once, without wasting any more time, from Tidbury in general to the High Street in particular, and to our present destination there – the commercial establishment of Messrs. Dunball and Dark' (ch. 1). Ruskin's description of the story as not merely an imitation but a theft is a significant one, because the story is all about the relation of imitation and theft, in which one act of theft – Wray's making a cast of the Shakespeare bust – turns out not to be theft at all and the other theft – of the cast from Wray – is one that destroys not just the object but also his follower's sanity. *Mr. Wray's Cash-Box*, for all its amiable benevo-lence, is a tale with a good deal of anxiety in it about the relationship of artists to their precursors. Wray is a doubly subordinate and influenced figure who uncritically worships both Shakespeare and the actor Kemble with whom he worked. The story explores in multiple ways the relationship between literary and theatrical celebrity and imitation, instigated by an act of disinterested devotion that may also be theft and deceit. It is deeply concerned with the nature of value, and the relationship of monetary value to artistic, representational and literary value – the mask is kept in a cash-box and is thought to be cash – but also about the unmasterable psychic forces of possession and haunting that are released through writing, imita-tion and representation. When Wray sees Shakespeare's bust, he says, 'I felt as if I'd seen Shakspeare himself, risen from the dead! . . . And this thought came across me, quick, like the shooting of a sudden pain: – I must make that face of Shakspeare mine; my possession, my companion, my great treasure that no money can pay for! And I've got it! – Here!' (ch. 4)

The result is what he calls later 'a Shakspeare . . . made with my own hands' and, perhaps most revealingly, 'my face of Shakspeare' (ch. 4). In the story the anxiety and the cycle of theft, guilt and destruction are allayed by two things: the law and mechanical reproduction. The benevolent squire tells Wray that there is no copyright in the image and that he should make many copies, which he can sell. The play of imitations and masks, the fears of theft and indebtedness, the threat of madness which occurs when the mask is broken, is ended through a Dickensian benevolence – the squire also gives them a house and money – but also through the destruction of the unique copy, and the beginning of a potentially endless and lucrative work of reproduction.

Mr Wray's Cash-Box is a rather untypical Collins story. He is much better known as the pioneer of detective fiction in English. But here, too, Collins is not free of influence, for Poe's brief but spectacularly inventive career left a legacy that was to affect Collins in significant ways. George Eliot, anonymously reviewing Collins's collection of stories *After Dark* in the *Westminster Review* of 1856, noted the effective blending of 'curiosity' and 'terror' that linked the two authors' works:

> The great interest lies in the excitement either of curiosity or terror . . . Instead of turning pale at a ghost we knit our brow and construct hypotheses to account for it. Edgar Poe's tales were an effort of genius to reconcile the two tendencies – to appal the imagination yet satisfy the intellect, and Mr Wilkie Collins in this respect often follows in Poe's tracks.[12]

Poe's transformation and revitalisation of Gothic modes and tropes and 'deliberate dedication to economy and consistency of effect' were enduring legacies to Collins, who 'almost singlehanded . . . effected the importation into England of the detective story on Poe's model'.[13] The complexities of this legacy can be seen particularly clearly in the ways in which Collins appropriates Poe's best-known story, 'The Purloined Letter'. At first, 'A Stolen Letter' appears to be simply purloined from Poe's earlier story: both texts are about writing, theft and detection and their central actions – the foiling of a blackmail attempt that centres on a stolen or purloined letter – are remarkably similar. But it is wrong to describe 'The Stolen Letter' as 'almost a crib' of Poe's work, for Collins strikingly reverses the most important aspects of what makes its precursor so celebrated and distinctive. Unlike 'The Purloined Letter', for example, 'The Stolen Letter' is not concerned with knowledge of an illicit sexual affair that is then used to blackmail a woman, but about a legitimate romance which is then put back on course for marriage. The act of detection is made by a lawyer, whose relationship to the case is very different from that of Poe's celebrated detective, Dupin. The process of detection is also very different: in Poe's story the police search the office of the Minister and fail to find the letter that is in front of their very eyes, albeit in disguised form. The traditional police methods, such as the search of the suspect's clothing and home, are fruitless and only after a lengthy lapse of time, some eighteen months, is the letter discovered. Collins reverses all, or nearly all, these assumptions: the search of the blackmailer's clothing is useful as it reveals a piece of paper which contains (in coded form) the location of the letter, which has been hidden under the floorboards of the inn at which the blackmailer is staying. It takes the lawyer less than forty-eight hours to find the stolen letter; he does this through the very methods that are seen to fail so spectacularly in Poe.

Collins's thefts or borrowings from Dickens and Poe, then, are anything but straightforward, and in both cases they enable vigorous fictional growth, in which Collins makes the very act of appropriation central to the subject matter of the fiction he creates. In *Mr Wray's Cash-Box*, for example, Ruskin's charge against Collins – that of theft from a major author – becomes precisely the subject matter of the story, which explores in complex ways relationships between earlier artists and their successors. But perhaps the most significant aspect of these two stories is the central role given to the figure of the lawyer, who in both stories enables the successful resolution of the plot. Dabbs's legal opinion in *Mr Wray's Cash-Box* is as surprising as it is clear. Wray has done nothing wrong at all. 'What does Mr. Wray take with him into the church? Plaster of his own, in powder. What does he bring out with him? The same plaster, in another form. Does any right of copyright reside in a bust two hundred years old? Impossible' (ch. 10). What gives the story a happy ending and rescues Wray is legal opinion. This becomes a recurrent emphasis in Collins's works, at the heart of which is a deep investment in and simultaneous scepticism towards the law. As the celebrated opening page of *The Woman in White* has it, 'As the judge might once have heard it, so the reader shall hear it now.' The law can at times, as in *Mr Wray's Cash-Box*, resolve the dangerous psychic and social conflicts that the vulnerability and interchangeableness of human identity, property and writing have released in the story. At others, as in 'The Stolen Letter', it can only achieve such resolutions by itself working at the margins or against the law. Throughout his fiction Collins leads his narrators, readers and characters through complex negotiations with, and evasions and imitations of, legal process. It may be what makes his work most original.

Death, desire and dreams

Many of Collins's shorter fictions are centred on a marriage or romance plot which is arrested or disrupted by a missing person, event or object, or by the appearance of some threat or danger. In 'The Stolen Letter' it is a document that can be used for blackmail; in 'Mad Monkton', an unburied corpse; in 'John Jago's Ghost', a missing man; in 'The Diary of Anne Rodway', the identity of a murderer. The threat is often identified with the 'low' and disgusting: in 'A Stolen Letter' the appearance of 'the ugliest and dirtiest blackguard I ever saw in my life' (p. 137); in 'Mad Monkton' the phantom of his 'shameless profligate' uncle (p. 36); in 'The Diary of Anne Rodway' a 'very old, rotten, dingy strip of black silk' (p. 205). Around the threatening presence and the missing item grows up a penumbra of deceit and criminality which bring in their train a deep dislocation of the customary and normal. Free will becomes weak and the stories full of self-destructive and addictive behaviour. Psychic life is characterised by sudden shock, compulsive repetition or dreamlike association; desire is fascinated by the mysterious and fatal; space becomes confined, temporal order confounded, identity doubled and haunted; rational and emotive ways of understanding no longer correspond. With their sexually charged content, associative leaps and enigmatic resolutions, the stories come to resemble nightmares.

We see many of these forces in one of Collins's most celebrated and successful stories, 'The Dream Woman', or 'The Ostler' as it was known on its first publication.[14] At the heart of 'The Dream Woman' is the obscure fear of the consequences of desire. An unmarried man, Isaac Scatchard, who lives with his mother, is alone in an inn one night when he suddenly finds (or imagines, or dreams) that a woman has come into his room and is trying to stab him to death. Terrified, he wakes but there is no sign of the woman and no possibility of her having gained entry. Exactly seven years later, he meets a young woman, Rebecca Murdoch, with whom he falls in love. His mother believes, from his earlier description of his experience at the inn, that this is the same woman that he dreamed of before and she warns her son to have nothing to do with her. As in *The Woman in White*, the object of male passion is first encountered as a sexualised, uncanny and threatening figure who is only belatedly recognised as identical or near-identical at a subsequent encounter. Scatchard is compulsively drawn to her, and they are married. The apparently prophetic nature of the dream is confirmed as she turns to drink, obtains a knife akin to that in the dream, and tries to stab her husband in his bed, in an uncanny repetition of the earlier scene in the inn. At the end of the story, she flees but Isaac lives on, in perpetual fear of her murderous return. It is a characteristic Collins mixture of paranoia and uncanniness, combined with the threat of a powerful, and potentially deadly, femininity. As often in his work, sexual desire, in its irrational intensity, seems to bring with it the threat of madness and loss of identity and self-presence. Its possible consummation in the heterosexual marriage plot is thus a profoundly disturbing matter in Collins's fiction, and the stories characteristically work through and ward off the threat that it seems to embody.

In 'The Dream Woman' the marriage of Isaac and Rebecca is strangely preempted by the earlier, apparently supernatural, encounter which their later lives seem strangely compelled to repeat. This dangerous anticipation or forestalling of desire is a common pattern in Collins's work, where romance and sexuality are often strangely haunted either by an earlier relationship which is secret or shameful, or by some supernatural force. His 1855 'Mad Monkton' tells the story of an aristocratic young man, Alfred Monkton, who is on the verge of marriage but suddenly believes himself to be haunted by the spectre of his unburied uncle, who has died in a duel in Italy. Monkton thus cannot look at the face of his fiancée without seeing his dead uncle also: 'Think of the calm angel-face and the tortured spectre-face being always together, whenever my eyes met hers!' (p. 53). This is one of Collins's most successful and innovative stories, which takes characteristically Gothic material – an ancient house and family, complete with prophecy, fatal inheritance and ghost – into a complex exploration of psychic life and fictional uncertainty. Like Collins's novel *Basil*, its central character is the 'son of an ancient family whose real economic force has waned but whose symbolic power is . . . internalised into a morbid inherit-ance'.[15] The story draws on the characteristic Gothic idea of a family curse but lays beside it alternative explanations of Monkton's behaviour derived from contemporary debate about the inheritance of psychological dispos-itions and the dangers of hereditary insanity. This double pattern of causal-ity leads to powerfully uncertain effects, a method, derived from Poe, of 'assimilating specific psychological techniques and "sensations" into the rhetoric of the narrative, and employing this consciousness as the means of generating suspense'.[16]

'The Dream Woman' and 'Mad Monkton' are two of the most successful and representative of Collins's stories, but he could also write in very different modes. 'The Fatal Cradle', for example, is a very funny story in which Mr Heavysides describes the accidental substitution of himself and another baby at birth, an event that he believes has blighted his life ever since. It was one of Collins's favourite stories, in which he took his custom-ary material – fatal inheritance and the fragility of legal identity – and made them joyfully absurd: 'Yes! I was the bald baby of that memorable period. My excess in weight settled my destiny in life . . . Such is destiny, and such is life' (p. 433). As I hope to have shown, Collins is a flexible and inventive writer of short stories, able to use his characteristic subject matter in a wide variety of ways, but his work in this form also has significance for the structure and plotting of his longer novels. Indeed, the most distinctive and original feature of *The Moonstone* (1868) and *The Woman in White* is that they are told not as unified narratives but as gatherings of narrative fragments or, to put it another way, as collections of short stories.

NOTES

1. Julian Thompson's recent *Wilkie Collins: The Complete Shorter Fiction* (London: Robinson, 1995) omits the longer stories 'The Yellow Mask' and 'Sister Rose' as well as novellas such as *Miss or Mrs?* (1871), *The Haunted Hotel* (1878) and *My Lady's Money* (1879) but contains forty-eight Collins stories, something over nine hundred printed pages. All references will be to this edition. Some of the most important of these stories are readily available in Norman Page (ed.), *Mad Monkton and Other Stories* (Oxford: Oxford University Press, 1994).
2. Henry James, 'Miss Braddon', *Nation*, 9 November 1865; *CH*, p. 122.
3. Sigmund Freud, 'The Uncanny', (1919), *The Standard Edition of the Complete Psychological Works of Sigmund Freud*, trans. and ed. James Strachey, 24 vols. (London: Hogarth Press, 1953–73), XVII, pp. 217–52.
4. E. T. A. Hoffmann, 'The Sandman', in *The Golden Pot and Other Tales*, trans. Ritchie Robertson (Oxford: Oxford University Press, 1992), pp. 85–118.
5. *Saturday Review*, 22 October 1859; *CH*, p. 76.
6. *Saturday Review*, 25 August 1860; *CH*, pp. 84–5.
7. Walter Benjamin, 'The Storyteller', in Benjamin, *Illuminations*, ed. Hannah Arendt, trans. Harry Zohn (London: Fontana, 1973), p. 87.
8. Page (ed.), *Mad Monkton and Other Stories*, p. 21. Thompson's *Wilkie Collins: The Complete Shorter Fiction* uses the slightly different text of *After Dark*.
9. Eve Kosofsky Sedgwick, *Epistemology of the Closet* (Brighton: Harvester Wheatsheaf, 1991), p. 186.
10. Julian Symons, cited in Thompson (ed.), *The Complete Shorter Fiction*, p. 131.
11. John Lewis Bradley (ed.), *Ruskin's Letters from Venice* (New Haven: Yale University Press, 1955), p. 270.
12. George Eliot, 'Arts and Belles Lettres', *Westminster Review* 9, April 1856, 640, cited in Jenny Bourne Taylor, *In the Secret Theatre of Home: Wilkie Collins, Sensation Narrative and Nineteenth-Century Psychology* (London: Routledge, 1988), p. 7.
13. Thompson (ed.), Introduction, *The Complete Shorter Fiction*, p. ix. Chris Baldick (ed.), *The Oxford Book of Gothic Tales* (Oxford: Oxford University Press, 1992), p. xviii.
14. First published in *The Holly Tree Inn*, the 1855 Christmas number of *Household Words*, lengthened for volume appearance as 'Brother Morgan's Story of the Dream Woman' in *After Dark*, then expanded by Collins again to make a reading for his American tour in 1873–4 and once more for its appearance in *The Frozen Deep and other Stories* (1874). Most critics agree that these expansions weaken the story and dilute its impact.
15. Taylor, *In the Secret Theatre of Home*, p. 74.
16. Ibid., pp. 93–4.

4

LYN PYKETT

Collins and the sensation novel

[I]t is only natural that art and literature should, in an age which has turned out to one of events, attempt a kindred depth of effect and shock of incident . . . Sir Walter [Scott] himself never deprived his readers of their lawful rest to a greater extent with one novel than Mr Wilkie Collins has succeeded in doing with his 'Woman in White'.
  – Margaret Oliphant, 'Sensation Novels'[1]

The serialisation of *The Woman in White* in Charles Dickens's new weekly magazine, *All the Year Round*, between 26 November 1859 and 25 August 1860 has been heralded as the birth of the sensation novel, a fictional phenomenon that has been particularly associated with the 1860s. But what exactly was the sensation novel? Did Wilkie Collins and his contemporaries – such as Mary Elizabeth Braddon, Mrs Henry Wood, Charles Reade, Rhoda Broughton, 'Ouida' (Marie Louise De la Ramée) and Charlotte Riddell – consciously think of themselves as sensation novelists? Was the sensation novel actually a distinct genre or subgenre, or was it rather a label applied to a range of novels by certain kinds of reviewer to express and amplify a particular kind of cultural anxiety? This chapter begins by addressing some of these questions before going on to look at Collins as a sensation novelist, focusing on *The Woman in White* and *No Name* (1862).

At the end of the decade that had been dominated by sensations and sensationalism of one kind or another, Thomas Hardy characterised the sensation narrative as 'a long and intricately inwrought chain of circumstance', which usually involved 'murder, blackmail, illegitimacy, impersonation, eavesdropping, multiple secrets, a suggestion of bigamy, amateur and professional detectives'.[2] A few additions – such as madness, wrongful incarceration, lost, concealed or forged wills, adultery (or a suggestion of it), and, as far as narrative form was concerned, a propensity to concealment and a tendency to emphasise 'incident' or plot rather than character – would more or less complete the list of sensation ingredients. Whatever their subject matter, it was generally agreed that sensation novels were, above all, exciting page-turners, which aimed to shock, thrill and surprise by 'preach[ing] to the nerves' of their readers.[3] These novels of nervous affect were also regarded as having deleterious moral effects; as *Punch* mockingly put it, they were devoted to '[g]iving shocks to the nervous system, destroying Conventional Moralities, and generally Unfitting the Public for the Prosaic Avocations of Life'.[4]

Some reviewers saw the sensation novel as an attempt to spice up a fiction market which had become a little dull and domestic or, alternatively, too preoccupied with social problems. Others, such as Henry Mansel in his much-quoted 1863 review of twenty-four sensation novels in the *Quarterly Review*, attributed the rise of the sensation novel to contemporary cultural decline, of which it was both the cause and the effect; it both created and fed a diseased appetite.[5] For many mid-nineteenth-century commentators (especially those writing in the middle-class quarterly reviews) the sensation phenomenon was a morbid symptom of modernity, the product of a commodified literary marketplace in which periodicals, serial publication, circulating libraries and the new railway bookstalls were the distribution chain for a factory-made, formulaic mode of literary production with an emphasis on the 'frequent and rapid recurrence of piquant situation and startling incident'.[6]

Seen by many commentators as a hybrid form, combining realism and romance, the exotic and the everyday, the gothic and the domestic, the sensation novel was also deemed to be a mutant or mutating form; the life-cycle of its 'butterfly existence' including serialised instalments in the rapidly expanding market of popular weekly miscellanies, the three-volume format required by the circulating libraries, and single-volume cheap reprints including yellowback (paperback) versions for sale at railway bookstalls for the diversion of the railway reader who required 'something hot and strong for the journey'.[7] The sensation novel not only blurred or crossed boundaries of genre and material form, it also crossed over between different readerships and different social classes, by making the 'literature of the kitchen the favourite reading of the drawing room'.[8] There was also traffic in the other direction, and Collins was not the only novelist of the 1860s who self-consciously sought to reach that 'unknown public', 'the monster audience', the 'unfathomable, the universal public', who avidly consumed the racy, soap-opera-like narratives in the penny weeklies which they purchased from 'small stationer's or tobacconist's shops' in 'second and third rate neighbourhoods'.[9]

Even when they were not being castigated as symptoms of cultural decline or social disease, sensation novels were often linked to social change and disruption. They were the literary expression of an age of 'events' and of the society of the spectacle: they were a reaction to disruptions (such as the Crimean War and the American Civil War) to the age of peace and progress which had been proclaimed in the year of the first Great Exhibition in London (1851).[10] Above all, sensation novels were modern; they were tales of 'our own times' whose attempts at 'electrifying the nerves of the reader' depended upon their settings 'being laid in our own days and among the people we are in the habit of meeting'.[11] So up to date were they that many sensation novels took aspects of their plots from the newspapers of the day. They were particularly indebted to sensational newspaper reports of crimes and their detection, and to reports of murder trials, such as those of Madeleine Smith, who was accused in 1857 of poisoning her lover by putting arsenic in his cocoa, and the sixteen-year-old Constance Kent, who stood trial in 1860 for the stabbing of her younger brother. Similarly, the divorce cases which resulted from the beginning of the reform of the divorce laws with the Matrimonial Causes Act of 1857 both created and fed interest in tales of marital misalliance, mistreatment, adultery and intrigue which were taken up in sensation novels. Newspaper reports of the long-running Yelverton bigamy-divorce case, which began in 1857, paraded the chaotic state of the marriage and property laws before the newspaper readers of England and provided novelists with potential plot situations. The plots and preoccupations of many sensation novels also owe something to the debates about the rights of (middle- and upper-class) women and their changing roles both within and beyond the family which filled the pages of newspapers and periodicals throughout the 1850s, and to press campaigns about their less fortunate sisters and the 'social evil' of prostitution in the 1850s and 1860s.

Another set of press campaigns that fed into the sensation novel concerned the diagnosis and treatment of mental illness and the wrongful incarceration of the vulnerable (especially women) in asylums.[12] Indeed, by the mid-1860s madness had come to be seen as almost synonymous with sensation fiction, both as a theme for investigation and as a means of achieving sensation effects. Sensation novelists in general, and Collins in particular, were seen as being disproportionately interested in exploring the social production and construction of madness and in investigating the questions of what made people mad and how society defined and labelled and treated madness and mad people. This reliance on disordered mental states was also seen by the author of a *Spectator* essay on 'Madness in Novels' (1866) as a literary device, a means by which the modern author could stretch probability to its extreme, or dispense with it altogether in order both to increase surprise and to transcend the limitations of a prosaic and materialistic modern age.[13]

Both mid-nineteenth-century reviewers and late twentieth- and early twenty-first-century cultural critics have examined sensation novels as either morbid symptoms or vital signs of Victorian responses to modernity. Sensation fiction was indeed the product of an age of rapid communication in which railways (and steam power in general), newspapers and the electric telegraph system changed the physical and social geography of Britain and transformed conceptions of time and space. It was both the symptom and expression of a modern age in which – to quote Dr Downward in Collins's *Armadale* (1866) – 'nervous derangement (the parent of insanity) is steadily on the increase' (Book 4, ch. 3). Sensation fiction both expressed and managed that nervous derangement, which, in our own time, and particularly in a cultural criticism shaped by the writings of Walter Benjamin and Georg Simmel, we have increasingly come to see as a 'specifically modern nervousness', which is bound up with the 'modernization of the senses effected by the technological revolutions of the nineteenth century'.[14]

The thrills of sensation fiction are also bound up with the secrecy and suspicion, spying and detection which some twentieth-century critics have associated with urban modernity, the culture of display, and the breakdown of what Raymond Williams described as the traditional 'knowable community'. In a time of rapid social change and growing urbanisation, people increasingly felt that they did not know their neighbours, nor did they necessarily know how to 'read' them or their place (or indeed their own place) in the social hierarchy. The sensation novel both fed on and fed nineteenth-century fears that one's respectable-looking neighbours concealed some awful secret or crime in their past or present, that under the 'pleasing outsides' of the 'man who shook our hand with a hearty English grasp half an hour ago' or 'the woman whose beauty and grace were the charm of last night

> might be concealed some demon in human shape, a Count Fosco or a Lady Audley! . . . He may have a mysterious female, immured in a solitary tower or a private lunatic asylum, destined to come forth hereafter to menace the name and position of the excellent lady whom the world acknowledges as his wife: she may have a husband lying dead at the bottom of a well, and a fatherless child nobody knows where.[15]

Despite the moral panic about sensation fiction in the 1860s, the sensation novel was not, in fact, a new phenomenon. As Mary Elizabeth Braddon noted in *The Doctor's Wife* (1864), her satire on the critical abuse of sensationalism: 'That bitter term of reproach, "sensation," had not been invented for the terror of romancers in the fifty second year of this present century; but the thing existed nevertheless in divers forms, and people wrote sensation novels as unconsciously as Monsieur Jourdain talked prose.'[16]

Although 'sensation' may not have existed as 'a bitter term of reproach' in 1852, Collins's novel *Basil,* published that year, had many features later labelled 'sensational'. A tale of modern life whose plot begins on a London omnibus, *Basil* revolves around a secret cross-class marriage, adultery and a tale of intergenerational revenge (fuelled by class envy) in which the deeds of the fathers continue to reverberate in the lives of their sons. Four years earlier, Anne Brontë had used many of the ingredients which were later associated with the sensation novel in *The Tenant of Wildfell Hall* (1848), which, like many of Collins's novels, is a complexly layered narrative made up of a variety of texts and voices – letters, the heroine's journal and an editorialising commentary by the hero. With its focus on a woman with a secret in flight from the tyranny of a bullying drunkard who seeks to exploit his legal rights over his wife and child, Brontë's novel anticipates the sensation novel's preoccupation with the consequences for women of the inequalities of the laws governing marriage and the custody of children. Brontë's protosensation novel is an example of that modernisation of the Gothic which Henry James noted in 1865 as a distinguishing characteristic of the sensation novel. Instead of the terrors of Italian castles or monasteries of a bygone age, James wrote, sensation novels dealt with 'those most mysterious of mysteries, the mysteries which are at our own doors . . . the terrors of the cheerful country-house and the busy London lodgings . . . [which were] infinitely the more terrible'.[17]

Domestic mysteries and the terrors of the English country house are also at the centre of *The Woman in White* and *No Name* as well as Collins's other novels of the 1860s, *Armadale* and *The Moonstone* (1868). These novels frequently employ devices which echo the Gothic, such as menacing villains (some of them 'foreign'), the incarceration of heroines, suggestions of the supernatural and the uncanny in the settings, the use of dreams and coincidence and so on, but they all have plots focusing on the implosion or disruption of domestic stability as a result of secrecy or concealment of one kind or another. The families at the centre of these novels are not what they seem; in each case the narrative is propelled by the irruption into the present of secrets from the past. The plot of *The Woman in White,* for example, turns on a series of interconnected family secrets and deceptions. When Sir Percival Glyde's marriage to Laura Fairlie fails to give him full access to her wealth, he exploits his wife's physical resemblance to Anne Catherick, the woman in white, to put in train a plot to switch the women's identities. This deception is made possible by a family secret and the answer to two questions which lie at the heart of the narrative – who is the woman in white and what is her secret? Fears about what Anne's secret might be and attempts to discover it lead to other deceptions and uncover other secrets, and the secrets of other families (notably those of Glyde's parents). The plot of *No Name* also originates in family secrets and questions of legitimacy, though in this case the secret and its consequences are revealed very early in the narrative.

The Woman in White

The Woman in White not only 'preaches to the nerves', but also represents and explores the nerves and nervousness, opening with the blood-stopping nighttime encounter on the edges of Hampstead Heath between Walter Hartright and the mysterious woman: 'in one moment, every drop of blood in my body was brought to a stop by the touch of a hand laid lightly and suddenly on my shoulder from behind me' (p. 20). Walter's nervousness is compounded by the woman's own agitated and distracted manner and his curiosity is 'excited' by her references to Limmeridge, where he is shortly to take up a much-needed post, a place for which he feels an inexplicable and self-confessedly 'perverse' aversion. The meeting leaves Walter disorientated, questioning his own actions, and in a thoroughly 'disturbed state of mind' (p. 29) – a condition exacerbated by his first encounters with Marian Halcombe and his employer Mr Fairlie, both of whom confound his gender expectations. As seen through Walter's eyes, Marian's voluptuous feminine form ('visibly and delightfully undeformed by stays'), belies her masculine facial features: the 'dark down on her upper lip' resembles a 'moustache', and, worse still, she had 'a large, firm, masculine mouth and jaw; prominent, piercing, resolute brown eyes' and a 'bright, frank, intelligent' expression which seemed 'to be altogether wanting in those feminine attractions of gentleness and pliability' (pp. 31–2). Frederick Fairlie, similarly, cannot be read satisfactorily in terms of the gender codes which Walter has at his disposal. Frederick is 'womanish', but his 'frail, languidly-fretful, over-refined look', makes him, in Walter's eyes, neither masculine nor feminine: rather, it suggested 'something singularly and unpleasantly delicate in its association with a man, and, at the same time, something which could by no possibility have looked natural and appropriate if it had been transferred to the personal appearance of a woman' (pp. 39–40). Frederick Fairlie seems to belong to an intermediate sex or gender. Combining an excess of sensibility and aesthetic overrefinement with the oversensitivity of the nervous modern subject, he is simultaneously overcivilised and degenerate – a combination which was at the centre of a significant cultural anxiety in the second half of the nineteenth century.[18]

Walter's nervous disturbance (and, by extension, the reader's) is also indicated in his reaction to Laura Fairlie: 'Among the sensations that crowded on me, when I first looked upon her', he writes in his opening narrative, was an 'impression, which, in a shadowy way, suggested to me the idea of something wanting. At one time it seemed like something wanting in *her*; at another, like something wanting in myself, which hindered me from understanding her as I ought' (pp. 50–1). Walter's articulation of his sense of 'something wanting' in Laura draws the reader into a growing sense of mystery, which is to be heightened by his later recognition of her resemblance to the woman in white. It also signals the process by which his involvement with Laura (and Anne) first confuses and then begins to undo the identity of the artist-drawing master – whose calling is not quite a masculine profession and whose social position is not entirely clear or secure – before rebuilding it as the properly gendered and classed identity of the middle-class husband and father.

This latter process is achieved by means of a period of self-imposed exile in a 'new world of adventure and peril' (p. 414) in Central America, where Walter 'tempered [his] nature afresh', and where 'my will had learnt to be strong, my heart to be resolute, my mind to rely on itself' (p. 415). Walter forges his identity as an Englishman by surviving 'death by disease . . . Indians . . . [and] drowning' in foreign parts (p. 415), and this process both equips him for and is continued by his quest to right the wrong that has been done to Laura. It is completed by his redefining of himself in relation to a Laura who, following her incarceration in the asylum and the removal of her legal and social identity (as the daughter of a philandering country gentleman and the niece of a degenerate aesthete), is also remade in the image of the middle-class domestic ideal.

Like many sensation novels, *The Woman in White* domesticates the Gothic and makes use of the natural supernatural. The 'ghosts' and spectral presences in this novel are always still living, and the uncanny aura which surrounds the white women, Anne and Laura, has both a psychological and social explanation. Premonitions and visions also function psychologically, revealing the unconscious hopes and fears of the characters – for example, in Marian's dreams about Walter's Brazilian adventures. Moreover, in this novel the 'madhouse' is not simply the conventional site of Gothic imprisonment, but rather is a target for social critique (rather like the articles on 'asylum abuse' which surrounded some of the serial parts of the novel as it first appeared in *All the Year Round*), or is part of an exploration of the techniques for the moral management of the mentally disordered which was replacing the restraint system in the mid-nineteenth century.[19]

The sensation novel was also noted for its unconventional or transgressive female characters. Marian Halcombe is an example of that phenomenon noted by E. S. Dallas in his review of *Lady Audley's Secret* (1862) in

The Times: 'if the heroines have the first place, it will scarcely do to present them as passive and quite angelic, or insipid – which heroines usually are. They have to be high-strung women, full of passion, purpose and movement.'[20] Marian is certainly full of passion and purpose. She rails against the restraints of her petticoat existence, engages in a battle of wits with Count Fosco (Glyde's fellow plotter and mentor in villainy), and joins forces with Walter to solve the mystery of Anne Catherick, and to restore Laura to health and reclaim her half-sister's social identity and property. Unlike Laura or Anne, Marian also has a role in telling her own (and their) story, as her journal is one of the several sources of 'testimony' from which the narrative is (re)constructed. It is noteworthy, however, that Marian's voice is not heard directly; rather it is mediated through a document which – we discover as the diary breaks off – has been appropriated and annotated by Fosco. Indeed, when we read Fosco's 'Postscript by a Sincere Friend' we have the uncanny impression that we have been reading Marian's journal over his shoulder. Her journal has also been edited by Walter, who notes that he has excised sections which are not of direct relevance to Laura' s story. In this last respect Marian's 'testimony' is treated no differently from many of the other narratives that make up *The Woman in White*. Hartright represents the novel's mode of narration as if it were a series of witness statements or sources of evidence presented to a judge in a court of justice. Like Marian, Walter is a source of testimony, but through his editing and organisation of the testimony of Marian and others he also, in effect, produces the 'summing up' of evidence usually reserved for the lawyers for the defence and prosecution and finally for the judge. In the end, the multiple narratives which make up *The Woman in White* are presented by the male editor as the single narrative of what a man's resolution can achieve (and a woman's patience can endure).

No Name

In the next sensation novel which Collins wrote for *All the Year Round*, in 1862, the transgressive woman is placed centre stage in the person of Magdalen Vanstone, the heroine who acts energetically on her own behalf to right the wrongs she suffers at the hands of a 'cruel law'. However, if Collins's representation of Magdalen challenges some gender stereotypes, it reproduces others. This heroine is full of purpose and passion, but she is also manipulative, scheming, duplicitous and histrionic – in short, she displays many of the negative traits often associated with femininity in the mid-nineteenth century. Magdalen is Collins's version of the 'girl of the period' – a term later used by the journalist and novelist Eliza Lynn Linton to name the restless young woman who longs for more action and pleasure than was usually afforded by the social routines of bourgeois life.[21] She is introduced into the narrative as a lovable and self-parodying sensation seeker, who embraces the role of the 'rake' and yearns for a life of pleasure: 'I want to go to another concert – or a play . . . or a ball . . . or anything else in the way of amusement that puts me into a new dress, and plunges me into a crowd of people, and illuminates me with plenty of light, and sets me in a tingle of excitement all over, from head to toe' (pp. 7–8).

Magdalen is a young woman who not only seeks sensations, but also causes them – for example, by her defiance of her family's resistance to her participation in the private theatrical performance of Richard Brinsley Sheridan's *The Rivals* and in the impact of her performance: to the consternation of her family, the stage manager pronounces her a 'born actress' (p. 38). Magdalen's exploits as an actress are a persistent source of sensation in a narrative which is set in train by a sensational event and a sensational revelation. The sensational event is the railway crash in which Magdalen's father, Andrew Vanstone, is killed, and which in turn leads to his wife's death following the premature birth of a son (and heir) who outlives her by only a few hours. Rail travel had become well established as a means of mass transport by the 1860s and the railway journey and the railway crash are often important plot devices in the sensation novel. Braddon's Lady Audley makes deft use of the railway timetable to dash around the country covering her tracks, and a railway crash deprives Wood's Isabel Vane of her looks – thus acting as both a form of retribution for her adultery and a disguise which enables her to return to her former marital home in the role of governess to her own children. This use of the railway is yet another example of the sensation novel's modernity. Indeed, the sensation novel's 'preaching to the nerves' can be linked to a general mid-nineteenth-century nervousness about the railways – a nervousness related to the railway crash (and various forms of railway injury both physical and psychological), and the nervousness produced by the railway's reorientation of time and space.[22]

The sensational revelation occasioned by the crash is that the apparently respectably and happily married Vanstones had not, in fact, been legally married until shortly before the birth of their son. The secret which had lurked in the bosoms of these respectable-looking people is revealed as a kind of sensation novel within the sensation novel. Having escaped from an early and unwise marriage to a disreputable older woman while he was serving as a soldier in Canada, Andrew Vanstone had returned to England to discover himself the beneficiary of his father's 'vindictive will' (p. 80), which had disinherited his elder brother. Cast aside by this brother and his outraged mother, Vanstone had fallen into a life of dissipation from which he was rescued by a chance meeting with a young woman with whom he fell in love and whom he persuaded to live with him as his wife. In recounting this story Collins has the solicitor, Mr Pendril, dwell on the irony that Andrew Vanstone was rescued from a life of degradation and his 'wife' was removed from a 'mean and underhand' family by joining in an illicit union: 'Let me not be misunderstood; let me not be accused of trifling with the serious social question on which my narrative forces me to touch. I will defend her memory by no false reasoning – I will only speak the truth . . . that she snatched him from mad excesses . . . [and] she restored him to [a] . . . happy home-existence' (p. 91).

Even more ironically, Vanstone's act of making an honest woman of his 'wife' by legally marrying her leads to the disinheritance of his daughters, Magdalen and her sister Norah: the marriage invalidates the will in which he had left his fortune to his daughters, and the death of his legitimate child has the effect of transferring the Vanstone estate to the next male heir – Vanstone's estranged elder brother. The consequence of this sensational revelation is very similar to the results of Glyde's plotting against Laura Fairlie: the Vanstone sisters are left with no name, no home and no income, and they are thrown on the mercy of a male relative, who denies them. This sudden shift in fortunes is a common feature of the sensation novel and reflects a real mid-nineteenth-century anxiety about the ease with which the family could be disrupted by danger, death or disease on the one hand, and the vagaries of the law, the banking system or the stockmarket on the other.

In Magdalen Collins creates a heroine who combines the roles of Marian Halcombe and Laura Fairlie. She is even more independent than Marian in seeking to escape the confines of petticoat existence and engage in an active campaign to retrieve the social and financial position which has been taken from her by a 'cruel law' and the callous disregard of her male relatives. However, like Laura, Magdalen collapses under the weight of circumstances and is rescued and restored by the domestic attentions of the 'manly' Kirke (coincidentally, the son of her late father's best friend). Like The Woman in White, No Name is a story of resolution and patience. Magdalen is resolute and active, refusing to accept the law's injustice, while her sister Norah patiently adapts to her changed and reduced circumstances by taking up a post as a governess. It is one of the many ironies that complicate the meanings of Collins's narrative that Norah achieves by passive endurance what Magdalen fails to gain by all her ingenious scheming: She regains the family name and fortune by being chosen as the wife of a cousin, who – in due course – inherits their father's estate.

While Norah plays the woman's part, Magdalen plays the parts of several women. First, having concluded that she has 'no position to lose, and no name to degrade' (p. 130), she quits the unbearably 'quiet life' offered to the sisters by their former governess, Miss Garth, in order to seek her fortune on the stage. Under the direction of her mother's relative, the professional swindler Captain Wragge, she learns to control her nervousness and tendency to hysteria and embarks on a successful stage tour of the provinces, delighting audiences with her 'knack of disguising her own identity in the impersonation of different characters' (p.180). Before long Magdalen exchanges the social and moral ambiguity of the actress's role for the role-playing of a swindler who attempts to regain her father's fortune by duping his heirs. Collins's depiction of the theatricality of Magdalen's career as a plotter and of Wragge's role in it is a vehicle for an exploration of issues of identity and a critique of social and gender roles. The novel's preoccupation with theatricality and performativity is underscored by its organisation as a series of directly narrated 'Scenes' and sections made up of letters and extracts from journals, entitled 'Between the Scenes'.

Wragge is an interesting creation. A rogue with a meticulously organised filing system and set of accounts, he organises his life and 'work' on the assumption that social identity is performative, a series of 'Skins to Jump Into', to borrow the title of one of the lists in the 'commercial library' which he has created to support his enterprises. This self-described 'moral agriculturalist', who likens his vocation to that of the writer who 'cultivates the field of human sympathy', is a dramatist, director and actor. His life history is also a satire on Victorian social mobility and the culture of speculation. He speculates to accumulate by 'investing' in Magdalen, in the railway mania, and finally in advertisements to launch a multipurpose (and utterly purposeless) pill. The moral agriculturalist who began by 'prey[ing] on the public sympathy' progresses to 'prey[ing] on the public stomach', and in the process becomes a 'Great Financial Fact . . . solvent, flourishing, popular – And all on a Pill' (p. 525).

Magdalen's various impersonations also serve to suggest that both social and gender roles are forms of impersonation or masquerade. The difference between a 'lady' and her maid is one of dress and bearing – as Magdalen 'bitterly' informs her maid when she is trying to persuade her to exchange places with her: 'A lady is a woman who wears a silk gown, and has a sense of her own importance' (p. 453). Like many sensation heroines, Magdalen is cast in the double role of heroine and villain. She is the wronged heroine who seeks to take control of her own life, but she is also the duplicitous female who plays different roles according to occasion, and exploits her sexuality in order to ensnare a husband. It is a moot point whether she is in her role of truth-telling heroine or duplicitous villain when she muses to Wragge's poor confused wife that 'Thousands of women marry for money . . . Why shouldn't I?' (p. 361). But such a declaration enables Collins to offer a critique of modern marriage customs and challenge his reader's comfortable certainties, while at the same time concealing that critique in the moral ambiguity of Magdalen's character. These are, after all, the words of a headstrong girl who reassures the bemused Mrs Wragge that she should not 'mind what I say, – all girls talk nonsense; and I'm no better than the rest of them' (p. 361).

No Name, like *The Woman in White*, is concerned with the modern nervous subject, notably in its representation of the perpetually confused Mrs Wragge and the querulous and effete Noel Vanstone, who, like Henry Fairlie, is both degenerative and overcivilised – a 'frail, flaxen-haired, self-satisfied little man, clothed in a fair white dressing-gown, many sizes too large for him, with a nosegay of violets drawn neatly through the button-hole over his breast . . . [and a] complexion . . . as delicate as a young girl's' (pp. 204–5). However, the novel's prime example of the modern nervous subject is its heroine, whose histrionic powers are linked to her hysterical tendencies and whose cool calculation is both driven and disrupted by her nervousness. Constantly driven by her highly strung nature, Magdalen collapses under the pressures that it imposes on her. Thus, in one of the most sensational scenes in the novel, she confronts the implications of the success of her plot to ensnare Noel into marriage and chooses suicide instead. It is an intensely melodramatic scene, but also an intensely dramatic one, which plots Magdalen's journey to and from the brink of self-slaughter through a highly wrought description of her changing sensations as she writes the final lines of a suicide note to her sister, carefully prepares a parcel of money to settle her debts to Wragge, contemplates her own pale image in the mirror, tidies her hair, and, finally, picks up the small bottle containing the laudanum with which she intends to dispatch herself. The sensation of seeing and touching this bottle, combined with the sensation of uttering the word 'DEATH!', propel her unsteadily across the room 'with a maddening confusion in her head, with a suffocating anguish at her heart', and she drops the bottle:

> The faint clink of the bottle as it . . . rolled against some porcelain object on the table struck through her brain like the stroke of a knife. The sound of her own voice, sunk to a whisper . . . uttering that one word, Death – rushed in her ears like the rushing of a wind . . . she dragged herself to the bedside.

> An interval passed . . . she started to her feet . . . In one moment, she was back
> at the table; in another the poison was once more in her hand.
> She removed the cork, and lifted the bottle to her mouth.   (p. 367)

This sensation leads to another: 'At the first cold touch of the glass on her lips, her strong young life leapt up in her leaping blood', and this action in the blood leads to action in the body, as Magdalen 'made for the window, and threw back the curtain' (p. 367). In the hands of a different novelist – George Eliot, for example – the curtains would have been thrown back to banish the nighttime world and reveal a new dawn in a life-affirming scene of nature or of human interaction.[23] In this novel however, the thrown-back curtains give Magdalen 'a sight of the sea' which activates the memory of the mental state which had led to her death wish, and, instead of embracing the new dawn, she 'resolved to end the struggle, by setting her life or death on the hazard of a chance' (p. 368). Collins prolongs the suspense, making the character and the reader wait for the 'sign' that Magdalen should not take the poison.

Magdalen's final nervous and physical collapse, when all her role-playing and plots are thwarted, anticipates the fate that was to befall the attempts of active and highly strung young women to flee the nets of restrictive gender and social roles in the New Woman writing of the 1880s and 1890s. The surgeon, who is summoned to treat Magdalen when she is about to be dispatched to the hospital or the workhouse, attributes her illness to 'some long-continued mental trial, some wearing and terrible suspense – and she has broken down under it . . . Her whole nervous system has given way; all the ordinary functions of her brain are in a state of collapse' (p. 521). Like Laura Fairlie, Magdalen is restored to herself by a period of domestic confinement which she shares with the solicitous Kirke. Magdalen's rest cure follows a similar pattern to the moral management practices of the new asylums, but it is a process in which both the man and the woman are domesticated and feminised.[24] Thus Magdalen delights in the fact that Kirke's hand 'that has rescued the drowning from death' and 'seized men mad with mutiny' now 'tenderly' rearranges her pillows and peels her fruit 'more delicately and more neatly than I could do it for myself' (p. 533).

Jenny Bourne Taylor has argued that *No Name* culminates with 'the restitution of identity and a legitimate social role'.[25] This is true, but the identity which is restored to Magdalen is not the one she had lost. Her identity has been transformed from that of a 'resolute and impetuous, clever and domineering [woman] . . . not one of those model women who want a man to look up to, and to protect them' (p. 52) into that of a weakened and dependent 'model' woman who has a man to look up to and protect her. Indeed, the novel ends by inserting both Magdalen and Kirke into a new identity and social role in which they share the complementary gender roles of the companionate genteel middle-class marriage. While the twenty-first-century reader might be disappointed by the transformation of the feisty Magdalen into the budding Victorian matron, some of the novel's first readers were shocked that the novel seemed to require its readers to accept that Magdalen's 'career of vulgar and aimless trickery and wickedness' should result in her being 'restored to society . . . and have a good husband and a happy home'.[26] In many of the novels that followed during the next quarter of a century, Collins returned to the ingredients of the sensation plot to unsettle his readers' social and moral certitudes by exploring the modern nervous subject and raising awkward questions about social, psychological and gender identities and about the relationship between respectability, wickedness and deception.

NOTES

1. Margaret Oliphant, 'Sensation Novels', unsigned review in *Blackwood's Edinburgh Magazine* 91 (May 1862), 564–84 (564).
2. Thomas Hardy, 1871 Preface to *Desperate Remedies*.
3. Henry Mansel 'Sensation Novels', unsigned review in *Quarterly Review* 113 (1863), 481–514 (482).
4. Anon., 'The Sensation Times: A Chronicle of Excitement', *Punch*, 9 May 1863, 193.
5. Mansel, 'Sensation Novels' (1863), 482.
6. Oliphant, 'Sensation Novels' (1862), 568.
7. Mansel, 'Sensation Novels' (1863), 485.
8. W. Fraser Rae, 'Sensation Novelists: Miss Braddon', *North British Review* 43 (1865), 180–204 (204).
9. Wilkie Collins, 'The Unknown Public', *Household Words*, 21 August 1858, reprinted in *My Miscellanies* (London: Chatto & Windus, 1875), pp. 262, 249.
10. Oliphant, 'Sensation Novels' (1862), 564.
11. Mansel, 'Sensation Novels' (1863), 486.
12. See Deborah Wynne, *The Sensation Novel and the Victorian Family Magazine* (Basingstoke: Palgrave, 2001), ch. 2.
13. 'Madness in Novels', *Spectator*, 3 February 1866, 134.
14. Nicholas Daly, 'Railway Novels: Sensation Fiction and the Modernization of the Senses', *English Literary History* 66 (1999), 461–87 (468).
15. Rae, 'Sensation Novelists: Miss Braddon', (1865), 203.
16. Mary Elizabeth Braddon, *The Doctor's Wife* (1864), ed. Lyn Pykett (Oxford: Oxford University Press, 1998), p. 11.
17. Henry James, 'Miss Braddon', *Nation*, 9 November 1865; *CH*, pp. 122–3.
18. See Richard Collins, 'Marian's Moustache: Bearded Ladies, Hermaphrodites, and Intersexual Collage in *The Woman in White*', in Maria K. Bachman and

Don Richard Cox (eds.), *Reality's Dark Light: The Sensational Wilkie Collins* (Knoxville: University of Tennessee Press, 2003).

19. See Jenny Bourne Taylor, *In the Secret Theatre of Home: Wilkie Collins, Sensation Narrative and Nineteenth-Century Psychology* (London: Routledge, 1988), pp. 30–45, 101–29.

20. *The Times*, 18 November 1862, 8.

21. Eliza Lynn Linton, 'The Girl of the Period', *Saturday Review*, 14 March 1868, 339–4.

22. See Nicholas Daly, *Literature, Technology and Modernity, 1860–2000* (Cambridge: Cambridge University Press, 2004), chs. 1 and 2.

23. See George Eliot, *Middlemarch* (1871–2) Book VIII, ch. 80.

24. See Taylor, *In the Secret Theatre of Home*, as in note 19 above and also pp. 145, 148.

25. Ibid., p. 132.

26. Margaret Oliphant, 'Novels', *Blackwood's Edinburgh Magazine* 94 (1863), 168–83 (170).

5

RONALD R. THOMAS

The Moonstone, detective fiction and forensic science

One source of the power of Wilkie Collins's *The Moonstone* (1868), like the diamond at its heart, is the complex range of interpretations the novel inspires.[1] If the diamond stands, alternatively, as a sign of religious devotion, imperial plunder, colonial revenge, capitalist desire, personal vengeance, sexual experience or psychological integration, the novel equally invites an array of interpretations: it is an orientalist romance, a critique of imperialism, an inheritance plot, an allegory of seduction and, as was most famously claimed by T. S. Eliot, the first and the greatest of modern English detective novels.[2] Regardless of the myriad interpretative meanings the novel offers, however, its narrative force and logic are clear: *The Moonstone* is an elaborate act of historical detection and reconstruction. By way of an intricate collective narrative performed by a series of individuals who explicitly present their case like witnesses in a trial, this novel dramatises a sustained effort to recover a lost incident, connecting contemporary circumstances with historical origins, and assembling a 'chain of evidence' that will link the present to the past by explaining the truth about a mysterious sequence of events (p. 342). In its complex narrative and in the unfolding of its even more complicated plot, *The Moonstone* did in fact become the prototypical English detective novel.

Whether it is the first or best of its kind is open to debate. Detectives had played more prominent roles in earlier texts, and novels that involved fairly elaborate if unofficial acts of amateur detection had been published previously, too, some of them written by Collins himself (as Anthea Trodd and John Bowen discuss in this volume). Detectives began to appear in popular fiction in England almost as soon as the detective branch of the Metropolitan Police was established in Scotland Yard in 1842. Collins's Inspector Cuff is thought to be modelled on the famous Inspector Whicher, one of the earliest and most sensational detectives to be added to the London police force, whose exploits earned him appearances in a series of stories in *Household Words* under the slightly fictionalised name of

'Sergeant Witchem'. In mid-century Dickens's *Bleak House* put a detective story at the centre of its many plots, creating in Inspector Bucket a brilliant and sharp-eyed detective based on another prominent figure in the Metropolitan Police, Inspector Field. As early as 1862, in a review of Collins's *The Woman in White* – several years before *The Moonstone* was published – Margaret Oliphant had already claimed to have read enough English detective stories in the press and in novels alike. She cautioned that novels that focused their attention on the detection of crime represented a significant threat to the integrity of Victorian literature: 'What Mr. Wilkie Collins has done with delicate care and laborious reticence, his followers will attempt without any such discretion,' she predicted. 'We have already had specimens, as many as are desirable, of what the detective policeman can do for the enlivenment of literature: and it is into the hands of the literary Detective that this school of story-telling must inevitably fall at last.'[3]

The Moonstone and the detective novels to which it gave rise are the direct heirs of the sensation novels that Collins played such an important role in advancing during the 1860s. The rise of detective fiction may also be traced to the 'Newgate' novels that romanticised criminal exploits, as well as to the numerous quasi-fictional reminiscences of detectives from earlier in the century. The well-recognised place that *The Moonstone* occupies as a watershed moment in the history of the genre, however, rests not on the fact that it was technically the first or the longest of its kind, or even on the quality of the investigation conducted in it. *The Moonstone*'s significance is due to the methodical way in which it reconstructs the past through deploying techniques of the emerging nineteenth-century science of forensic criminology and the practices of criminal investigation it inspired.

The defining characteristic of this detective novel is that the master detective is not even primarily responsible for solving the mystery. That privilege falls to an obscure scientist working at the forefront of Victorian forensic medicine. When the initial investigator of the sensational theft of the Moonstone, the inept local police superintendent, Mr Seegrave, was replaced by the famous expert from London, Detective Sergeant Cuff, the principals in the case were confident that the mysterious disappearance of the gem would be soon resolved. But Cuff's arrival on the scene was just the beginning of things, not the end. Like Seegrave, he, too, proved inadequate to the task. In the course of his doomed investigation, Sergeant Cuff proposes that a 'bold experiment' (p. 168) be performed on the victim, Rachel Verinder, to elicit more information from this reluctant witness about the circumstances of the crime. He knows she is hiding something and he is confident that his experiment will expose it.

This experiment in surprise interrogation, however, does not succeed in producing the desired results. Sergeant Cuff does manage to advance the case considerably by piecing together some important clues in the mystery and making some canny predictions about its eventual solution; but he fails to elicit the information from Rachel or to provide an explanation for the crime. He is summarily dismissed from the case and fades into the background of the novel, retiring to his garden to cultivate rare varieties of roses. Even though all agree that '"when it comes to unraveling a mystery, there isn't the equal in England of Sergeant Cuff"' (p. 95), the arrival of this expert detective on the scene in fact begins a train of other mysteries and investigations, unleashing a widespread epidemic of 'detective-fever' among the victims and suspects in the crime (p. 300). As the fever of detection spreads from the protagonist Franklin Blake to the house steward Gabriel Betteredge, to the domestic (and former felon) Rosanna Spearman, to the family solicitor Matthew Bruff, to the colonial explorer Mr Murthwaite, to the mysterious trio of Indian nationals who seek to return the sacred diamond to its rightful place, the intervention of the master detective in this case widens the net of suspicion rather than narrowing it.

The primary responsibility for solving the mystery of the diamond's disappearance ultimately goes to a controversial scientist and physician, the mysterious half-breed Ezra Jennings. At the climax of the story, he, too, proposes a 'bold experiment' (p. 384) to solve the case, an experiment that in this case is rigorously scientific in nature, is based on the most recent research and theory in forensic medicine, and involves an elaborate chain of physical, physiological and chemical interactions. This second bold experiment echoes the failed one performed by the master detective; but it succeeds where the other failed because this experiment is sanctioned by a science that focuses on the body of the suspect as a text to be read. The expert interpretation of the material evidence provided by the criminal body succeeds in challenging, correcting and making sense of the string of sometimes conflicting testimonies offered by the suspect witnesses who are involved in the case. The reason that *The Moonstone* might qualify, as Eliot claimed it did, as the first and best of *modern* English detective novels is that it is the first novel of any kind to demonstrate in a compelling way the emergence of the modern field of forensic science and its growing importance to a new science called criminology.

In his 1865 review in the *Nation*, Henry James maintained that the complexity of sensational plots like those written by Collins and other sensation novelists qualified them as 'not so much works of art as works of science'.[4] Although James was referring to the intricate technology of the structure of these texts (and none illustrates this feature better than

The Moonstone), the claim might equally apply to their character and content as well. Indeed, in the great sequence of novels that Collins published through the 1860s (beginning with *The Woman in White*, extending through *No Name* (1862), and *Armadale* (1866), and leading up to *The Moonstone*) physicians and men of science become an increasingly powerful force at the heart of the plots. Scientific knowledge is put to both good and ill uses in these texts, from the infamous Count Fosco's application of his considerable chemical knowledge to perpetrate a grand crime in *The Woman in White* to the charlatan Dr LeDoux using his sanatorium for the treatment of nervous diseases in women as a scene of imprisonment and attempted murder in *Armadale*.

But in *The Moonstone* – regarded by many as Collins's greatest work, and, coincidentally, as the work in which he moved from writing in the sensation mode to inventing the modern detective novel – the medical man Jennings puts science to more benign purposes, managing to succeed where the detective and the legal experts fail because he possesses specialised knowledge and is committed to scientific theory. In this he appropriates the prophetic scientism of Edgar Allan Poe's Dupin stories and anticipates the mixture of the legal with the medical-scientific that Arthur Conan Doyle's Sherlock Holmes pursued in his Baker Street laboratory at the height of the detective genre's popularity at the century's end. The establishment of the centrality of science in this novel is especially impressive given that *The Moonstone* begins as the most apparently political of Collins's novels, with its detailed account of the bloody plundering of a colonial village in India by occupying British troops and the conspiracy of vengeance that violence produces. In the context of the legendary curse of revenge that the diamond is said to carry, we (like the victims) are immediately made to suspect that the three shadowy Indians who frequent the Verinder household before the theft are responsible for the crime. But the sacred Moonstone, first stolen from its murdered owner in that originary political crime in the colonies, eventually becomes the focus of intense scientific scrutiny and speculation rather than political commentary. The climax of the novel comes when, once suspicion is turned back upon the members of the household, the body of the most unlikely (and very English) suspect is made into a theatre of scientific observation that tells its own story to the medical expert and to the gathered community (as well as the subject himself). Franklin Blake's body tells the tale that no witness, not even he himself, could tell.

In 1841 Poe invented in the person of Chevalier Dupin the reclusive, bohemian detective genius who is a master of observation, logic, intuition and esoteric knowledge. He is the direct predecessor not only of Holmes, but also of fictional detectives such as Dr R. Austin Freeman's John Thorndyke and Agatha Christie's Hercule Poirot, along with the long line of forensic pathologists in twentieth-century crime fiction. As would be the case in *The Moonstone*, Dupin's acts of analysis sometimes juxtaposed the political and the scientific. In 'The Murders in the Rue Morgue', the 1841 tale widely acknowledged as the first modern detective story, Dupin puts these powers on display to solve a pair of brutal murders that had stymied the Parisian police. For Dupin, the case came to centre on two linked acts of diagnosis and interpretation: the first was the elaborate anatomical examination of the victims' bodies and the unusual physiology of the perpetrator that the wounds implied; the second was the interpretation of the perpetrator's undetermined nationality and voice, a subject on which no two of the witnesses could agree. The first analysis raised a set of scientific issues, the second a set of political concerns. The identification of the criminal could take place only when Dupin juxtaposed these two forms of analysis to produce the evidence that he alone – as the expert – could read.

Dupin does so by declaring to his astonished partner that the criminal is not a person at all, but an orangutan from Central Asia. As proof of this outrageous hypothesis, Dupin produces physical evidence of the criminal body: a tuft of orange hair, the traces of an extraordinary handprint, and a passage from the palaeontologist Georges Cuvier's *Regne Animal* on the anatomical features of the orangutan (and its resemblance to human beings). He stages a bold experiment of his own to flush out the owner of the orangutan and confirm his theory. In reconstructing what would seem to be a political mystery (the perpetrator as a foreigner of unknown language and nationality) through the authority of scientific principles (an anatomical examination of the traces of the body at the scene and the recourse to a scientific expert), Dupin makes the bodies of the victims and the criminal tell their own tale. In this he provides a hermeneutic precedent for the detectives invented by Collins, Conan Doyle, Christie, and the long line of popular detectives who would solve cases that no one else could because they possessed specialised knowledge, often addressing political issues through scientific means.

The rise and widespread adoption of one of the most enduring of forensic techniques demonstrate this juxtaposition of science and politics vividly, and its history relates directly to the political-scientific dynamic in *The Moonstone*. Long before fingerprinting was used in law enforcement, the British had employed the technique as a method to identify criminals in India in response to the same events in the Empire that first moved Collins to write *The Moonstone*: the Indian Mutiny. As early as 1858, the year after the initiation of the bloody uprising in the Indian colonies and the British troops' brutal response, Sir William Herschel, the chief magistrate of the Hooghly district in Jungipoor, began using prints of the palm, the forefinger and the thumb on contracts with Indians to authenticate and, eventually, identify them. The system that Herschel put in place was later employed by Sir Edward Henry (former Inspector General of police in Nepal and Inspector General of Bengal) as a means of registering (and distinguishing) criminals in Indian prisons as well as a means of identifying them in investigations and trials. The science that provided evidence for the uniqueness of skin patterns in each individual was still in development, but the juridical application of those principles was already in place in British India. After successfully implementing the system in the colonies, Henry would then be recruited by Scotland Yard to take charge of the Metropolitan Police forces in London to establish the fingerprint method there, largely because he had used so effectively it as a criminological tactic in India.

Ironically, a form of fingerprinting had been in place long before as a matter of everyday practice in Bengali culture to seal letters and documents with the mark of the sender as a sign of authenticity. This personal expression of good faith was then taken over by British imperial administrators as a form of biological monitoring and control. Sir Francis Galton, who would publish the most comprehensive scientific study of the subject in 1892, studied these Indian applications as part of his research. Galton advocated the universal adoption of the procedure for criminological applications and even tried (unsuccessfully) to trace distinguishing racial characteristics in fingerprints, expecting to find among Indian tribes a more primitive and 'monkey-like pattern' of print than in whites.[5] Just as theories of evolution were appropriated by criminologists and empire-builders to further political agendas, native custom and scientific theory alike were appropriated by law enforcement agencies to mark individuals biologically and confer an identity on them.

Unlike Poe's Dupin before him and Sherlock Holmes after him, Jennings is a scientist by profession. Like Dupin and Holmes, however, his act of analysis implicitly embodies the 'juxtaposition' of the scientific and the political in his use of scientific literature and material evidence to solve his case. Jennings is introduced to us as a mystery himself, with something 'unaccountable' about him (p. 321). He is the author of a controversial theoretical text on the functioning of the nervous system and an expert on the physiological basis of behaviour. He is also the assistant to the senior physician in the novel, Dr Candy, whose argument with Blake about the precision and power of chemistry and the medical profession was the cause of much of the mystery. In setting out to solve that mystery, Jennings designs and conducts the experiment that confirms to the protagonist, Blake, a fact that was as shocking as Dupin's hypothesis in 'The Murders in the

Rue Morgue': that Blake himself, the man most fervently pursuing the investigation, had committed the theft of the Moonstone unconsciously, under the influence of a combination of chemical stimulants, physiological drives and nervous impulses. To defend his proposed course of action and provide proof of this theory, Jennings asserts, simply, 'Science sanctions my proposal, fanciful as it may seem' (p. 385). Jennings states explicitly here what the novel asserts over and over: science is the sanctioning authority in *The Moonstone*, superseding and eventually collaborating with that of the law to reveal the truth. Through this experiment, what does indeed begin as the most political of Collins's novels (investigating the criminal implications of a plundering colonial policy in British India and the vengeance of the Empire), ends by being the most scientific (shifting the focus of the investigation from international politics to a laboratory experiment).

But this was science with powerful political origins and implications. First, much of the chemistry behind the crime and the experiment that solves it is rooted in the effects of opium, the substance from India that had taken a hold of Colonel Herncastle's body and Jennings's as well. Like the diamond, this powerful drug brings its own curse of vengeance back upon the colonisers in England. At once an illicit substance and a legitimate medical treatment, opium is an apt representation of the Empire's complex and controversial place in nineteenth-century Britain, and in the novel. It is worth noting that Collins himself was under the drug's influence during the time he wrote *The Moonstone*, as was Blake (unknowingly) when he took the diamond from Rachel's room (thanks to Dr Candy's own 'experiment' performed upon Blake). The presence of opium in their bodies connects all these figures with the political story of India, where, like the diamond, the drug had originated (as Lillian Nayder's essay in this volume discusses). Further, in addition to his own opium addiction, Jennings's connection to the novel's political intrigue is evidenced by his being part Indian and part English. He is, quite literally, a child of the Empire, with a 'gipsy darkness' and face that 'presented the fine shape and modelling so often found among the ancient people of the East, so seldom visible among the newer races of the West' (p. 319). Jennings occupies a mysterious intersection point between two worlds, carrying with him to his grave a secret wound and a secret malady that locates him at the very centre of the book's imperial intrigue as well as at the heart of its detective story. Like the drug that was agent of both rehabilitation and dissipation, Jennings represents two sides of the same coin. His bold experiment reveals that the suspicion the English cast upon the Indians should be returned upon themselves, a conclusion that is confirmed when the central role in the crime played by the imposter Godfrey Ablewhite is discovered at the end, as the body of this hypocrite-philanthropist is unmasked in the disguise of a Lascar sailor.

In the light of these details, the scientific story of the novel (like the story of the origins of forensic science) is not so much a displacement of its political content as it is an elaboration of it. After he returned to England with the diamond from his adventures in India, Colonel Herncastle became known for two things: being 'given up to smoking opium' and 'trying strange things in chemistry' (p. 31). His interest in science was such that, even as he had 'dissipated the greater part of his fortune in his chemical investigations', he determined in his will that his legacy should be to bequeath the Moonstone to his niece and to establish a professorship of experimental chemistry at a northern university. The diamond and experimental science are from the beginning presented as the two principal aspects of the 'legacy of trouble' that Herncastle gains for himself in his imperial plundering and leaves behind him in his will for his heirs (pp. 32–3).

The emergence of the discipline of criminology in the mid-nineteenth century was also implicated with social and political developments during this period: the reform of the criminal code, the rise of professional 'expert' classes as a new elite, the increasing interest of an expanding middle class in protecting property, and the gathering of restive working classes and foreigners in large numbers into urban centres. Criminology was still in its infancy when Collins wrote *The Moonstone*, but these and other factors had brought it to a critical point of development. In the Preface to the first edition of the novel, Collins notes that 'the physiological experiment' that occupies such a 'prominent place' in the novel was the product of his own research in books from 'living authorities'. In the course of explaining his theory of the crime, Jennings would cite two of these prominent authorities as sources for his own more original ideas on the subject: Dr Carpenter, a respected professor of forensic medicine, and Dr John Elliotson, the noted physiologist who had written a highly regarded text on *Human Physiology* (1840). Forensic science was at the time a mixture of science and pseudoscience, of human physiology and social prejudice, with theories about criminal types emerging from the traditions of physiognomy and phrenology from early in the century combining with advances in diagnostic medicine, new knowledge about the human body, and a growing interest in racial typing, genetics and, eventually, eugenics. Based on the work of American theorists from earlier in the century (such as Benjamin Rush), the English phrenologist M. B. Sampson published perhaps the most influential early book on the subject in 1846, entitled *The Rationale of Crime, and its Appropriate Treatment; Being a Treatise on Criminal Jurisprudence Considered in Relation to Cerebral Organization.*

The emergence of professional detective police forces during this same period brought another important element to the dynamic, with the demand for more systematic and 'scientific' methods not only to identify individual criminals, but also to recognise criminal characteristics and types, a line of thinking deeply informed by the racial and political theories of the time. Dickens, in his great admiration for the detective police, would publish one of many popular articles on the subject in *Household Words* in 1850, called 'The Modern Science of Thief-Taking', in addition to creating his own great fictional detective in Inspector Bucket at about the same time.[6] The popular admiration for the detective police that Dickens helped to promote had, by the 1870s, begun to wane in the face of some infamous incidents of police corruption and ineptitude. The desire for a more rigorous and scientific approach to catching criminals that would be fulfilled in Sherlock Holmes in the popular imagination and by criminology in public policy was already in place by the time Collins wrote *The Moonstone*.

Collins sets the primary action of *The Moonstone* in 1848–9, though he wrote and published the book about two decades later, in 1868. In the interim between these two dates, the field of criminal anthropology was born as a serious discipline in Europe and America, with Italy's Cesare Lombroso taking the lead as the most prominent and prolific of the discipline's founders. As early as 1863, Lombroso began publishing essays that he would later collect into his magnum opus, *Criminal Man* (1876). His theories may be understood as direct applications of the principles of evolutionary biology to the study of social behaviour. Indeed, it was in 1859, the year of the publication of *On the Origin of Species*, that Lombroso first proposed that the criminal represented a distinct 'human variety'.[7] Darwin provided the theoretical justification and method by which Lombroso elaborated the notion, and evolutionary theory encouraged him to identify the physical characteristics of the criminal with earlier incarnations of the human species, which he invariably associated with the nonwhite races of Asia and Africa, with what he and his followers referred to as the 'lower human races' or the 'primitive savage'. Claiming to have discovered in their new discipline 'the Natural History of the Criminal', nineteenth-century criminologists considered the criminal type, like the primitive races it resembled, to 'belong to earlier times' and to be 'reversions to far more ancient days'.[8]

While *The Moonstone* evinces some of these racialist representations of the Indians (even Jennings is described as a member of the 'ancient people of the East' as opposed to 'the newer races of the West'), its more significant debt to early forensic science is in its invention of the criminal body as a text that can be read only by the scientific expert. The action of the novel is finally directed towards mounting Jennings's elaborate scientific demonstration, that 'bold experiment' that places the spectacle of Blake's body at its centre. The young physician theorises that Blake had in fact unconsciously engaged in the theft for purely physiological reasons, acting under the influence of a precise mixture of alcohol and opium combined with a nervous condition brought on by deprivation of sleep and tobacco, all of which conspired to produce his body's mysterious behaviour against his own will. The physician theorises, therefore, that an exact replication of these precise physiological conditions in Blake's body will cause him to replicate his actions on the night in question and reveal the fate of the stolen object. Moreover, this dramatic restaging of Blake's physiology and body chemistry, the physician stipulates, must be performed before 'witnesses whose testimony is beyond dispute' (p. 384). Blake's body must become a public spectacle, an object of suspicion and observation, a field of scientific investigation for the entire community.

The assembly and construction of the complicated machinery and personnel to complete this bold experiment form the main event of the novel, transforming the novel's interest in the political crime of colonial conquest into a story of scientific triumph. D. A. Miller has shown how *The Moonstone* and other Victorian novels demonstrate the dispersal of the regulatory function of the police into the everyday activities of ordinary life.[9] But here, in this moment of scientific theatre when Blake's body is submitted to the surveillance of the community, the reduction of the patient to a body subject to the biological and chemical conditions of his own physiology has its most dramatic demonstration in an event that is anything but ordinary. The remarkable achievement of this novel is to convince Blake (and us) to approve of this bold experiment as an acceptable practice and to submit to the sanctions of science for determining our guilt or innocence. This assumption forms the foundation of modern forensic science, the discipline in which Jennings was a shadowy and intriguing fictional pioneer.

The sequence of events that leads up to the experiment on Blake convinces him that we must all 'become objects of inquiry to ourselves' (p. 357). This is the realisation in which this detective story is most deeply invested, a conclusion reinforced by the experiment on Blake's body and reflected in the novel's unusual narrative form. At the moment when Blake realises that we must all suspect ourselves, he determines the unusual manner in which this story must be told: 'I resolved – as a means of enriching the deficient resources of my own memory – to appeal to the memory of the rest of the guests; to write down all that they could recollect of the social events of the birthday; and to test the result, thus obtained, by the light of what had happened afterwards' (p. 357). Any single representation of events, he concludes, is deficient and therefore suspect; likewise, these other testimonies, like his own, must also be subjected to inquiry and tested against material evidence – the sanctions of science. Such notions are not merely the unfortunate effects of Blake's continental education. They represent emerging ideas in nineteenth-century psychology that became the basis not only for the birth of forensic science, but for fundamental changes in legal theory and practice as well.

Over the course of the century, the lawyer becomes a much more powerful presence in criminal trials, superseding in many ways that of the individual witness. This development is attributable to the rising power of the professions in bourgeois culture and to corresponding changes in the conception of subjectivity during the period. Psychological theory began to define individual character as something constructed by the accumulation of sensations and impressions, effectively rendering all human perception 'subjective' and therefore suspect from an evidentiary point of view. In courts of law, accordingly, the application of rational principles of evidence to verbal testimony increasingly required substantiation by material and circumstantial evidence. Guidelines for a new 'science of proof' received their most ambitious reformulations at the beginning of the nineteenth century from Jeremy Bentham in England (in *The Rationale of Judicial Evidence*, 1825) and at the end of the century from the American John Wigmore (in *The Principles of Judicial Proof*, 1913).

Both works offered critiques of the value of direct testimony by pointing out the ways in which the psychology of the witness demanded that testimony be corroborated by circumstantial evidence. 'Things furnish what is called *real evidence*', Bentham maintained in his analysis of direct testimony, and 'all real evidence is circumstantial'.[10] Wigmore would go further in raising the value of material evidence over testimony, affirming that 'science tells us that the traits which affect the probative value of testimony are numerous and subtle'.[11] In the century spanning this scholarship, the lawyer's role gradually changed from being a master of legal tradition and precedent to acting as rhetorical specialist skilfully managing information. Blending the testimony of witnesses with corroborating material evidence, the lawyer's task was to make an argument that turns even false testimony to account. In the same period in which the probative force of circumstantial evidence over testimony was being championed by theorists and practitioners of the law, moreover, the attitude of English novelists towards the fictionality of their work underwent an analogous change: namely, according to Alexander Welsh, 'the claim to represent reality in novels was expressed by their internal connectedness of circumstances' rather than by the dependability of the narrator or the trustworthiness of a character – which were held in more and more suspicion.[12]

If the experiment on Blake's body in The Moonstone is a dramatisation of the key assumptions of the emerging science of criminology, the novel's narrative form is a demonstration of these developments in legal theory and practice. Solicitors like Matthew Bruff play key roles in the novel to lend legitimacy to the effort 'to trace results back, by rational means, to natural causes' (pp. 282–3). But the figure of the nineteenth century that most elaborately stages the transformation of 'testimony' into 'things' to produce 'real evidence' is not the lawyer, but the scientific detective, as we see in the more prominent role of the scientist in Collins's novel. Indeed, in the Anglo-American detective story, the official agents of the law often prove themselves inadequate to deal with the deceit that the detective figure, equipped with his scientific knowledge, invariably exposes. This pattern illustrates a growing rift within the legal community with respect to the gathering claims of scientific criminology upon legal practice. The Adventures of Sherlock Holmes (where Holmes's science constantly upstages Scotland Yard's police work) was published in the same decade in which the lie detector was developed (by Lombroso and Hugo Munsterberg) to challenge personal testimony and Sir Francis Galton published his landmark book on finger-printing to challenge self-representation. Holmes's first appearance also came two years before the publication of Henry Havelock Ellis's The Criminal (1890), the first systematic English work on criminology. There Ellis would echo Holmes's arguments for the necessity of a more scientific approach to policing, making a vigorous case for the legitimacy of his discipline: 'The day when criminal anthropology needed to justify itself has gone by', Ellis affirmed, 'and it may well be hoped that this is the last occasion on which it will be necessary to point out that Great Britain has fallen short in furnishing her quota to the scientific study of this problem.'[13] This was a time calling for extraordinary efforts in forensic science, he maintained, in the light of the 'extensive literature which is growing up concerning the nature and fallacies of verbal evidence, and the influences which affect the credibility of witnesses'.[14]

As the detective genre developed, the detective increasingly explained what seemed to be his uncanny act of second sight as the simple application of a scientific technique to the variables of the present occasion. The literary detective's power, that is, came to be consistently represented as a new kind of diagnostic device ('bold experiments' of various kinds) with a new kind of authority, just as the genre which produced him is regarded as a new kind of writing. The systematic medicalisation of crime during this period corresponded to the literary detective's development into a kind of master diagnostician, an expert capable of reading the symptoms of criminal pathology in the individual body and the social body as well. For all his exotic and even tragic characteristics, Jennings – as physician and theoretician – embodies these very talents.

The Moonstone dramatically demonstrates that the techniques that make up the new discipline of forensic science, however scientifically represented, often prove to have a political genealogy that becomes inflected into the act of analysis. It may be the detective's matching of a suspect with a fingerprint left at the scene of the crime that suggests a racial or even national set of differences. It may be the discovery of a chemical substance in the body that could only have originated in an exotic colonial setting. It may be the recognition of certain features in a foreigner's image that correspond to the facial characteristics of a 'typical' criminal as delineated in current anthropological data. In Jennings Collins created the forerunner not only of the modern forensic scientist, but also of the practice of medical science as a form of surveillance and discipline, of police work as a form of therapy. Two decades before Sherlock Holmes would appear as the master scientific detective and subject the world to his masterful, scientific gaze, *The Moonstone* successfully moved the setting for criminal investigation from the teeming streets of the crime scene to the chemical interactions that take place in the scientific laboratory.

NOTES

1. This essay draws some of its material from several works I have published earlier on the subjects of Collins, detective fiction and the rise of forensic science, including: *Detective Fiction and the Rise of Forensic Science* (Cambridge: Cambridge University Press, 1999); 'Minding the Body Politic: The Romance of Science and the Revision of History in Victorian Detective Fiction', *Victorian Literature and Culture* 19 (1991), 233–54; 'The Fingerprint of the Foreigner: Colonizing the Criminal in 1890s Detective Fiction and Criminal Anthropology', *English Literary History* 61 (Autumn 1994), 653–81; 'Wilkie Collins and the Sensation Novel', in John Richetti (ed.), *The Colombia History of the British Novel* (New York: Colombia University Press, 1994), pp. 478–507; and 'Detection in the Victorian Novel', in Deirdre David (ed.), *The Cambridge Companion to the Victorian Novel* (Cambridge: Cambridge University Press, 2000), pp. 169–91.
2. T. S. Eliot, 'Wilkie Collins and Dickens', *Selected Essays of T. S. Eliot* (New York: Harcourt, Brace and World, 1960), p. 413.
3. Margaret Oliphant, 'Sensation Novels', unsigned review in *Blackwood's Edinburgh Magazine* 91 (May 1862), 564–84 (568).
4. Henry James, 'Miss Braddon', *Nation*, 9 November 1865; *CH*, pp. 123–4.
5. Francis Galton, *Finger Prints* (London: Macmillan and Company, 1890), pp. 26, 195–6.

6. *Household Words*, 1:16 (13 July 1850).

7. Henry Havelock Ellis, *The Criminal* (1890) (Montclair: Patterson Smith, 1973), p. 38.

8. Gina Lombroso-Ferrero, *Criminal Man According to the Classification of Cesare Lombroso* (1911) (Montclair: Patterson Smith, 1972), p. 5. See also Ellis, *The Criminal*, pp. 208–9.

9. D. A. Miller, *The Novel and the Police* (Berkeley: University of California Press, 1988).

10. Jeremy Bentham, *A Treatise on Judicial Evidence* (London: J. W. Paget, 1825), p. 143.

11. John Wigmore, *The Principles of Judicial Proof* (1913), 2nd edn. (Boston: Little Brown, 1931), p. 938.

12. Alexander Welsh, *Strong Representations: Narrative and Circumstantial Evidence in England* (Baltimore: Johns Hopkins University Press, 1992), p. 42.

13. Ellis, *The Criminal*, p. 32.

14. Ibid., p. xxv.

6

JENNY BOURNE TAYLOR

The later novels

What brought good Wilkie's genius nigh perdition?
Some demon whispered – 'Wilkie! Have a mission.'[1]

At the beginning of November 1889, just over a month after Wilkie Collins's death, a lengthy retrospect by Algernon Swinburne appeared in the *Fortnightly Review*. Surveying the long sweep of Collins's career, Swinburne praised the novelist's narrative flair: 'far beyond the reach of any contemporary, however far above him in the loftier and clearer qualities of genius' (*CH*, p. 254). However, 'there are many', he went on, 'who think that Wilkie Collins would have a likelier chance of a longer life in the memories of more future readers if he had left nothing behind him but his masterpiece *The Moonstone* and one or two other stories' (*CH*, p. 259). Although much of the later fiction had real merit, Swinburne concluded, and 'nothing can be more fatuous than to brand all didactic or missionary fiction as an illegitimate or inferior form of art' (*CH*, p. 262), Collins's tendency to engage explicitly with social issues after 1870 could often be heavy-handed.

Swinburne's parody of Alexander Pope stuck stubbornly to Collins's later writing through most of the twentieth century: the last two decades of his life are generally regarded as a long-drawn-out creative twilight, punctuated by 'fitful gleams' (Peters, p. 313). The loss of the steadying hand of Charles Dickens in 1870 has been one explanation of this decline, alongside the continuing influence of Charles Reade, whose minutely researched polemical novels and plays addressed topical issues such as prison reform. Collins's failing health, his growing dependence on laudanum and a host of other medications to relieve the agonising pain of ocular gout and rheumatic illness, together with the demands of two families and his theatrical activities have added to this picture, as literary influence, bodily and mental fragility, a complicated personal and professional life, and a more explicit ideological stance have blended into an overarching narrative that has dominated readings of his later work.

Yet Collins published thirteen full-length novels (the last, *Blind Love* (1890), completed posthumously by Walter Besant), three novellas and numerous short stories after 1870, and as Graham Law discusses in this volume, continued to negotiate an increasingly complex and globalised literary market until the end of his life. And while the critical response to his later fiction could be thoroughly hostile, it was more often ambivalent. Even when they were appalled by Collins's latest offerings, reviewers still found them intriguing and disturbing, at once highly readable and hard to pin down. 'Is a noble warmth of the heart, or a creepy sensation down the spine, the commoner consequence of reading one of [his] novels?' asked the *Spectator*, reviewing *Jezebel's Daughter* in 1880. 'Is Mr Collins . . . a moral reformer, or is he merely an ingenious story teller?'[2] Collins attempted to be both, adapting his earlier methods to engage in specific topical debates and to probe the workings of modern institutions after 1870; but he also extended his abiding concern with the complexity and ambiguity of psychic life, and his later narratives steer an uncertain path between opening up new kinds of questions and closing meaning down.

'The limits of modern fiction'

Wilkie Collins had always regarded himself as both a 'serious' and a 'popular' writer, using his Prefaces to confront 'Readers in Particular', critics who found that his fiction 'oversteps in more than one direction the narrow limits within which they are disposed to restrict the development of modern fiction', as he put it in the Preface to *Armadale* (1866). But his ideal of an enlightened mass audience became increasingly elusive as the century advanced, and while Collins shared the frustrations of Thomas Hardy, George Moore and George Gissing with the repressive power of circulating libraries, his work seems to have little in common with these younger writers. Hardy had described his own first published novel *Desperate Remedies* (1867) as a sensation novel, and late nineteenth-century fiction was heavily indebted to the genre. But although generic boundaries remained permeable and writers would move between them, the mixed elements of sensation fiction that Lyn Pykett's essay discusses in this volume tended to separate into distinct strands of popular fiction as the literary landscape became increasingly fragmented during the last third of the century.[3] It was Mary Elizabeth Braddon, Ellen (Mrs Henry) Wood, Rhoda Broughton, Florence Marryat and 'Ouida' who took the sensation novel itself forward as a predominantly female mode; detective short stories would exploit the methods of induction and forensic science; and R. L. Stevenson, Bram Stoker, Oscar Wilde and H. G. Wells would transform Gothic and uncanny forms, using science to explore the disintegration of the body, the mutability of identity, the possibilities of the future and the limits of the human.[4]

Collins's writing mirrors this process of fragmentation, but obliquely. His later writing was often regarded as 'illegitimate' because it wound up sensation conventions to an increasingly strained pitch, so that what had been a culturally dubious hybrid now became an unsettling montage: 'His new book is an outrageous burlesque upon himself', the *Athenaeum* noted of *The Law and the Lady* in 1875.[5] The later novels span a wide generic spectrum, from the Gothic *Jezebel's Daughter* to the domestic melodrama *Poor Miss Finch* (1872). Many address particular issues – marriage law and women's lack of control over their property in *Man and Wife* (1870); the treatment of the insane in *Jezebel's Daughter*; vivisection in *Heart and Science* (1883); prostitution in *The New Magdalen* (1873) and *The Fallen Leaves* (1879) – and Collins's critique of the absurdities and iniquities of modern society is not confined to specific abuses. Yet all of his late novels pose interpretative challenges, and each manifests its own peculiar form of generic indeterminacy.

The Preface to *Man and Wife*, for example, makes it clear that this is a 'fiction founded on facts', its twin targets the failure of parliament to reform the Scottish rules on irregular marriage in the late 1860s and 'the mania for muscular cultivation' among upper-class youth. But Collins dramatises his critique of the law, as he does in *The Woman in White* (1860), by transposing the late eighteenth-century Gothic motif of the vulnerable and incarcerated woman to a modern setting to highlight Anne Silvester's absolute vulnerability as the brutish Geoffrey Delamayne's lawful wife in ways that stretched the grounds of credibility. Collins 'unintentionally shows the limits' of the abuse of these laws, Margaret Oliphant noted in *Blackwood's Magazine* in November 1870, 'by proving that only a thoroughly heartless and unscrupulous villain could make them work real harm', adding that Hester Dethridge, the working-class woman driven to insanity at the hands of a feckless and violent husband, 'belongs to the category of sprites and demons' (*CH*, p. 190).

In contrast, it is Scottish divorce law that is criticised in *The Evil Genius* (1886) for accepting the husband's adultery as adequate grounds for legal separation (unlike English law) and thus allowing what may have been a passing male fancy to destroy family bonds.[6] With its lurid title and theme of marital infidelity centring on the well-worn figure of the governess, this promises to be a highly strung sensation novel. Instead, the narrative progresses in a deliberately low-key way, sympathetically balancing the perspectives of the mistress and the wronged wife and showing the husband (like so many of Collins's male figures) to be weak and vacillating rather than villainous; the 'evil genius' of the title is neither seductress nor mad wife nor wicked husband, but meddling mother-in-law. Yet even here there are some odd disjunctions. The lengthy Prologue describing the bleak and loveless childhood of the governess Sydney Westerfield has the making of a detective story, featuring an insurance fraud, a missing diamond, codes and ciphers, together with a brother lost in America; but these mysteries are left open-ended once the story itself begins and they are never really resolved.

This uneasy mixture of modes, in which earlier methods and motifs are both stretched and transformed, is echoed in the oddly solipsistic, disconnected quality that pervades so much of Collins's later writing. It is reflected, too, in shifts in narrative method. After 1870, Collins rarely achieved the textual complexity of *The Woman in White* or *The Moonstone* (1868), with their interwoven testimonies and juggling of narrative authority and time. Although they use a range of devices to create mystery, this work generally lacks the tightness of the earlier fiction, focusing – with some notable exceptions – more on generating foreboding and suspense than on the disclosure of secrets or origins. At the same time, the narrative self-consciousness that had marked Collins's fiction from the days of *Basil* (1852) becomes if anything more pronounced, as personal testimony and narrative embedding are put to various uses. *Poor Miss Finch*, for example, is primarily narrated by 'the curious foreign woman' Madame Pratalungo, a widow of 'ultra-liberal' republican principles who makes comic or debunking asides to the story she watches unfold; within this is embedded the blind heroine Lucilla's diary (ch. 1). Conversely, Valeria, the feisty heroine of *The Law and the Lady*, tells her own story, disclosing and using letters, diaries and trial transcripts as a central part of her detective method as she tries to prove her husband's innocence. *The Two Destinies* (1876), with its use of dreams, mesmeric influence and second sight, is an embedded story which contains a further series of inset narratives, as do, for instance, *Jezebel's Daughter* and *The Black Robe* (1881). In *The Guilty River* (1887) the dreamy voice of the protagonist at times has the quality of an interior monologue: 'In the silence and the darkness I lay down under a tree, and let my mind dwell on itself and on my new life to come' (ch. 1). In *Heart and Science* the narrative opens by following the chain of events leading to the meeting of hero and heroine with naturalistic clarity as Ovid Vere, at once doctor and 'dreamer in daylight' (ch. 1), wanders round the London streets and squares.

The limits of the self

This generic instability takes Collins's abiding interest in the fragility of identity to a new pitch. For all his hostility towards doctrinaire evangelicalism, Collins never completely repudiated the idea of the individual soul, that immaterial core of being that many faculty-based psychologists continued to support through the century.[7] At the same time, his writing depended for its uncanny effects on everything that eroded such unified subjectivity: masking, doubling and performativity; the slippery line between 'legitimate' and 'illegitimate' selves. Indeed, since the early 1850s Collins had played on precisely those psychological theories that stressed the unpredictable and unconscious workings of the mind as a key method of creating anxiety, suspense and cognitive uncertainty in his narratives.[8] His fascination with the fluidity of the boundary between sanity and madness, with perverse or unconscious motivation, and with the visible and hidden legacies of the past becomes more overt in the later writing, as he reworks these earlier concerns and places them in wider, socialised, contexts. Collins thus participates in the increasingly pervasive and professionalised sciences of the mind and forensic medicine after 1870 – the description of Oscar Dubourg's seizure in *Poor Miss Finch*, for example, directly echoes contemporary neurological accounts of focal epilepsy. But he does so with growing ambivalence. Collins exploits the most striking features of psychological science, but he also questions and satirises its authority as an overweening and at times repressive form of modern knowledge.

The dominant feature of both psychological and social theory after 1870 was the growing stress on inheritance and degeneration, as the notion that morbid features accumulate through families (developed by the French psychiatrist B. A. Morel) came to dominate British sociology, criminology and psychology by the 1880s.[9] But while 'degeneration' supplied the overarching framework for studies of the brain and mind, it did not provide the whole story. Mid-century mental scientists had tended to regard the self as a battleground between reason and passion. They had appropriated phrenology's materialist mental mapping and combined it with the associationist tradition's stress on the formative influence of memory and habit to underline the importance of self-control, underpinned by the internalised surveillance of moral management. At the same time, mental physiologists were fascinated by various kinds of psychological disorder – insanity, dreams, states of mesmeric trance – which they regarded as a key to the working of the 'normal' mind as much as a sign that it had gone awry. This combined stress on *locating* mental properties within the brain and exploring how *memory* shapes the subject played a crucial role in developing theories of the mind after 1870, particularly in the increasingly professionalised arenas of medicine and neurology.

This dual emphasis can be seen above all in the theme that fascinated Collins throughout his career – that of doubling. The idea of 'double consciousness' had been explored since the 1840s, and the question of how to map mental and motor function on to the brain's physical hemispheres gained further force after 1860, when Pierre Paul Broca's discovery of the physical seat of language sparked a series of specialised discussions, particularly in France and Germany. By 1870 the desire to map the precise workings of the nerves and the brain had become completely framed within the parameters of inductive, experimental science. This experimental model dominated the laboratory, in tests on the brains and motor capacities of dogs and monkeys. It permeated the clinic, where cases of double personality such as that of Felida X and Louis Vivé reinforced the argument that the brain was divided into a rational, civilised left and a primitive, anarchic right side. It pervaded J. M. Charcot's use of hypnotism to study the physical spasms of his hysterical patients. It even spread to the séance: the Cambridge classicist F. W. H. Myers, who made developments in French neurology available to an English readership, attempted to link clinical studies of 'multiplex personality' to his wider investigation of trance states and the 'subliminal consciousness'.[10]

However, studies of hysteria and traumatic neurosis would raise questions that could be answered only by regarding the mind as a dynamic set of associations and mental representations in which splits and gaps in memory were seen as a response to terrible events in the past. The notion that memory always incorporates forgotten traces or latent capacities that might be revived under particular conditions had been a central aspect of associationism and mid-century physiological psychology, but the specific concept of trauma was a more direct product of industrial modernity. It first took the form of 'railway spine' – the realisation in the 1860s that the inexplicable symptoms of many railway accident victims broke down any distinction between physical symptom and psychological reaction. 'Railway spine' helped to shape the notion that symptoms of hysterical patients, including the splitting of the personality, might represent a response to the repressed memory of a traumatic event in the past, a notion that would be taken up in different ways by Pierre Janet and Sigmund Freud in the 1890s.[11] British psychology in the 1870s and 1880s thus formed a complex web of reworked older traditions such as associationism, continuing debates (the key figures of mid-nineteenth-century physiological psychology, Alexander Bain, William Carpenter, Herbert Spencer and G. H. Lewes, carried on writing in the 1870s) and the growing influence of experimental and clinically based models developed within a European context.

Deception, displacement and confinement

This unevenness is reflected in Collins's work after 1870. He owned a copy of F. B. Winslow's luridly written *On Obscure Diseases of the Brain and*

Disorders of the Mind (1860) and several of the figures in his later fiction could well be based on the bizarre cases of disordered memory and moral insanity graphically described there.[12] But Winslow also raised a more disturbing question: 'What heart has been, at all times, free from malevolent passion, revengeful emotion, lustful feeling, unnatural and, alas! devilish impulses?' he asked.[13] This stress on perversity now becomes more intense in Collins's writing. The theme of literal doubles that drove *The Woman in White* persists – in *Poor Miss Finch*, for example, Nugent Duborg impersonates his twin brother, and Collins's final novel, *Blind Love*, features the substitution, with the aid of photography, of a living man by a corpse. But often, as in *No Name* (1862), multiplicity is reconfigured within the self as much as being set against a defining other. Collins often clings explicitly to the mid-nineteenth-century belief in moral management and individual agency in the later fiction, as experimental science and medicine become sources of horror; but his unstable narratives also push the resources of contemporary psychology to a tighter pitch, focusing on states of anxiety, delusion and divided identity in pursuit of ever more intense effects.

This ambiguity is played out in different ways in *The New Magdalen, The Haunted Hotel* (1879), *Jezebel's Daughter*, and *Heart and Science* – all case studies of female deception or villainy. Opening in the immediate present, during the Franco-Prussian War of 1870–1, *The New Magdalen* turns a key device of 1860s sensation fiction on its head by making the imposter the figure who gains our sympathy. Mercy Merrick, a reformed prostitute turned Red Cross nurse, steals the identity of Grace Rosebury, appropriating her name and papers after Grace is apparently killed by a German shell; the novel traces the fallout of Mercy's deception when Grace recovers following innovative brain surgery and tries to reclaim her 'legitimate' place. In taking a reformed prostitute as his heroine – Mercy is set against her unsympathetic victim Grace – and resorting to the polarities of melodrama, Collins at first seems to close down the ambiguity and mutability of the self. Mercy not only describes herself as 'a Magdalen of modern times' (ch. 2) but is an idealised extension of the 'Magdalenist' discourse which was still a dominant if well-worn element within the predominantly Anglican rescue movement in the late 1860s. Portraying fallen women as the innocent victims of male lust, this rhetoric had domesticated the radical melodrama of the 1830s and 1840s, reframing it within New Testament narratives of individual reformation and redemption, and Mercy echoes this – with her noble bearing and perfect speech, she is an impossible figure in realist terms. But this idealised person is literally a performance conjured up by the radical preacher Julian Gray who holds an almost mesmeric power over Mercy: 'Be the woman I once spoke of – the woman I still have in my mind,' he exhorts her (ch. 22). Celebrity preacher and revolutionary philanthropist, Gray is the first of a series of subversive Christians who stringently attack social inequality in the late fiction, thus reviving (if rather absurdly) some of the older radicalism of melodrama itself.

The New Magdalen's investigation of what it means to have an authentic social identity hinges on this tension between essence and performance. The dramatised version was a great success and the novel is highly visual, with detailed 'scene directions' clearly written with an eye to immediate adaptation. The narrative, too, relies heavily on the older codes of physiognomy, in which the soul is revealed to the observer through clearly visible signs. Mercy's 'noble nature' is conveyed through her face, and Grace's moral degeneracy is signalled by specific physiognomic clues: 'the forehead was unusually low and broad; the eyes unusually far apart' (ch. 3). Yet Mercy also reveals that she has been brought up in the world of the theatre and has been an actress since childhood. We never know her 'real' name: she is given a new identity as part of her rehabilitation at the Refuge and changes this herself to 'Mercy Merrick' – her assumption of 'Grace Rosebury' ('mercy' and 'grace' have overlapping meanings) is not only a response to social intolerance but recapitulates the rescue process itself. One of the twists of the novel is that Mercy plays the role of adoptive daughter so naturally that her sponsor, Lady Janet Roy, spurns the real Grace even after the subterfuge is revealed – she finally rejects Mercy because Mercy herself rejects her too-successful role.

Mercy's redemption thus lies in refusing the rhetoric of rescue and reform and the novel closes with her and Julian renouncing 'English Society' for the authenticity of the New World. But in highlighting Mercy's own inner struggle between the desire for legitimacy and the guilt of imposture, *The New Magdalen* also plays on contemporary images of double and multiple selves. Mercy's confession is continually delayed, first by circumstance, then by Grace's tormenting lack of sympathy, but her better nature is finally aroused when Grace – whom everybody believes to be suffering from an insane delusion – is threatened with incarceration, in an inverted recapitulation of Laura Fairlie's fate in *The Woman in White*. Grace's apparent condition carries the authority of modern neurological science, and it is telling that the diagnosis – that she is suffering from a kind of traumatic neurosis as a result of her head injury – takes the form of a conflict between French and German surgeons, since the Franco-Prussian War had intensified the struggle between the two nations in the field of neurophysiology.[14] Grace's 'low nature' puts her beyond the pale of narrative sympathy, but we are given few clues to her history or character before the bombing, and her self-possession does indeed seem pathological – a psychic response to physical trauma. In contrast, Mercy unsuccessfully strives to forget an abusive past, and her inner conflict, shaped by suppressed memory, takes the form of irritability, lethargy, fainting and inexplicable weeping: the symptoms of neurasthenia and hysteria. 'Is she suffering in mind, or suffering in body?' the narrator asks (ch. 6). Mercy's unsuccessful attempt to assume a 'second self' shows that a line cannot be drawn between them.

Mercy's benefactress, Lady Janet Roy, is at one end of a spectrum of older women, usually widows, who dominate many of Collins's novels after 1875, acting out various forms of transgressive female power within male-dominated culture. The Countess Navona in *The Haunted Hotel* and Madame Fontaine in *Jezebel's Daughter* are among the most striking – both are exotic foreign widows who self-consciously perform the role of villainess while remaining ultimately enigmatic. *The Haunted Hotel* is probably Collins's most gruesome work, featuring substituted corpses and a ghostly severed head – either vision or hallucination – suspended in mid-air at the climax; and in hovering on the cusp of the rational itself, the story harks back to the uses of 'natural magic' (where ghost-seeing is explained as 'spectral delusion') earlier in the century. But the story also plays on sensation as well as supernatural motifs. Set in 1860, it almost parodically transposes Gothic tropes into a modern setting with the conversion of the gloomy Venetian mansion into a luxurious hotel, using an insurance fraud as motivation behind the substitution plot (like the later *Blind Love*) together with the fruits of modern knowledge – chemistry and forensic science – to conceal the murder and to reveal the victim's identity. It also plays on the use of insanity as a sensation device, but now more self-reflexively. *The Haunted Hotel* opens in the consulting room of a fashionable doctor, whose expertise in nervous disorders and brain disease is challenged by the medical mystery of the Countess, who wishes to be told that she is suffering from intellectual delusion to escape her own diagnosis that her wickedness is predetermined. The Countess's attempt to evade her doom means that fate 'is no longer merely a wire jerking the figures', as T. S. Eliot noted in 1927: 'The . . . fatal woman is herself obsessed by the idea of fatality.'[15] The climax of this process is the Countess's own obsessive writing of a sensation drama, a play that turns into a replay of the crime – part memory, part delusion, part confession, part performance.

Jezebel's Daughter, on the other hand, radically reworks Collins's own earlier lurid melodrama *The Red Vial*, which had been ridiculed when it was performed at the Olympic Theatre in 1858. Twenty years later, Collins stressed that he aimed to produce 'two interesting studies of humanity' in the reformed lunatic Jack Straw and the villainess, Madame Fontaine, noting that the Gothic motif of live burial that had caused such hilarity sprang from careful research into the Deadhouse in Frankfurt, a model secular institution for classifying and disciplining death itself (Preface).[16] The novel thus again reframes Gothic motifs in a modern scientific setting, as the narrator, a former clerk in the firm of merchants, looks back at the late 1820s from the standpoint of 1878. But *Jezebel's Daughter* also draws heavily on this older Gothic, in a mix of genres that dramatise clashing models of identity by tracing how two widows, Mrs Wagner and Madame Fontaine, appropriate their husbands' knowledge and power.

Mrs Wagner, English widow of one of the firm's German partners, is presented as the direct extension of her husband's liberalism. A 'restless reforming spirit' (ch. 16), embodying the most optimistic aspects of mid-century meliorism, she plans to employ vulnerable single women as clerks in the firm, and applies the innovative methods of moral treatment to a lunatic, Jack Straw, whom she rescues from the horrors of Bedlam and brings home to rebuild as a social being. Madame Fontaine, in contrast, turns her husband's chemical research on the use of poisons in curative medicine to her own ends as she pushes the liberal rhetoric in which she is framed to its limits: her letters knowingly place her in the well-established tradition of the female poisoner. 'I can understand the murderess becoming morally intoxicated with the sense of her own tremendous power,' she writes of a famous case as she rails against her 'Animated Mummy' of a husband and her dreary life as a faculty wife (ch. 15).[17] Making use of poison's indeterminacy, Madame Fontaine drugs one of the firm's partners – first to bring him to the verge of death, then to cure him before poisoning Mrs Wagner.

The two women thus embody and polarise two of the strands that contributed to mid-century medicine: the therapeutic treatment of insanity and the analysis of the body as a set of chemical processes. These strands converge in the figure of Jack Straw, whose treatment is introduced as a 'merciful experiment' (ch. 16), modelled on Samuel Tuke's 1813 classic of lunacy reform, *A Description of the Retreat*. Jack's basket-weaving demonstrates how he has internalised the codes of moral management, though he also retains the 'Gothic' image of the unreformed asylum, and can be read as a case of double personality. He first appears as a victim of amnesia, but is later revealed to be 'Hans Grimm', a 'poor half-witted friendless creature' and the human subject of Madame Fontaine's chemical experiments. As a liminal figure who resists stable classification, Jack throws open a range of boundaries – between insanity and idiocy, between moral and medical treatment, even between human and animal: 'In administering the antidote I had no previous experiments to guide me except my experiments with rabbits and dogs' Madame Fontaine notes ('Between the Parts', 2).

Jack/Hans's uneasy combination of sensation and Gothic modes acts out the tension between these concepts of the self within the narrative. It is he who finally administers the antidote that will revive Mrs Wagner, but unconsciously, in an inversion of Madame Fontaine's knowing adoption of the role of villainess.

The unease about women entering the public sphere is taken further in *Heart and Science*, Collins's most explicit attack on the pretensions of modern scientific knowledge. The female savant Mrs Gallilee has none of the redeeming maternal affection of Madame Fontaine. At once chilling and comic, her amateur passion for science is shown to be a means of displacing her frustrated social and sexual ambitions, as she discourses on the interspatial regions, the conversion of energy, Thompson's theory of atoms, and the nervous systems of bees. *Heart and Science* again adapts the older Gothic motif of the 'death-in-life' confinement of a vulnerable heiress, but with a difference. Carmina, the sensitive half-Italian heroine, falls into a mysterious catalytic trance (combining the symptoms of hysteria and neurasthenia) when confined in her aunt's claustrophobic household, and becomes an 'object of medical inquiry, pursued in secret' for the sinister physiologist, the vivisector Dr Benjulia (ch. 33). Nicknamed 'the living skeleton', excessively tall and racially ambiguous, working secretly in a laboratory on the desolate fringes of the city, Benjulia, like Mary Shelley's Frankenstein and Wells's Dr Moreau, is a figure of modern Gothic, who forms the extreme limit of the novel's satire of scientific utopianism as he pursues knowledge for his own vainglorious ends. Desensitised to all emotion by his research on animals, Benjulia moves from vivisection, to experimentally tickling a child, Zo (another liminal figure between human and animal in the novel's evolutionary scheme), to studying Carmina's nervous collapse as an abstract medical problem.

Subtitled 'A Story of the Present Time', *Heart and Science* is a highly topical novel, its most obvious purpose being to intervene in the vivisection controversy that raged in the press during the 1870s and 1880s. A central tool of neurological research, vivisection had entered mainstream medicine in Britain in the 1870s, giving rise to widespread opposition which peaked with the passing of the Cruelty to Animals Act in 1876. However, the abolitionists' campaign met with increasingly confident medical resistance after the International Medical Congress was held in London in 1881 and the eminent neurologist David Ferrier, author of *The Localisation of Cerebral Disease* (1876), was acquitted of performing vivisection without a licence later that year.[18] Picking up the controversy in the early 1880s, Collins engages with contemporary arguments as well as harking back to a longer humanitarian tradition – the Preface quotes 'Walter Scott's Opinion' that science 'hardens the heart'. Collins corresponded with both the anti-vivisection campaigner Frances Power Cobbe and the Surgeon-General Charles Gordon during 1882, and the novel dramatises the point, often made in the contemporary press, that vivisection represents 'bad science' and cannot lead to the genuine understanding of complex problems. The arguments against vivisection are forcefully expressed by Benjulia's brother, but they also come from within medicine itself – from the surgeon hero Ovid Vere, who represents the voice of orthodox science, and from the unnamed, mixed-race brain doctor, an echo of Ezra Jennings in *The Moonstone*, whose research leads to Carmina's cure. They even come from Ferrier himself, whom Collins cheekily quotes in both the Preface and the text to underline the difficulty of establishing causality in research on the brain.

Heart and Science therefore undercuts the polarities of its title, transposing the stark opposition between 'heart' and 'science' into a more complex relationship between legitimate and illegitimate knowledge. And in stressing the limits of medical understanding, the novel is perhaps Collins's most powerful exploration of the difficulty of comprehending the workings of the mind.[19] For in contrast to *The New Magdalen*'s melodramatic use of physiognomy, the naturalistic narrative constantly stresses the limitations of using the face as the index of the self, while demonstrating how psychic trauma is somatically expressed. Carmina's illness forms the central medical mystery, but while the cure is finally framed as an organic illness within the parameters of orthodox inductive science, it is triggered by psychic shock – the trauma of being called '"an impudent bastard"' by Mrs Gallilee – which carries links to a buried past (ch. 45). The nameless doctor's notes stress that medical results are 'not infrequently obtained by indirect and unexpected means' and that his theories were based on two case histories of young women, 'each one having been hysterically affected by a serious moral shock; terminating . . . in simulated paralysis' (ch. 59).

Moreover, almost every character in the novel – male and female – exhibits some form of mental pathology. Mrs Gallilee finally degenerates into insanity and imbecility triggered by her husband's desertion as much as by the physical violence of Carmina's Italian nurse, Teresa, who savagely defends her charge. Teresa therefore represents 'primitive' passion and superstition. The governess Frances Minerva struggles with the pathological impulses generated by repressed sexual desire: 'If Inquisitive Science, vowed to medical research, could detect firmness of will, working at its steadiest repressive action – then the mystery of Miss Minerva's inner nature might possibly have been revealed,' the narrator comments ironically. 'As it was, nothing more remarkable exposed itself to view than an irritable temper; serving perhaps as safety-valve to an underlying explosive force' (ch. 5). The men, too, provide a range of case studies. Benjulia is fascinating for all his moral degeneracy – the *Spectator* found him a 'curiously interesting psychological study' – and his overweening professional ambition is presented as monomania leading to a nihilism that finally drives him to suicide.[20] Mr Gallilee, the family lawyer and the incompetent Dr Null are all pathologically weak and indecisive, while Ovid Vere is victim of that key condition of late-Victorian modernity – nervous depletion and exhaustion from overwork.

Detecting buried memory

The Law and the Lady and the oddly titled *'I Say No'* (1884) overturn the 'Gothic' figure of the passive heroine. Both feature resolute young women determined to reveal the secrets of the past, and in both cases apparent murder turns out to be suicide. But in the later novel, the mystery is finally solved by the diffident hero, as the final resolution merges into the marriage plot. In contrast, *The Law and the Lady* opens with Valeria Brinton's marriage to a man whose own mother describes him as '"one of the weakest of living mortals"' (ch. 23). Her discovery that Eustace Macallen had been tried for the murder of his first wife and her determination to overturn the Scottish 'Not Proven' verdict is driven by her desire to base her marriage on equality and trust: in the process she radically redefines the balance of power within matrimony itself.

With her 'strongly marked' eyebrows and 'aquiline' nose (ch. 1) Valeria bears a passing resemblance to Marian Halcombe, and she replaces Walter Hartright's opposition between masculine resolution and feminine patience with 'a woman's fortitude and a woman's sense of duty' (ch. 44). Yet even as she controls the narrative, Valeria presents herself as unstable and perverse. 'I seemed in some way to have lost my ordinary identity,' she notes, after assuming the disguise of conventional femininity to visit the ageing roué Major Fitz-David (ch. 8), and she becomes 'a new woman, with a new mind' after reading the report of her husband's trial (ch. 21). Moreover, as her quest develops Valeria comes to recognise her own murky motives in suspecting a sexual rival of committing the crime, and this forms one aspect of the novel's investigation of unconscious motivation and the difficulty of defining guilt. 'What do we know of our own lives? What do we know of the fulfilment of our dearest wishes?' she finally concludes (ch. 50).

In *The Law and the Lady*, as in *The Moonstone* (as Ronald R. Thomas discusses in this volume), it is the combined methods of psychological investigation and forensic science that establish the truth as much as law alone. The novel also complicates this process by splitting the investigation between different subjects and forms of knowledge, all of which are linked by the interpretative challenges posed by various forms of representation. Valeria stumbles on the depth of the mystery when she first discovers a photograph of her husband's mother, then, as she searches the Major's study, another of Eustace with Sara, his first wife. She is first led to the trial transcript as a sensational story: it is presented as a 'judicial drama' and draws on a range of testimonies: the evidence of the nurse and Miserrimus Dexter, Eustace's diary – the unreliability of which leaves the clear forensic evidence that Sara was poisoned inconclusive. Conversely, Valeria describes both her first interview with Dexter, and her later stratagem of noting his spontaneous associations, as 'experiments', in a transcription of a dreamlike memory which leads to the palimpsest of the dust-heap (the forgotten detritus of the household) and thus to Sara's confession of suicide. As in *The Moonstone*, the truth is finally verified by forensic science (a professional chemist pieces together the torn fragments of Sara's letter) supplemented by literary interpretation as the family lawyer fills in the gaps.

Miserrimus Dexter himself stands at the centre of this process. The most bizarre of Collins's creations, Dexter embodies the most excessive elements of sensation fiction and exaggerates them into a decadent aestheticism in his figure as well as his art: 'Persons who look for mere Nature in works of Art . . . are persons to whom Mr Dexter does not address himself with the brush,' he writes of his gruesome paintings (ch. 27). The subject of Valeria's experiments who sadistically experiments on his own mentally challenged servant, Dexter is presented as an outlandish case study, in whom it is impossible to draw a line between the mental and the physical, and who not only challenges all notions of a coherent self, but also moves between contemporary psychological frameworks and hints at a realm beyond all of them. 'This most multiform of human beings' (ch. 29), Dexter is a case of what F. W. H Myers would term 'multiplex personality', an intriguing case study who subsumes his personality into a range of historical heroes, and veers wildly between abject melancholy and narcissistic excess. He is clearly placed within a degenerative framework, reinforcing the links between genius and degeneration that were becoming increasingly prevalent. Yet as Kate Flint stresses in this volume, he is never completely other; Valeria's observation that he 'openly expresses . . . thoughts and feelings which most of us are ashamed of as weaknesses' (ch. 26) emphasises the continuum between the normal and deviant mind. It is Dexter, too, who perceives the disturbing similarity between Valeria and Sara, suggesting a pattern of perverse behaviour in Eustace's choice of his second wife that the resolution of the novel is unable to dispel.

Hidden legacies

Although Valeria is sidelined from the detective process in *The Law and the Lady* by her pregnancy, her quest is ultimately driven by her fear of the transmission of a shameful legacy from father to child. This question of how social and psychological legacies are transmitted between generations is taken up most explicitly in *The Fallen Leaves* and *The Legacy of Cain* (1888). Both novels rework the well-worn 'fairytale' trope of abandoned or substituted children into explorations of origins and the meaning of hidden inheritance. Both, too, set the family within a wider social fabric, and incorporate elements of the increasingly dominant degenerative discourse they explicitly attempt to resist. *The Fallen Leaves* is Collins's most overt attack on contemporary capitalism and a study of the interaction of social and psychic repression. The Prologue opens with John Farnaby, epitome of competitive individualism, stealing and disposing of his illegitimate child for the sake of respectability, and the family romance of separation and return is continually disrupted by the clashing of generic modes within the novel as a whole. *The Fallen Leaves* was widely regarded as a monumental failure ('ludicrously loathsome' Swinburne called it (*CH*, p. 261)); it veers between utopianism and naturalistic social investigation, domestic realism and lurid melodrama.[21] Yet this dissonance allows different forms of representation to coexist uneasily, refusing any clear resolution to the problems of social transmission that the novel probes, above all in the contrast between the emblematic hero Amelius Goldenheart and the lost child's mother Emma Farnaby.

The Christian Socialist Amelius highlights the hypocrisy of social conventions as he moves between polite society and the East End and embodies the possibility of a better world. However, his 'fatal lecture' links a recognition of the need to overcome structural economic divisions to the fear of social degeneration, and while his own home community in America practises an egalitarian communism, it allows only the healthy to reproduce. Amelius is another impossible figure – the product of utopian aspiration, without history or memory. While he unwitting discovers Emma's daughter Sally – now a prostitute – the very fact that he is innocent of the morbid legacies of the Old World means that he is unable to survive in it: the story ends, as in *The New Magdalen*, with emigration. Sally is also an impossible figure who 'looked as though she had passed through the contamination of the streets without being touched by it' (Book 6, ch. 1); her apparant feeblemindedness protects her from the degeneracy that surrounds her rather than expressing it. Instead, the legacy of her exclusion and repression is born by her mother Emma, an extraordinary study of frustrated maternity, whose pathology lies not in neurasthenic weakness, but perverse bodily strength.

Collins's final completed novel, *The Legacy of Cain* is explicitly set up as a debate with the post-Darwinian theories of hereditary criminality and insanity that had become so pervasive by the late 1880s – indeed, the novel can be read as an extended meditation on Henry Maudsley's gloomy assertion that 'no one can escape the destiny that is innate in him and which unconsciously and irresistibly shapes his ends'.[22] Opening in a prison, the Prologue sets up three representative types – the prison governor (the narrator), the doctor and the minister – whose contrasting concepts of criminality and the relative power of heredity and environment are focused on the case of a convicted murderess; their hypotheses are tested in the story when the minister, Gracedieu, agrees to adopt the murderess's daughter and bring her up alongside his own child (this novel is perhaps the clearest instance of Collins's use of overtly emblematic names). However, he is secretly opposed by his wife, whose degraded character is briefly revealed to the prison governor before her death, and this means that the story traces a double process, as the two girls' natures are revealed in their diaries, and the social experiment takes the form of an exploration of consciousness. It soon becomes clear that Helena, Gracedieu's natural daughter, has incubated and developed the latent pathological tendencies of her apparently respectable mother; she is a full-blown case of 'moral insanity', pathologically self-possessed, who finally plots to poison her lover. Eunice, the adopted daughter whose birth mother was the convicted murderess, is, in contrast, naive and trusting, allowing her suitor to be stolen by her sister. Eunice's unconscious response to her mother's criminal legacy takes the form of a double consciousness in which a 'second self' is revealed in states of trance, but which Eunice is able to control and ultimately overcome.

Reviewing *The Legacy of Cain* in the *Spectator*, J. A. Noble compared the novel's 'intellectual scheme' with that of *Armadale* (1866): both works are 'implicit protests against the fatalism which is more or less bound up with . . . the modern doctrine of heredity'.[23] But the later novel lacks *Armadale*'s exploration of how legacies are internalised by the next generation (neither Eunice nor Helena is aware of her mother's history), and in exploiting the degenerationist assumptions he explicitly rejects, Collins is writing both in and against his time. The novel finally harks back to a belief in a moral management that is underpinned by an older notion of the individual soul. Helena's wickedness ultimately springs from herself rather than her mother, while Eunice is able to resist *her* criminal mother's unconscious admonitions. Yet for all its tendentiousness, there is still something undecidable about *The Legacy of Cain*. Helena's narrative takes on an increasingly melodramatic tone, and while both girls' diaries are framed by the prison governor's memoirs, there is ultimately no absolute narrative authority. Collins 'may occasionally have a theory to illustrate, but he always has a story to tell, and the story is more important, both to him and his readers than the theory', Noble noted (*CH*, p. 221). The later fiction dramatises just how unstable Collins's stories, theories and, resting on both, identities, remain.

NOTES

1. A. C. Swinburne, 'Wilkie Collins', *Fortnightly Review*, 1 November 1889; *CH*, p. 262.
2. *Spectator*, 15 May 1880; *CH*, p. 208.
3. Peter Keating, *The Haunted Study: A Social History of the English Novel 1875–1914* (London: Secker & Warburg 1989), ch. 1.
4. See Kelly Hurley, *The Gothic Body: Sexuality, Materialism and Degeneration at the Fin de Siècle* (Cambridge: Cambridge University Press, 1996).
5. *Athenaeum*, 20 February, 1875, 258.
6. See the Introduction to Graham Law (ed), *The Evil Genius* (Peterborough, Canada: Broadview Literary Texts, 1994), pp. 9–17.
7. See Rick Rylance, *Victorian Psychology and British Culture 1850–1880* (Oxford: Oxford University Press, 2000), ch. 1.
8. See Jenny Bourne Taylor, *In the Secret Theatre of Home: Wilkie Collins, Sensation Narrative and Nineteenth-Century Psychology* (London: Routledge, 1988).
9. See William Greenslade, *Culture, Degeneration and the Novel* (Cambridge: Cambridge University Press, 1994), ch. 1.
10. See Ann Harrington, *Medicine, Mind and the Double Brain* (Princeton: Princeton University Press 1987).
11. See Jill L. Matus, 'Trauma, Memory and Railway Disaster: The Dickensian Connection', *Victorian Studies* 43:3 (2001), 413–36, and Mark S. Micale and Paul Lerner (eds.), *Traumatic Pasts: History, Psychiatry and Trauma in the Modern Age, 1870–1930* (Cambridge: Cambridge University Press, 2001).
12. See William Baker, *Wilkie Collins's Library: A Reconstruction* (Westport, CT: Greenwood Press, 2002).
13. F. B. Winslow, *On Obscure Diseases of the Brain and Disorders of the Mind*, 2nd edn., (London: John W. Davis, 1861), p. 201.
14. Harrington, *Medicine, Mind and the Double Brain,* p. 74.
15. T. S. Eliot, 'Wilkie Collins and Dickens' (1927), in Eliot, *Selected Essays 1917–1932* (London: Faber and Faber, 1932), p. 415.
16. See Laurence Talairach-Vielmas, 'Mad Scientists and Chemical Ghosts: On Collins's "Materialist Supernaturalism"', *Wilkie Collins Society Journal* 7 (2004), 3–20 (10–11).
17. See Piya Pal-Lapinski, 'Chemical Seductions: Exoticism, Toxicology and the Female Poisoner in *Armadale* and *The Legacy of Cain*', in Maria K. Bachman and Don Richard Cox (eds.), *Reality's Dark Light: The Sensational Wilkie Collins* (Knoxville: University of Tennessee Press, 2003), pp. 94–130.

18. See the Introduction and Appendix to Steve Falmer (ed.), *Heart and Science, A Story of the Present Time* (Peterborough, Canada: Broadview Literary Texts, 1996), and Richard D. French, *Antivivisection and Medical Science in Victorian Society* (Princeton: Princeton University Press, 1975).

19. C. S. Wiesenthal, 'From Charcot to Plato: The History of Hysteria in *Heart and Science*', in Nelson Smith and R. C. Terry (eds.), *Wilkie Collins to the Forefront: Some Reassessments* (New York: AMS Press, 1995), pp. 257–68.

20. Unsigned review, *Spectator*, 26 May 1883; *CH*, p. 217.

21. Ann-Marie Beller, '"Too Absurdly Repulsive": Generic Indeterminacy and the Failure of *The Fallen Leaves*', in Andrew Manghan (ed.), *The Topical Wilkie Collins: Interdisciplinary and Historical Essays in a Victorian Writer* (Newcastle: Cambridge Scholar Press, 2006).

22. Henry Maudsley, *Body and Mind, An Inquiry into their Connection and Mutual Influence, Specially in Reference to Mental Disorders*, 2nd edn. (London: Macmillan & Co., 1873), p. 76.

23. J. A. Noble, unsigned review, *Spectator*, 26 January 1889; *CH*, p. 221.

7

GRAHAM LAW

The professional writer and the literary marketplace

The defining moment of Wilkie Collins's career occurred at the turn of the 1860s with the runaway success of *The Woman in White*. The novel's striking combination of respectable settings and illicit events launched the fashion for 'sensation fiction' which prevailed through much of the next two decades, thus marking a breakthrough in the marketing of fiction as a commodity form. Running as a serial in Charles Dickens's new family weekly *All the Year Round* from November 1859, the narrative aroused wide interest with its eerily enigmatic opening and deft manipulation of suspense, causing queues on publication day and raising the circulation into six figures. When the novel appeared from Sampson Low in three volumes for the lending libraries in mid-August 1860, it was widely advertised, sold 1,350 copies within the week and received its eighth impression before the end of the year. When the single-volume edition appeared from the same publisher in April 1861, embellished with a signed likeness of the author, Collins had to sit several times for the photographer to keep pace with the demand.

The popularity of *The Woman in White* was not limited to Britain. Translations into German and French, for example, were already in train before the end of 1860, while copy had been sold early to Harper & Brothers in America so that the novel was issued simultaneously in London and New York.[1] Although the author's own dramatisation of *The Woman in White* was not produced until ten years later, unauthorised theatrical productions began to appear as early as November 1860, and theatrical pirates were by no means the only commercial operators to cash in at the peak of the novel's popularity. Then, as attested by advertising in papers such as the *Illustrated London News*, 'every possible commodity was labelled "Woman in White". There were "Woman in White" cloaks and bonnets, "Woman in White" perfumes and . . . toilet requisites, "Woman in White" Waltzes and Quadrilles'.[2] While there was little direct financial reward to Collins from much of this exploitation of his narrative, the publicity helped to boost his bargaining power so

97

that he could boast to his mother in July 1861 that he had 'got to the top of the tree' (*B&C* I, 197–8). By this time, in addition to a substantial sum for a cheap edition of the earlier fiction, Sampson Low had offered £3,000 to lease the volume rights to *No Name* (1862), while Smith, Elder & Co. had put up £5,000 to purchase the entire copyright of *Armadale* (1866). The need to negotiate deals such as these encouraged Collins gradually to seek more professional assistance in the business of authorship, while the flow of income from *The Woman in White* itself prompted him to open a personal account at Coutts Bank for the first time.[3]

The opening and closing stages of Collins's career were inevitably less of a triumph. His youthful first novel, the exotic romance *Ioláni*, went the rounds of the London publishers in 1845 but never saw the light of day. His first published book was the modestly successful *Memoirs of the Life of William Collins Esq., RA*, his painter father, published in 1848 by Longmans on a subscription basis, so that many of Collins's early extant business letters take the form of obsequious appeals to his father's aristocratic patrons. In 1850, after the completed historical novel *Antonina* was rejected by Smith, Elder (despite the recommendation of John Ruskin), Collins was concerned that he might be forced to finance its publication personally. Thus the author jumped at an offer of £200 for the copyright from Richard Bentley, who went on not only to publish a series of Collins's short pieces in his house monthly, *Bentley's Miscellany*, but also to issue the author's next two triple-decker novels, both rather daring in their social and sexual themes. The copyright of *Basil* (1852) brought the author £350, but in the middle of the Crimean War the price for *Hide and Seek* (1854) fell back to £150. Less than 500 copies of the three-volume edition of the latter work were sold, and there was to be no single-volume edition for seven years. The opening decade of the author's career thus offered few hints of the extraordinary success to follow. It was not until Collins had proved his worth to Dickens as a resourceful contributor to *Household Words*, and had been rewarded with the chance to write his first full-length serial novel (*The Dead Secret* of 1857), that conditions were right for a palpable hit like *The Woman in White*.

Yet Victorian print culture continued to undergo rapid change and Collins's period at 'the top of the tree' was in fact to last little more than a decade. *The Woman in White* represented a breakthrough in middle-class publishing, with success measured by sales in tens of thousands; by the 1880s there were already clear signs of the emergence of a mass market for fiction creating access to an audience in hundreds of thousands in Britain alone. Among the major developments there were the syndication of fiction in popular weekly newspapers, and the rise of the 'shilling shocker', a compact novel of mystery and suspense sold especially at railway stations and in the holiday seasons. Collins was by no means averse to exploring these new publishing media: he composed the first of a series of newspaper serials with *Jezebel's Daughter* of 1879–80 and in 1886 produced *The Guilty River* for one of the popular Christmas annuals. Yet evidence both literary and economic suggests that Collins was unable to respond to the demands of these new markets with quite the same verve as, in the case of the newspaper serial, women sensationalists like Mary Braddon, or, in the case of the cheap thriller, younger exponents of suspense like Arthur Conan Doyle.[4] Although the ageing Collins was often annoyed when billed simply as 'Author of "The Woman in White"', he was himself prone to invoke the comparison when his literary standing was in question. 'My own vainglorious idea is that I have never written such a first number since "The Woman in White"', he wrote to Andrew Chatto of *Heart and Science* in June 1882 (*BGL&L*, III, 344). Yet *Heart and Science* was far from topping the bestseller lists of 1882–3, when larger headlines were being made by newcomers like 'F. Anstey', with his comic fantasy *Vice-Versâ*, or 'Hugh Conway', with the political thriller *Called Back*.

Nevertheless, from its beginnings amid the vestiges of the patronage system to the clear signs of the rise of a mass fiction market accompanying its close, the literary career of Wilkie Collins offers extraordinary insights into contemporary developments in print-capitalism. These related changes include:

- the gradual commodification of the literary work, resulting from the introduction of methods of production, packaging and promotion similar to those used to market new brand household goods such as Pear's Soap or Bird's Custard Powder;
- the increasing legal codification of copyright at both the national and international level, including new serial and performance rights, thus serving to enhance the concept, and raise the value, of literary property;
- the growing professionalisation of authorship, marked by the creation of organisations such as the Society of Authors, incorporated in 1884, to represent and defend the interests of those making a living by their pens; and
- the widening divide between 'popular' and 'serious' readerships, which Wilkie Collins himself had been quick to note in 'The Unknown Public', a leading article written for *Household Words* as early as 1858.

Although Collins was generally keen to exploit new publishing trends, his reactions to these developments were often complex and contradictory. This is well illustrated in the author's correspondence, where nearly half of the surviving letters concern the business of publishing and performance.[5] This chapter will consider how the author negotiated the changing world of publishing through the different stages of his career, focusing on five distinct areas: periodical publishing and serialisation; volume publication and the lending libraries; the dramatisation of narrative for theatrical performance; the internationalisation of the fiction market; and the emergence of the professional literary agent. Together these constitute a fascinating case study in the sociology of literature in the second half of the nineteenth century.

Periodical publishing and serialisation

Nineteenth-century bourgeois culture was especially receptive to the expansive, cumulative rhythm of narrative in serial form.[6] Almost throughout the Victorian period, the rigidity of the market for new books – geared to expensive multivolume editions in small print runs for the circulating libraries – encouraged a mode of prior part-publication characterised by variety and innovation. By the second half of the century, there were few novelists who did not issue their work initially in instalments of some kind. But Collins has a special place in the development of the serial market because of his enthusiastic response to the shift from the more leisurely monthly number to the compact weekly instalment.[7] In the early Victorian decades, the predominance of monthly serialisation had been reinforced by the startling success of Dickens's first two instalment novels – *Pickwick Papers* (1836–7) in independent fascicles and *Oliver Twist* (1837–8) in the columns of *Bentley's Miscellany*. Dickens always preferred the open spaces of the monthly number, but in the 1860s it was Collins who experienced a sense of exhilaration in 'winning the battle against the infernal periodical system', as he wrote to his mother (26 July 1860, *B&C* I, 184), and who learnt most adeptly to exploit the mechanics of enigma and suspense encouraged by the weekly number. These included the striking opening to increase the chance of a serial's 'taking' with the subscribers, the episodic integrity of the short instalment, and frequent 'climax and curtain' endings to make readers come back for more. But with *The Woman in White* Collins also added a strikingly original use of multiple narration, refusing the 'hearsay evidence' of a third party and instead stipulating that the text be inscribed by 'more than one pen, as the story of an offence against the laws is told in Court by more than one witness' (p. 5).

From 1857 onwards, therefore, Collins's novels and short stories were all published initially in periodical form, with the majority appearing in weekly journals. Exceptions were *Armadale* in Smith, Elder's *Cornhill Magazine* from 1864, and a handful of late novels in literary monthlies of lesser standing such as *Temple Bar*. But Collins felt most at home in Dickens's weekly papers, where shared editorial responsibilities and collaboration with his mentor on the special Christmas issues often imparted to the writing a spirit of camaraderie or rivalry.[8] Dickens was not only happy to allow *The Moonstone* (1868) to stretch to thirty-two parts though only twenty-six had been originally planned, but had even offered assistance with his own pen for *No Name*, when illness threatened Collins's 'advance on the press'. After Dickens's death, though, Collins was forced to explore new weekly venues, which could be less hospitable as well as more lucrative. Unlike many of his fellow sensation novelists – notably Mary Elizabeth Braddon with *Belgravia*, Ellen (Mrs Henry) Wood with *Argosy*, and James Payn with *Chambers's Journal* – he had refused offers to act as the editor of a journal which would provide a vehicle for his own serials.[9] Thus most of his new fiction appeared in popular penny miscellanies such as *Cassell's Magazine*, illustrated middle-class family papers such as the *Graphic*, and, most importantly, syndicates of provincial newspapers via organisations such as Tillotson & Son's 'Fiction Bureau' of Bolton, Lancashire.

The results were often uncomfortable. Like Dickens, Collins came to find the demands of the weekly instalment physically debilitating, and there was now much less flexibility as regards shortening a number or extending the run. For example, although he earned a record sum for the sale of the serial rights for *The Evil Genius* (1885–6) to Tillotson & Son, Collins was exasperated when his instalments fell far short of the minimum word-count stipulated in the contract, provoking loud complaints from syndicate members like the *Chicago Daily News*. At the same time, he found that the owners of the weekly journals tended to treat the products of his labours in a less respectful manner than the literary publishing houses: *Cassell's Magazine* wanted a 'damn it' deleted from *Man and Wife* (1870) (25 September 1869, *BGL&L* II, 152), and the *Graphic* peremptorily censored what it saw as 'an attempted violation of the heroine' of *The Law and the Lady* (1875) (20 March 1875, *B&C* II, 391), while a livelier opening and a more striking title were demanded by the 'curious savages' who comprised the newspaper syndicate for *Heart and Science* (8 February 1882, *B&C* II, 442). By the turn of the 1880s, authors like Collins were earning significantly more from serial than book rights, but the concomitant stresses and strains represented a substantial hidden cost.

Volume publication and the lending libraries

The priority given to periodical publication must be seen as a principal reason for Collins switching so restlessly between imprints when his works were issued in volume form. Another was the influence of his mentor Dickens, who taught the young writer that publishers' agreements must be treated with suspicion if authors' rights were to be secured. As we have seen, in the early stages Collins was content to sell his copyrights outright to a single firm. But by the mid-1850s Bentley was in dire financial straits, which forced him not only to sell the *Miscellany* (with its circulation now down to a few thousand) but also to try discreetly to trade back copyrights acquired from authors such as Collins. So at the height of his success, the author tended rather to auction his forthcoming work to the highest bidder, preferring to lease the copyright but still willing to sell if the price seemed high enough, and not infrequently opting for agreements combining serial and volume rights. There were sometimes errors of judgement, as with the decision to entrust the book publication of *Man and Wife* on commission to the antiquarian bookseller F. S. Ellis. Ellis had never before issued a novel and, Collins wrote to William Tindall, kept the appearance of the book 'as profound a secret' as possible (26 June 1870, *B&C* II, 343). The restlessness with publishers is revealed in Collins's surviving letters: there are extensive correspondences with Richard Bentley, Sampson Low, Smith, Elder, and Chatto & Windus, all of which carried at least three of his works, as well as more limited exchanges with the likes of Hurst & Blackett or Tinsley Brothers, which published only one. The largest charts the relationship with Chatto & Windus beginning in the mid-1870s; thereafter the firm issued virtually all Collins's new fiction in volume form and gradually acquired the rights to earlier work. The Bentley correspondence, however, covers a far longer time span and offers the clearest insight into the evolution of the author's thinking concerning the luxury editions dictated by the circulating libraries.

Led by Mudie's 'Select Library' with its increasingly prim notions of literary propriety, these institutions offered major financial incentives to the London publishers to resist the temptations of either a popular or a progressive audience. Collins did not live to see the final sinking of the triple-decker in the mid-1890s, but his distrust of the monopolistic conservatism of the library owners is apparent from the start. While working on *Hide and Seek*, Collins offered his support to Bentley in a bold but finally abortive plan to bypass the libraries by 'lowering the present extravagantly absurd prices charged for works of fiction' (17 August 1853, *BGL&L* I, 87). Those feelings had hardened to disgust and anger by the early 1870s, when the poor sales of *Poor Miss Finch* (1872) were put down to 'the present insanely-absurd system of Circulating Library publication' (22 March 1872, *BGL&L* II, 335), or when there was an attempt to censor the title of *The New Magdalen* (1873) by that 'ignorant fanatic' Mudie (18 March

1873, *BGL&L* II, 387). However, by the last decade of his career, in the face of often indifferent reviews, and with the sales of work both new and old in decline, Collins often had reason to be glad of the protection offered by the library system. In a late letter to George Bentley he still railed against the 'rubbish in three volumes, which Mr Mudie buys cheap, and forces on his customers' (6 January 1885, *BGL&L* IV, 79), but the complaint was by then something of a ritual. New novels in a single volume were no longer a rarity, whether naturalist experiments by George Moore or exotic romances from Rider Haggard. But Collins's only effort at a short thriller, *The Guilty River*, left the Bristol publisher Arrowsmith with thousands of unsold copies of his Christmas Annual on his hands, while his more substantial new work remained in the by now safe grooves of sensationalism and thus raised no objections from Mudie.[10]

Moreover, Collins was never entirely comfortable with the most obvious solution to the Mudie monopoly – to sell cheap books to the mass of the population rather than loan luxury editions to the select few. If he always disliked the sumptuous library edition, he also became suspicious of the glossy yellowback. This was aimed principally at the railway market and sold typically at two shillings, not a small sum, but the cheapest format in which reprint fiction was issued until the gaudy sixpenny paperback appeared shortly before his death. Collins believed that Sampson Low had damaged his long-term interests by flooding the market with yellowback copies of *The Woman in White* in 1865, and thereafter insisted on a clause in his publishing agreements significantly delaying issues in railway format. Collins remained fondest throughout of the solid cloth-bound reprint, but his constant switching of publishers effectively prevented the creation of a uniform edition until late in his career. Such editions, it should be remembered, encouraged repeat purchases and customer loyalty in a similar way to serial publication. Here there is an instructive contrast with the case of Ellen Wood. Following the success of *East Lynne*, the hit of the year after *The Woman in White*, Bentley continued to issue all Wood's fiction in volume form until the house was sold at the end of the century, more than a decade after the author's death. In the mid-1870s Collins was astounded to learn by quite how far the sales of his reprinted novels were outstripped by those of his more conservative rival. This helps to explain his decision to establish a permanent relationship with Chatto & Windus – though by then it was too late to catch up. This must also be at least part of the reason why Wood's *post mortem* literary reputation remained in good repair for a good deal longer. It is difficult to avoid the conclusion that Collins's short-term success in the periodicals was purchased at the expense of long-term prosperity through his reprinted novels.

Dramatisation of narrative for theatrical performance

In defending the melodramatic qualities of *Basil* (1852), Collins argued in the Preface that the novel and play were 'twin-sisters in the family of Fiction'. The idea should be familiar to a generation accustomed to novelists turning their hands to screenplays (or even composing fiction with an eye already on the cinematic adaptation), and certainly the sisters are often conflated in the course of Collins's own career. Yet, given that his role as a professional dramatist began in spectacular failure with *The Red Vial* of 1858, and ended in humiliating farce in 1883 when *Rank and Riches* was laughed off the stage, we need to consider why he spent so much time writing for the theatre.

In the late 1840s the young Collins brothers had regularly turned the family's back drawing room into the 'Theatre Royal, Blandford Square' for domestic performances. Whether in London or Paris, Wilkie was an inveterate theatregoer, and among his duties on the *Leader* in the early 1850s was reviewing the latest plays. It was again the author's love of things theatrical that first brought him into contact with Dickens in 1851: as well as performing together, Dickens and Collins worked closely on Wilkie's early playscripts *The Lighthouse* (1855) and *The Frozen Deep* (1856). Collins's first effort at dramatising his own fiction was also with Dickens on the 1860 Christmas story *A Message from the Sea*, while his decision to make a reading tour of North America in 1873–4 was widely interpreted as a misguided attempt to follow again in his master's footsteps. Yet it would be a mistake to see Collins's writings for the theatre merely as an expression of a juvenile passion for footlights and grease paint. For there is a lengthy period from the late 1860s when more of his energy goes into the play than the novel; indeed, on several occasions, he threatens to abandon fiction altogether. Within ten years, in addition to collaborations with Dickens on *No Thoroughfare* (1867) and Charles Fechter on *Black and White* (1869), plus the long American reading tour, we see Collins creating adaptations of all his great sensation novels of the 1860s, and cutting corners by simultaneously working on the narrative and dramatic versions of *Man and Wife* and *The New Magdalen*.

Clearly, one attraction of theatrical performance was that it seemed to promise escape from the Grundyish interference of publishers, editors or librarians, and offer relatively unmediated access to a wide audience. (Collins seems to have been less anxious about the threat of stage censorship, in part because from 1874 this was in the hands of his friend Edward Pigott, at the Lord Chamberlain's office.) At the same time, success at the box office then promised profits on a scale no longer in prospect from his new fiction. During this period there are moments of triumph and elation for the author. A couple of weeks into the six-month run of *No Thorough-fare*, for example, Collins crows to his mother, 'Every night the Theatre is crammed. This speculation on the public taste is paying, and promises long to pay me, from fifty to fifty-five pounds a week' (17 January 1868, *BGL&L* II, 105). The specific pressure inciting Collins to make plays out of his fiction, however, was the sense of outrage at the inadequacy of legal protection for the plots and characters created by the Victorian novelist. From almost the beginning of his career Dickens's novels had been subject to unauthorised dramatisation, while another intimate literary friend, Charles Reade, was not only a regular dramatiser of his own fiction, but also an inveterate litigant in defence of his rights as author. But a series of legal actions by Reade in the early 1860s served mainly to confirm that 'representing the incidents of a published novel in a dramatic form upon the stage, although done publicly and for profit, is no infringement of copyright'.[11] Since there were plenty of managers ready to take advantage of loopholes in the law which remained unplugged until the end of his career, the ageing Collins could sum up the situation in a single curt sentence to Hall Caine: 'the stupid copyright law of England allows any scoundrel possessing a pot of paste and a pair of scissors to steal our novels for stage purposes' (8 February 1888, *BGL&L* IV, 299).

The only recourse for the novelist, it emerged, was to issue a dramatic version in which copyright would pertain – if it were duly registered at Stationer's Hall and/or given a public performance. Here timing was of the essence and there was often an unseemly scramble for precedence, resulting in the bizarre practice of one-off performances without costumes or scenery for copyright purposes only. And the situation was complicated by the lack of reciprocal legal protection for theatrical works between the United Kingdom and the United States, and thus the danger of losing domestic copyright through prior performances across the Atlantic.[12] Near the end of his career Collins made a final, forlorn attempt to compose narrative and dramatic versions of a single plot with *The Evil Genius* (1886), writing to Henry Pigott:

> Alack-a-day the barbarous copyright laws of England, and no laws of America, force me to write a play as well as a novel this time – and have this play acted *first* otherwise (the story I am now writing being essentially dramatic in subject) I shall be robbed here and in the U. S. and lose (literally) thousands of pounds. The loss I can suffer with some patience – but when I think of the pockets into which the ill-earned money goes, I am not far from going distracted.　　　　　　　(13 October 1885, *BGL&L* IV, 122)

But in the end there was neither loss nor gain but only distraction: although the still incomplete play underwent a ritual 'copyright performance', it seems never to have been professionally produced, with or without the author's permission, either in Britain or overseas. Since Collins had recognised early 'the misleading influence . . . of following the story of a novel in writing a play' (16 February 1859, *BGL&L* I, 173), it is unsurprising that his attempts to control the dramatic realisations of his own narratives led as often to frustration as fulfillment.

Internationalisation of the fiction market

The appearances of Collins's work in New York theatres or Chicago newspapers are among many reflections of the internationalisation of the literary market which occurred during the later nineteenth century, with London and Paris functioning as the dominant metropolitan centres.[13] His novels were quickly translated into French from the mid-1850s, either as *romans feuilletons* or as volumes from the house of Hachette – and not only into French. Referring to the serial run of *The New Magdalen* in *Temple Bar*, Collins sent a cocky apology to George Bentley:

> I'm really quite ashamed of the number of copies of the Magazine which I circulate among my translators . . . Dutch, German, and Russian translations are all in progress – and now I am told that there is likely to be a 'market' for me in Sweden, Poland, and (I think) Denmark. (12 February 1873, *BGL&L* II, 378)

But the picture was not always so rosy: earlier, when *Poor Miss Finch* was about to be serialised, the author had written exasperatedly to Cassell's:

> I am getting so weary of the vexatious and absurd regulations which these foreign laws impose on English literature, that I am strongly disposed to let myself be robbed, as the preferable alternative to letting myself be worried. (2 August 1871, *BGL&L* II, 265)

The French Republic had been the pioneer in defining the concept of *droit moral* and extending its protection to foreign citizens, while Britain had taken a more commercial approach in a series of bilateral copyright conventions established from the beginning of Victoria's reign.[14] Together these two were the leaders among the Western European nations which created the International Copyright Union through the Berne Convention of 1886 – perhaps unsurprisingly given that the interests of French and British authors were those most at stake. Several smaller European states – notably the Netherlands – were slow to sign up and insisted on domestic manufacture if the rights of outsiders were to be secured. Again following Dickens, Collins was vigorous in his denunciations of what he saw as acts of international piracy. In late 1869 he launched a heavy-handed publicity stunt when Belinfante Brothers of The Hague carried an unauthorised Dutch translation of *Man and Wife* in their house journal. With the benefit of hindsight, the blame might just as fairly have been laid at the door of the British government for failing to propose a treaty with the Netherlands. Nevertheless, the buccaneers promptly capitulated and became thereafter Collins's official Dutch publishers.[15]

In economic terms, however, continental Europe – where the profits were eaten into by the costs of translation – was far less important than the current and former imperial dominions where English prevailed. However, in North America in particular the complexities and inadequacies of colonial and international copyright conventions were a major source of anxiety and loss. Despite campaigns by local authors like William Cullen Bryant and the advocacy of eminent visitors like Dickens, America resisted all reciprocal copyright arrangements until after Collins's death. Even the Chace Act of 1891 remained heavily protectionist, in that the work of foreign authors had to be physically produced in the country for copyright to pertain. In spite of the barriers, Collins went to great lengths to tap the potential of the vast North American marketplace. He soon took a personal hand in forwarding to his approved American publishers the required 'advance sheets' – early proofs designed to give them a lengthy start over unauthorised rivals.[16] In the case of *The Woman in White*, for example, the first American book edition – Harper's single paper-covered volume with plates by John McLenan – cost only 75 cents, less than a tenth of the guinea and a half charged for the unillustrated triple-decker from Sampson Low in London, and we can be certain that the publishers' sales, if not the author's receipts, were considerably higher on the other side of the Atlantic.

In theory British copyright legislation extended throughout the Empire, but the long open border with America meant that imperial legislation was in practice unenforceable in Canada. Collins was a pioneer in establishing contacts there with the Toronto publishers Hunter, Rose and in arranging for domestic editions to protect his interests. Yet this move led to unforeseen problems, since the cheap Canadian imprints were promptly exported across the open border, causing Harper's to cry foul. Collins conducted an extended correspondence with his authorised publishers in both New York and Toronto, letters which constitute a unique record of the working out of these complex tensions in an early phase of what we have since learnt to call globalisation. But these documents also suggest that Collins failed to recognise that the circulating library monopoly, which he had so often attacked for its socioeconomic effects at home, caused quite as much damage abroad.

Although he was not alone in this, there were other British authors like Matthew Arnold who saw clearly that 'the highly eccentric, artificial, and unsatisfactory system' of the British book trade was a major barrier to copyright reciprocity; unlike Collins, Arnold was thus convinced that the people of North America 'ought not to submit to our absurd system of dear books; . . . as a lover of civilisation, I should be sorry, though I am an author, if they did'.[17]

Emergence of the professional literary agent

Throughout the Victorian period British copyright law was confusing even to specialists. The 1842 Copyright Act had left many earlier provisions in force and was itself subject to many amendments, so that its interpretation in the courts became something of a lottery. In 1878 the Royal Commission on Copyright damned the existing legislation as 'wholly destitute of any sort of arrangement, incomplete, often obscure, and even when it is intelligible upon long study, it is in many parts so ill-expressed that no one who does not give such study to it can expect to understand it'.[18] The situation was particularly fraught concerning periodical publication and theatrical performance. The Commission commented that conflicting judgements left in doubt the question of whether the contents of newspapers were subject to copyright; at the same time, noting the dual nature of dramatic works, it proposed that the publication of a play should simultaneously confer performance rights, and vice-versa. But none of the recommendations was taken up with any urgency and it was not until the Copyright Act of 1911 that there was comprehensive reform of domestic law. And, as we have already seen, international copyright conventions remained in flux throughout the later decades of the century. These legal complexities presented authors who wished to exploit their literary capital to the full with a clear set of alternatives: either they must themselves develop greater legal and business acumen, or else employ professional agents to act on their behalf.

Wilkie Collins attempted consistently to do both. From the early 1850s we see him turning increasingly to his friend Charles Ward, a banker at Coutts, not only for fresh supplies of cash but also for advice in legal and financial questions regarding his writing. After the success of *The Woman in White*, he confers more regularly with Benham and Tindell, solicitors with experience in the business of publishing. From the early 1870s, he also begins to utilise a number of specialist representatives overseas, such as the Wall Street lawyer William D. Booth who handles theatrical problems in America, or the translator Alberto Cacchia who also acts as his registration agent for Italy. And in late 1881 he becomes the first major client of

A. P. Watt, the pioneer British professional literary agent. In the extensive surviving correspondence between Collins and Watt we can see the work of the literary agent being gradually and tentatively defined. While there are one or two engagements which turn sour, Collins's relations with his business representatives are generally amicable, and those with Tindell and Watt in particular gradually evolve into warm friendships. Yet the letters to his various agents suggest that, with his early legal training, Collins was often better informed than they were. In other words, he tends to keep a dog but still bark himself.

At other times we sense damaging conflicts of interest, as when Watt's firm (registered simply as 'The Literary Agency') acts simultaneously for both author and publisher or itself takes on the role of syndicating Collins's fiction in direct competition with Tillotson & Son. Often it seems that there are too many middlemen in the space between author and reader, and that the growth of agency generates as many stresses as it removes. Thus not all authors were convinced of the benefits of representation. Not long after Collins's death, the correspondence columns of the *Times* carried a heated exchange on 'New Literary Factors', that is, literary agents like Watt, syndicators like Tillotson & Son, and organisations representing the writing profession like the Society of Authors. The romantic novelist 'Ouida' was vehemently against all three, arguing that 'everything which assimilates literature to a trade . . . injures its quality and dwarfs its standard'.[19] As founding chairman of the society, Walter Besant briskly defended the activities of the new agencies, on the grounds that they enhanced the value of literary property and advanced the profession of authorship.[20] As one of the honorary vice-presidents of the society, Collins would surely have found more to support in Besant's position, but there was also a side of him in sympathy with Ouida's outcry.

The tensions noted in each of these five spheres of literary business are reminiscent of those encountered in Collins's prescient article 'The Unknown Public', which, in discussing the extensive proletarian readership of the popular 'penny-novel-journals' in 1858, had predicted that 'the readers who rank by millions will be the readers who give the widest reputations, who return the richest rewards, and who will, therefore, command the service of the best writers of their time'.[21] Nevertheless, Collins clearly felt no temptation to engage at once with such an audience, though fellow sensationalists like Braddon or Reade were already prepared to take the plunge. Indeed, Collins's article as a whole reveals a curious embarrassment at the prospect of a popular readership: the tone is comic, yet the laughter is directed uniformly downwards at 'the habits, the tastes, and the average intelligence of the Unknown Public'. It is then perhaps not surprising that his later encounters with the controllers of the new literary media, and indeed with the emerging mass audience itself, were often uncomfortable. Collins's uncertain reactions can thus be seen as symptoms of the growing divide between romantic and professional views of authorship, between 'gentlemanly' and 'commercial' modes of production, and between 'popular' and 'serious' readerships. Despite earlier triumphs like *The Woman in White*, it is apparent that, amid these rapid changes in the fiction marketplace, Collins became increasingly anxious about his literary income and unsure of his literary status.

NOTES

1. On the publishing history of *The Woman in White*, see Andrew Gasson, *Wilkie Collins: An Illustrated Guide* (Oxford: Oxford University Press, 1998).
2. S. M. Ellis, *Wilkie Collins, Le Fanu and Others* (London: Constable, 1931) pp. 29–30.
3. Throughout the 1850s Collins had continued to share an account at Coutts with his mother and brother.
4. See Graham Law, 'Yesterday's Sensations: Modes of Publication and Narrative Form in Collins's Late Works', in Maria K. Bachman and Don Richard Cox (eds.), *Reality's Dark Light: The Sensational Wilkie Collins* (Knoxville: University of Tennessee Press, 2003), pp. 329–60.
5. See Introduction, *BGL&L* I, xxiii–xxviii.
6. See Linda K. Hughes and Michael Lund, *The Victorian Serial* (Charlottesville: University Press of Virginia, 1991), ch. 1.
7. See Graham Law, *Serializing Fiction in the Victorian Press* (Basingstoke: Palgrave, 2000), ch. 1.
8. See Lillian Nayder, *Unequal Partners: Charles Dickens, Wilkie Collins, and Victorian Authorship* (Ithaca: Cornell University Press, 2002).
9. Notably from the publisher Alexander Strahan in 1862–3; see the letter to John Hollingshead, 15 January 1863, *BGL&L* I, 288–9.
10. Compare George Moore's virulent attack on Mudie in his pamphlet *Literature at Nurse, or Circulating Morals* (London: Vizetelly, 1885).
11. From the judgement in the case of *Reade v. Conquest* of 1862; see John Russell Stephens, *The Profession of the Playwright: British Theatre 1800–1900* (Cambridge: Cambridge University Press, 1992), pp. 97–105.
12. See Stephens, *The Profession of the Playwright*, pp. 105–13.
13. See Franco Moretti, *Atlas of the European Novel, 1800–1900* (London: Verso, 1998).
14. See David Saunders, *Authorship and Copyright* (London: Routledge, 1992), chs. 3 and 5.
15. See James Payn and Wilkie Collins, *A National Wrong*, (1869) ed. Andrew Gasson, Graham Law and Paul Lewis (London: Wilkie Collins Society, 2004) pp. 1–8.
16. See Saunders, *Authorship and Copyright*, ch. 6.

17. Matthew Arnold, 'Copyright', *Fortnightly Review* 159 (March 1880), 319–34.
18. Cited in Victor Bonham-Carter, *Authors by Profession: From the Introduction of Printing until the Copyright Act 1911* (London: Society of Authors, 1978), p. 98.
19. *The Times*, 22 May 1891, 3.
20. Ibid., 8.
21. [Wilkie Collins], 'The Unknown Public', *Household Words* 18 (21 August 1858), 217–22.

8

CAROLYN DEVER

The marriage plot and its alternatives

Wilkie Collins wrote novels of love and marriage which rigorously challenge the privileged status of marital love in both Victorian culture and modern fiction, even as he resolves sensational plots driven by deception, disguise, doubling, secrecy and criminal manipulation into the familiar conclusion of loving wedded bliss. Marriage is both a formal and a thematic concern in a Collins text: his novels explore the grey areas created by shifting social and legal expectations about love, property and the domestic sphere. His interventions range widely. *Man and Wife* (1870) and *The Black Robe* (1881) investigate whether a marriage took place legally, for example, and *The Woman in White* (1860) and *Armadale* (1866) whether it took place at all. The novel *Basil* (1852) includes an unconsummated marriage and an adultery plot; *The Two Destinies* (1876) a bigamy plot; *Miss or Mrs?* (1873) a clandestine marriage; and *The Evil Genius* (1886) adultery and divorce. The novel *No Name* (1862) alone features a bigamous love-match legitimised too late for the financial security of the offspring, an abortive engagement, two rather tepid marriages, and the blockbuster plot, a marriage contracted for the sole purpose of revenge.[1]

As the example of *No Name* might suggest, the domestic ideal is far from the forefront in a Wilkie Collins text. His novels situate violence and intrigue at the heart of domestic life, even as they probe the legal boundaries of the marriage contract in the period that witnessed the Divorce and Matrimonial Causes Act (1857), the Married Women's Property Bill (1856) and the 1868 Royal Commission attempt to regularise English, Irish and Scottish marriage laws.[2] Collins's concern with marriage, moreover, goes deeper than attacking legal abuses. In addressing different meanings of 'marriage' itself – as a legal contract, as a means of regulating sexual desire, as a method of property transmission, as a set of emotional bonds – he undermines the fundamental presumption that the concept is founded on the union of a man and a woman. Collins's heterosexual marriages often accompany equally strong or stronger affective and erotic relations between same-sex couples. Even as novelistic form all but requires a climactic wedding, Collins ingeniously subordinates heterosexual bonds to same-sex loyalties. Those same-sex relations far surpass the established conventions of romantic friendship to become an element of the sensation plot. Through the examples of *The Woman in White*, *Armadale* and *Man and Wife*, I will suggest that Collins's same-sex couples walk a fine line between affective convention and erotic transgression. In doing so, they smuggle sensation fiction's titillating agenda into the bourgeois comfort of novelistic form.

Sisterly love in *The Woman in White*

The Woman in White presents two of the key strategies that Collins uses to deconstruct the marriage plot. First, its melodrama pivots on a case of marital irregularity, in this instance Sir Percival Glyde's falsification of his parents' marriage. Second, and more subtly, the novel distributes the emotional intimacy ordinarily credited to marital love among three figures, rather than the conventional two.

Collins's novels are full of characters coping with implications of their parents' pre- or extramarital relations. In *The Woman in White*, Glyde, to whom the heiress Laura Fairlie is promised by her father, holds a legitimate claim on neither his name nor his property. Walter Hartright cracks Glyde's secret when he looks in the church marriage register for the record of the Glydes' marriage: where the record should appear, he discovers only a 'blank space'. Glyde kills himself in the attempt to burn this evidence of his illegitimate birth; but his attempts at forgery 'succeeded in the end', as Mrs Catherick writes, '– and made an honest woman of his mother, after she was dead in her grave!'(p. 544). Glyde's great 'Secret', moreover, is linked with the novel's other underlying topos of illegitimacy. Anne, Mrs Catherick's daughter, the novel's 'woman in white' and certified as a lunatic, is gripped by the belief that she understands Glyde's secret. Yet the second secret that this displaces – unbeknownst to Anne and only finally surmised by Hartright – is that she herself is the illegitimate half-sister of Laura. The sisters' identical appearance allows Glyde to incarcerate Laura in an asylum – under Anne's name – in a scheme to steal her riches; but the mystery of the resemblance is revealed, almost as an afterthought, only at the end of the novel, and Anne is never perceived or assimilated as Laura's kin.

Here *The Woman in White* differs from Collins's sympathetic representation of illegitimate children in other novels, *No Name* in particular. Collins uses the mental instability of Glyde and Anne to build sympathy for his narrator, Walter Hartright, as he circles around the text's legitimate heiress, Laura. The novel reinforces the exclusion of Anne and Glyde – both socially ostracised and killed – in order to anchor legitimate marriage and to align illegitimacy with lunacy. Serving as a force of sexual regulation, the novel hints that extramarital sex might produce a new generation of Glydes and Annes. Yet *The Woman in White*'s central romance is far from conventional in either its development or its resolution. At the end of the book, Walter marries the widowed Laura Glyde; but the climactic marriage is oddly anticlimactic, as Laura has effectively lost her mind in the struggle for her legal identity and her property. Into the breach steps Marian Halcombe, Laura's masculine and intelligent half-sister on her mother's side.

The union of Laura and Marian is the novel's most fully realised 'marriage', if we consider marriage a union based on emotional depth, mutual trust, and the presumption of permanence. Collins frequently maps the positive components of companionate marriage on to same-sex sibling or sibling-equivalent relations, or on to relationships that are for one reason or another not recognised by the law. In contrast, he often presents legal marriage as a sinkhole of deception, hostility, abuse and grubby materialism at worst, and at best a site of placid, jog-trot boredom. By distilling positive affect from legal marriage, Collins produces erotically pluralist novels under the protective, authorising cover of the conventional marriage plot. He uses the form against itself, turning the marriage plot inside out to feature affirmative, loving, nonmarital bonds.

Nowhere is this more vividly true than in the triangulated marriage that concludes *The Woman in White*. Marian and Walter are similarly dedicated to Laura. They band together to protect her from Glyde and Count Fosco, going so far as to join households in order to care for her and reclaim her shattered identity – and, not coincidentally, her lost inheritance.[3] Thus when Walter wishes to propose to Laura, he triangulates that proposal through Marian, reporting that 'Marian's eyes met mine affectionately – I could say no more. My heart was full, my lips were trembling' (p. 575). Conjoined by the masculine Marian – '"Can you look at Miss Halcombe"', asks Fosco, '"and not see that she has the foresight and the resolution of a man?"' (p. 330) – Walter and Laura enter a marriage anchored by its essential bisexuality. Providing a masculine companion for Walter and a feminine one for Laura, Marian is a full partner in this marriage of three.

Brotherly love in *Armadale*

Like *The Woman in White*, *Armadale* retains the formal structure of the marriage plot while triangulating marital intimacy through primary same-sex bonds. In *Armadale* Collins shifts the gendered plot of *The Woman in White* to investigate relations between two men presented as 'brothers'.

He gives these men a shared name, 'Allan Armadale', though in order to avoid impossible confusions, one goes by his assumed name, 'Ozias Midwinter'. With the name Allan Armadale comes a shared history of violence and intrigue about which only Midwinter knows, and which even he understands only partially. Drawn together by fate, the two Armadales stay together because of the 'perverse interest', the 'perverse fancy', that each holds for the other (Book 2, ch. 1).[4]

Collins adapted *Armadale* for the French stage in collaboration with the French actor Régnier soon after its publication, in 1867. While it is unlikely that this was actually staged, a later dramatisation of the novel, based on the Régnier collaboration, was renamed *Miss Gwilt* and performed at the Globe Theatre in London at the height of Collins's most successful decade in the theatre, in April 1876.[5] As its title implies, *Miss Gwilt* makes Lydia Gwilt the central figure, turning her into a melodramatic victim rather than a villain; but the play also highlights Collins's experimental approach to marriage by strengthening even further the dyad of Armadale and Midwinter. In *Miss Gwilt* Lydia is jealous of the bond between the two men, which motivates her violent revenge on Armadale: 'Who divided my husband's love with me, when I *had* a husband? Armadale! Who suspected my past life, and talked of secrets and mysteries before me in my husband's presence? Armadale! . . . Who took my husband away to sea, and told him my miserable secret? Armadale!' Lydia's rage notwithstanding, the play ends with a tableau of two men: '*As ALLAN bends over MIDWINTER and takes his hand the curtain falls.*' This dramatic conclusion reflects Collins's familiar triangular pattern: realising the novel's narcissistic implications, the curtain falls just as Allan Armadale bends over and takes the hand of . . . Allan Armadale.

Similarly, in the novel, Collins deploys what Sigmund Freud described as narcissistic identification as a way of writing into being the primary affective bond between his two male protagonists.[6] With their identical names and the commingled family histories that produced two baby boys named for fathers who were themselves two previous Allan Armadales united in tragedy, these Allan Armadales offer Collins a medium for the contemplation of abstract ideas of sameness and difference. This is an extension of the opportunity offered him by the twinned blondes of *The Woman in White*, Laura Fairlie and Anne Catherick. Yet *Armadale*'s two Armadales are remarkably dissimilar in their physical characteristics and in their personalities: Armadale is fair, flighty and bourgeois; Midwinter, his would-be protector, a man of mixed race, swarthy skin and uncertain background. Yet as he did with Laura Fairlie and Marian Halcombe, Collins uses the contrast of fairness, darkness and personality to deepen the bond between two men joined in a friendship sustained in the context of their differences. Further, Collins subtly underscores the concept of sameness between the Allans by giving them a name united by alliteration both between the names 'Allan' and 'Armadale' and internally within each of those names. Thematically and poetically, the differences that distinguish Allan Armadale from Allan Armadale occur within a primary matrix of sameness, of self-identity.

In *Armadale* Collins explictly probes questions of free will and destiny: are individual men and women bound to a predetermined fate, or are they free to create their own futures? He also implicitly credits the affective intensity between Allan Armadale and Ozias Midwinter to a shared history that binds over sons as payment for their fathers' sins. The Allan Armadales of the previous generation, both wild and violent youths, were bound in a relationship of mutual deception and destruction. Armadale's father was disinherited from the Armadale West Indian estates by *his* father after disgracing himself beyond redemption; his name and his inheritance were taken by Matthew Wrentmore, Midwinter's father. In revenge, Armadale's father returned under the name of Fergus Ingleby and (with the help of the pubescent Lydia Gwilt) seduced and eloped with Wrentmore/Armadale's intended bride, Armadale's mother, Miss Blanchard. Thus the name 'Allan Armadale' serves as a marker of predestination, of incarceration within a violent, tragic, male homosocial plot-loop seemingly set to continue for ever.

In fact, the name 'Allan Armadale' is so overdetermined that it seems to serve more as a floating signifier than a means of identification. This very looseness is significant in the context of the novel's plot because it indexes, semiotically, men's bonds with one another, underscoring unity, sameness and connection, and presaging the affective intimacy that flourishes between the novel's Armadale and his Midwinter. In this novel 'Allan Armadale' verges on a gender-identity in its own right. That gender identity draws powerfully on male homosocial bonds that orient the Allans not centrifugally towards heterosexual marriage or the capitalist model of production that modern heterosexuality serves, but inwards, centripetally, towards men – which means, in this novel, towards Allans and Armadales.

Emotional intimacy thrives in such extramarital contexts. In the present day of the text, Midwinter and Armadale grow fascinated with one another soon after the indigent Midwinter collapses near Armadale's comfortable home. For the sheltered Armadale, the exotic, swarthy Midwinter was the first 'outsider' in his world: 'What had Allan seen in him to take such a fancy to? Allan had seen in him – what he didn't see in people in general. He wasn't like all the other fellows in the neighbourhood' (Book 2, ch. 1). In turn, Midwinter's unflinching loyalty towards Armadale originates in the loving care that Armadale gave him during his recuperation. Midwinter describes the redemptive quality of '"My love for Allan Armadale"':

> '[A]sk your own heart if the miserable wretch whom Allan Armadale has treated as his equal and his friend, has said too much in saying that he loves him? I do love him! It will come out of me – I can't keep it back. I love the very ground he treads on! I would give my life – yes, the life that is precious to me now, because his kindness has made it a happy one – I tell you I would give my life –' (Book 2, ch. 2)

Midwinter breaks off here, choked by the overwhelming task of explaining his 'perverse attraction' to Armadale, of rationalising his seemingly irrational attraction to his friend. Brock, Armadale's tutor and surrogate father, is convinced by Midwinter's emotional display: '"I believe you love Allan . . . and I believe you have spoken the truth. A man who has produced that impression on me, is a man whom I am bound to trust. I trust you"' (Book 2, ch. 2). Yet even in the midst of this exchange, Midwinter and Brock know that fate has forecast a tragic ending to the Midwinter-Armadale bond. Brock endorses the bond nonetheless and Midwinter finds himself incapable of walking away, even to avert certain tragedy. Instead, he chooses to fight fate with love: '"I should never have torn myself from the hold which this letter fastened on me, if I had not loved Allan Armadale with all that I have in me of a brother's love . . . I can't believe – I won't believe – that a friendship which has grown out of nothing but kindness on one side, and nothing but gratitude on the other, is destined to lead to an evil end"' (Book 2, ch. 2).

Midwinter defensively explains his love as 'perverse' and while this may not directly anticipate Freud's later development of the notion of perversity as a primary mode of erotic subjectivity, it is symptomatic of the prevailing and unconventional nature of this bond.[7] Because both Midwinter and Armadale are forced to articulate the terms of their attraction, their union is invested with an emotional depth and texture entirely absent from the rest of the novel. Precisely because it is odd, is it uniquely authentic. Precisely because it is embattled, it runs true and deep. No heterosexual attraction in the novel is subjected to such justification. In heterosexual relations love is determined either before or immediately upon first sight. Midwinter falls in and out of love with Lydia Gwilt; Armadale decides before meeting Neelie Milroy that he will fall in love with her: he does, then throws her over for Lydia. Heterosexual bonds are flimsy matters of proximity and convenience. In the heterosexual context, 'love' signifies expediency far more than compatibility, much less emotion; at one point Armadale says to himself, '"The question is whether I hadn't better set myself right with my neighbours by becoming a married man?"' (Book 3, ch. 4).

In contrast, the novel puts its homoerotic bonds to the test. Fate itself is against the knowing Midwinter in his love for Armadale, and against the clueless Armadale in his reciprocal adoration of Midwinter. Yet repeatedly Midwinter and Armadale return to their primary loyalty to one another. The connection is physical, emotional, psychological: 'Struggling with the all-mastering dread that still held him, Midwinter laid his hand gently on Allan's forehead. Light as the touch was, there were mysterious sympathies in the dreaming man that answered it. His groaning ceased, and his hands dropped slowly' (Book 2, ch. 4). This burden of his bond with Armadale makes Midwinter an anxious mass of twitching, almost hysterical symptoms, which he attempts to control through self-imposed prohibitions on seeing his friend. As Cox and Bachman note:

> [T]he chaos that engulfs Midwinter – his hysteria and panic as well as his apparent inability to utter the unspeakable truth about Armadale – must not be interpreted simply as sexual repression. Midwinter is not conflicted about his 'uncomfortable affection' for Armadale; rather, his hysteria, his perpetual anxiety and feelings of terror, stem from an unconscious awareness that his 'love' for Armadale signifies death.[8]

This anxiety, however, originates in Midwinter's personal history of 'brotherly love'. Alone in the world from early in his childhood, the only affective connection he forged before meeting Armadale was with his 'dog-brothers': the dogs that belonged to an abusive master for whom he once worked as a performer. '"The dogs and I lived together, ate and drank, and slept together. I can't think of those poor little four-foot brothers of mine, even now, without a choking in the throat. Many is the beating we three took together; many is the hard day's dancing we did together; many is the night we have slept together, and whimpered together, on the cold hill-side"' (Book 2, ch. 2). Midwinter's loyalty to his dog-brothers contrasts with the cold world's stark dehumanisation. Only in brotherly bonds – with dogs, with Armadale – does Midwinter find the love and companionship he so desperately craves, and which the world gives him in no other form. Again, as with Armadale, Midwinter's dog-brothers function as his domestic unit, combining the bodily intimacies of eating, drinking, working and sleeping with emotional intimacies and loyalties. Midwinter and Armadale, like Midwinter and the dog-brothers of his childhood, are in no uncertain terms a family.

Strong though these unions are, they are vulnerable to forces outside the brothers' control: the boy and the dogs live at the whim of their brutal master, while Midwinter and Armadale are beholden to the destiny of their shared name. Although they could not be more different physically or temperamentally, Collins is insistent in his construction of them as *the same*: they are both named Allan Armadale; they are passionately dedicated to one another; they are both men. Like their fathers before them, they share a common heterosexual love object: this generation's Miss Blanchard is Lydia Gwilt. Yet just as Eve Kosofsky Sedgwick might suggest, the men's hetero-sexual desire works efficiently to consolidate their dyadic, homosocial relationship. Interest in Lydia is yet one more trait that Armadale and Midwinter share.[9] Collins eroticises this homosocial bond by means of the affective intensity that Armadale and Midwinter retain for one another. In the context of the novel's plot, 'fate' operates as the engine drawing the two ever closer to one another. Yet the mere fact of their interlocked histories and destinies alone does not fully explain how fascinating Armadale and Midwinter are to one another, nor does it explain their emergence as the novel's central couple, or their turbulent union as the novel's central marriage plot.

Collins's homosocialisation of the marriage plot occurs within a larger context of normative homosociality. This context emerges in the opening scene, where inhabitants of a German spa town await the new season's visitors. Here Collins attributes to the Mayor's wife 'a woman's insatiable curiosity about other women' (Prologue, ch. 1). This global statement about women serves a rhetorical function. As the bond of sameness between Armadale and Midwinter would suggest, Collins is interested in sameness within the genders – and especially with characteristics shared among women. 'Don't I know by experience that I am the sort of woman about whom other women are always spitefully curious?' Lydia asks of herself in her diary close to the novel's end. Later, she continues: 'Who can understand women? – we don't even understand ourselves' (Book 5, ch. 2). Earlier in the novel, Mrs Oldershaw has concurred: "How curiously hard it always seems to be for women to understand each other – especially when they have got their pens in their hands' (Book 3, ch. 1). Soon afterwards, Dr Downward chides Lydia: '"So like a woman!" he remarked, with the most exasperating good-humour. "The moment she sees her object, she dashes at it headlong the nearest way. Oh, the sex! The sex!"' (Book 5, ch. 2). The private eye Jemmy Bashwood, son of Lydia's aged abject ad-mirer, reflects the novel's pervasive misogynist sentiment: '"Women are queer creatures"' (Book 3, ch. 15). And the narrator himself chimes in on many occasions: 'The consciousness of guilt acts differently on the two sexes. In nine cases out of ten, it is a much more manageable consciousness with a woman than with a man' (Book 3, ch. 8).

Indeed, *Armadale* persistently characterises women in negative terms. Bored, manipulative, avaricious, amoral creatures, women send men, who are relatively benign, fleeing into the safe haven of one another's arms. In the world of the Armadales, the brotherly bonds of male unity far surpass heterosexual relations as the site of emotional intimacy. By this means, Collins distinguishes the novel's form from its content. At the end of the text, Armadale stands poised to marry the rather insipid Neelie Milroy. Midwinter, on the other hand, has paid the price of marriage plots in this world: having married Lydia, he nearly died in a rescue attempt when she tried to kill the other Allan Armadale. Lydia killed herself to save him, and Midwinter is now a widower seemingly poised to make it big somewhere in the world out there. In parting, Armadale reifies the eternal connection that will survive whatever adventures await Midwinter: '"You have promised me, I know, that if you take to Literature, it shan't part us, and that if you go on a sea voyage, you will remember when you come back that my house is your home"' (Epilogue, ch. 2). The novel ends not with a marriage but with a separation that reaffirms emotional bonds between the men. In its last lines Midwinter 'rose, and walked to the window. While [Midwinter and Armadale] had been speaking together, the darkness had passed. The first light of the new day met him as he looked out, and rested tenderly on his face' (Epilogue, ch. 2).

Women in love: *Man and Wife*

If the marriage plot represents the repository of a novel's affective and material investment, then the story of the relationship between Allan Armadale and Allan Armadale is surely the marriage plot of *Armadale*. In the same vein, the story of the relationship between two young women, Anne and Blanche, constitutes the marriage plot of Collins's 1870 novel *Man and Wife*.

This is only a slight exaggeration. *Man and Wife* follows structural principles identical to those of *Armadale*: the young women Anne and Blanche are the daughters of two women named Anne and Blanche. Unlike the previous generation's Allan Armadales, though, the previous Anne and Blanche were girlhood best friends, and when the first Anne dies, the first Blanche solemnly vows to raise the child she leaves behind. The first Anne describes this stable, continuous, familial love:

> 'We two mothers . . . seem literally to live again in our children. I have an only child. My friend has an only child. My daughter is little Anne – as *I* was. My friend's daughter is little Blanche – as she was. And, to crown it all, those two girls have taken the same fancy to one another, which *we* took to each other, in

the bygone days at school. One has often heard of hereditary hatred. Is there such a thing as hereditary love as well?'　　　　　　　(Prologue, part 1)

In *Man and Wife* as in *Armadale*, Collins distributed hereditary passions across multiple generations of same-sex couples. In contrast with *Armadale*, however, in *Man and Wife* he also pits this conception of a loving, positive 'marriage plot' directly against the dysfunctional heterosexual model. Collins felt that the 1868 Report of the Royal Commission on the Laws of Marriage failed to resolve the 'scandalous condition of the Marriage Laws of the United Kingdom', and offered the novel as a critique of what he saw as the Commission's fudged compromises.[10] The novel follows the 'fallen' governess Anne Silvester to a Scottish hotel where she plans to undertake a clandestine marriage with her seducer, the athlete and playboy Geoffrey Delamayn. When Delamayn sends in his place the guileless Arnold Brinkworth, suitor to Anne's beloved Blanche, Arnold and Anne are forced to present themselves as a married couple in order to preserve their respectable reputations. They face a problem, however. As Anne puts it to Delamayn, '"A man and a woman who wish to be married (in Scotland) have only to declare themselves married – and the thing is done"' (Scene 1, ch. 5).

And perhaps it is. The novel plots out the implications of Anne's inadvertent possible marriage to Brinkworth: it addresses Delamayn's abuse of Anne in a psychotic state fueled by his excessive devotion to athletic training; it witnesses the unwitting Brinkworth's marriage to Blanche – and the revelation soon afterwards that he might be a bigamist and sweet, virtuous Blanche a ruined woman. The novel chafes at the prospect that the state has reduced the culture's sacred ideal of marriage to a thin legal technicality. Yet Collins does not simply reify the marriage ideal to support his legal critique. As he does elsewhere, he represents affective bonds between human beings in the most positive terms. And as in his other work, he locates positive affective union both within and outside of conventional heterosexual marriages.

The longest lasting and most fully tested emotional bond in *Man and Wife* is the one that exists between Anne and Blanche, and which has indeed existed between Annes and Blanches throughout most of the nineteenth century. The fact of Anne's possible accidental marriage to Blanche's beloved future husband – or to put it the other way, Blanche's love-match with the man who may have inadvertently married her best friend – reflects the triangulated marriage plot familiar to readers of *The Woman in White*. As it does for Laura and Marian, the relationship between Anne and Blanche nourishes both women: Anne, in desperate straits, muses that, 'Her whole future depended on Geoffrey's making an honest woman of her. Not her future with *him* – that way, there was no hope; that way her life was wasted. Her future with Blanche – she looked forward to nothing now, but her future with Blanche'. (Scene 2, ch. 9). Indeed, Anne does find her way into a future with Blanche. Unlike her mother, who died in the arms of Blanche's mother, Anne does not die in her beloved's arms or at the hands of Geoffrey Delamayn. She survives – to marry Blanche's uncle, Sir Patrick Lundie, thus becoming aunt to her best friend, whose husband she once accidentally may have married. Like the relationship among the multiple Allan Armadales, Anne's relationship with Blanche is prolifically overdetermined. It is this relationship between two women that every episode of the novel tests and ultimately consolidates. The same-sex bond embodies a positive and constant emotional continuum.

Man and Wife offers this positive model against a running commentary on the superficiality and instability of many marriages. Well before he forms an attachment to Anne Silvester, Sir Patrick Lundie warns young Brinkworth of the marketing practices of the 'marriage-shop':

> 'You bring her home; and you discover that it's the old story of the sugar all over again. Your wife is an adulterated article. Her lovely yellow hair is – dye. Her exquisite skin is – pearl powder. Her plumpness is – padding. And three inches of her height are – in the boot-maker's heels. Shut your eyes, and swallow your adulterated wife as you swallow your adulterated sugar – and, I tell you again, you are one of the few men who can try the marriage experiment with a fair chance of success.' (Scene 1, ch. 6)

Even the narrator's account of the propitious-seeming marriage of Blanche and Arthur reflects Sir Patrick's cynical sense of doom:

> Then, the service began – rightly-considered, the most terrible surely of all mortal ceremonies – the service which binds two human beings, who know next to nothing of each other's natures, to risk the tremendous experiment of living together till death parts them – the service which says, in effect if not in words, Take your leap in the dark: we sanctify but we don't insure it! (Scene 7, ch. 39)

If marriage is a 'leap in the dark', the novel's concluding love matches are perhaps less stable than they seem to be on the surface. They are sanctified morally and sanctified legally. Yet the genre of sensation fiction itself posits that neither the moral nor the legal insures success or happiness in this unpredictable modern world. What does seem certain, for not only *Man and Wife* but for *The Woman in White*, *Armadale* and Collins's oeuvre more generally, are those affective bonds consolidated between same and same: the love of men for men, the love of women for women. These bonds stand the test of time; they weather turbulence and betrayal and the uncertainties that plague the gender-exogamous marriages that come and go against their monumental backdrop. As I have argued here, there is no question that Wilkie Collins is not invested in the comic, happily-ever-after form of domestic fiction: his novels invariably conclude at the altar of convention. His radical innovation involves the plots that get a man and a woman to the altar – and a third person who almost always stands up with the bridal pair. Marriage, for Collins, is but one mode of love among many. In these novels Collins suggests that heterosexual marriage is just one way, and perhaps not always the best way, to comprehend the lasting power of loving human devotion.

NOTES

1. See Ann Cvetkovich, *Mixed Feelings: Feminism, Mass Culture, and Victorian Sensationalism* (New Brunswick: Rutgers University Press, 1992); Tamar Heller, *Dead Secrets: Wilkie Collins and the Female Gothic* (New Haven: Yale University Press, 1992); Lillian Nayder, *Wilkie Collins* (New York: Twayne, 1997); and Marlene Tromp, *The Private Rod: Marital Violence, Sensation, and the Law in Victorian Britain* (Charlottesville: University Press of Virginia, 2000).
2. See Lillian Nayder, 'Sensation Fiction and Marriage Law Reform: Wives and Property in *The Woman in White*, *No Name*, and *Man and Wife*', pp. 71–99 in her *Wilkie Collins*; Mary Poovey, 'Covered But Not Bound: Caroline Norton and the 1857 Matrimonial Causes Act', in Poovey, *Uneven Developments: The Ideological Work of Gender in Mid-Victorian England* (Chicago: University of Chicago Press, 1988), pp. 51–88; and Mary Lyndon Shanley, *Feminism, Marriage, and the Law in Victorian England* (Princeton: Princeton University Press, 1989).
3. It is interesting to recognise that the novel leaves open the possibility that Laura Fairlie did in fact die. If this is the case, then the 'Laura' whom Walter marries is really Anne Catherick. If so, Marian and Walter have fiendishly reversed the sensation plot, using Anne in order to get their hands on the dead Laura's considerable property.
4. On homoeroticism in *Armadale*, see Maria K. Bachman and Don Richard Cox, 'Wilkie Collins's Villainous Miss Gwilt, Criminality and the Unspeakable Truth', *Dickens Studies Annual* 32 (2002), 319–37, and Carolyn Oulton, '"Never Be Divided Again": *Armadale* and the Threat to Romantic Friendship', *Wilkie Collins Society Journal* 7 (2004), 31–40.
5. Peters, pp. 277–9, 378–9. On the various dramatisations of *Armadale*, see the Appendix to John Sutherland's edition of *Armadale* (London and New York: Penguin, 1995), pp. 711–14.
6. Sigmund Freud first theorised male homosexuality through an analysis of the Narcissus myth in 'On Narcissism: An Introduction' (1914), *The Standard Edition of the Complete Psychological Works of Sigmund Freud*, ed. and trans. James Strachey, 24 vols. (London: Hogarth Press, 1953–73), XIV, pp. 73–102.

7. See Freud, *Three Essays on the Theory of Sexuality* (1905), in *The Standard Edition*, VII, esp. pp. 149–62. For a wonderful account of the theoretical flexibility offered by perverse eroticism, see Teresa de Lauretis, *The Practice of Love: Lesbian Sexuality and Perverse Desire* (Bloomington: Indiana University Press, 1994).

8. Bachman and Cox, 'Wilkie Collins's Villainous Miss Gwilt', 329. Sodomy was a capital crime in Britain until 1861, and as Cox and Bachman point out, "During the years 1856–59 alone, fifty-four men were sentenced to death for sodomy" (322). In *Armadale* the present-day plot takes place in 1851.

9. See Eve Kosofsky Sedgwick, *Between Men: English Literature and Male Homosocial Desire* (New York: Columbia University Press, 1985), on how patriarchal heterosexual conventions help to consolidate homosocial bonds, and to contain homosocial desires, between male subjects. On the covert signifying practices of homoeroticism, see Sedgwick's *Epistemology of the Closet* (Berkeley: University of California Press, 1990).

10. See Philip O'Neill, *Wilkie Collins: Women, Property and Propriety* (Basingstoke: Macmillan, 1998), pp. 125–52, and Nayder, *Wilkie Collins*, pp. 92–9.

9

JOHN KUCICH

Collins and Victorian masculinity

Wilkie Collins's novels abound in melancholic male protagonists. These dispirited heroes are an important key to Collins's conception of gender difference, since they dramatise what he saw as an identity crisis plaguing mid-Victorian men. It may not be the case, as D. A. Miller once famously argued, that Collins saw all sensation as feminine, or that he set his heroes the task of conquering emotionalism of any kind.[1] But in order to act, Walter Hartright, Franklin Blake, Ozias Midwinter and other Collins protagonists must at the very least overcome their persistent wallowing in sadness, loss, dejection and self-criticism. Such struggles can tell us a great deal about the psychological and cultural dynamics within which Victorian masculinity was constructed, about the historical shifts in gender norms that Collins helped both to articulate and to modify, and about the social transformations that his melancholic men portend.

Collins grappled most strenuously with a particular type of melancholia, a form of the malady that seemed – somewhat paradoxically – to fuel narcissistic excess. Although it may seem counterintuitive to believe that melancholia has an affinity with exaggerated narcissism, such an affinity has a long history in British cultural assumptions about male cultural elites. At least since the Renaissance, melancholia had been associated in British culture – and in European thought generally – with the man of genius. Borrowing lofty, flattering images of male melancholia from the Italian poets Torquato Tasso and Francesco Petrarch, sixteenth- and seventeenth-century British writers construed such images as signs of male creative and intellectual power. William Shakespeare's *Hamlet* (1603) is, perhaps, the most powerful work in the British tradition to have lionised the philosophical prowess of the male melancholic. Robert Burton's enormously influential 'Anatomy of Melancholy' (1621) also defined melancholia as the disease of great men, if not the source of their inspiration.[2] These exalted views of male melancholia persisted through the Romantic period, so much so that by the early nineteenth century a melancholy temper had become nearly synonymous with poetic genius. Samuel Taylor Coleridge, George Gordon Lord Byron, John Keats, Thomas De Quincey, and other Romantics all proudly laid claim to being melancholics.[3] As Julia Kristeva has observed, these traditional associations of melancholia with exceptional men removed it from pathology and enshrined it as a privileged cultural ethos.[4]

During this same period of history, by contrast, female melancholia was consistently diagnosed as an illness, and often associated with hysteria. Medical and other writers tended to regard it as a forerunner of madness. Modern-day researchers have not, in fact, identified any inherent difference in the ways men and women experience demoralisation. But the traditional association of male melancholia with genius is built on well-known psychological mechanisms that can bring any individual's melancholia into relationship with narcissistic grandiosity. Such mechanisms have been codified by modern psychiatry in a variety of ways. In 'Mourning and Melancholia' (1917), for example, Sigmund Freud defined a certain kind of melancholia as a 'disturbance in self-regard'.[5] The melancholic, according to Freud, reacts to losses in the external world with seemingly undeserved, exaggerated self-accusations. But these attacks on the self actually assuage grief through narcissistic identification. In other words, by redefining the self as the cause of one's sadness – a sadness that was originally provoked by the disappearance of a real person or thing – the melancholic comes to feel that the lost object has been incorporated, and thus preserved. As Freud puts it, a libidinal cathexis with the object is replaced by a libidinal cathexis with the subject's own ego. One symptom of the pleasurable self-sufficiency that results, Freud claimed, is that melancholia alternates, surprisingly, with mania – a euphoric state in which subjects experience themselves as tremendously powerful, perhaps invincible.

Traditional British attitudes toward male melancholia drew on these affinities between melancholia and narcissism, but they did so in historically and culturally specific terms. As we have seen, in British culture from the Renaissance through the Romantic period, melancholic self-aggrandisement was linked to intellectual, artistic and other culturally elite modes of male power. The crisis in Victorian masculinity that Collins's protagonists dramatise stemmed from a sudden disruption in this psychosocial system. By the 1850s and 1860s, for a variety of reasons, melancholia was sharply devalued as a sign of male cultural authority. Rather than signalling the creative power of the rarefied genius, it seemed to have become widespread, mundane and déclassé – a conventional attribute of middle-class commercial, leisured and professional men. In the course of this demographic diffusion, male melancholia became associated with inaction, indecisiveness, inhibition and other forms of emotional debility traditionally reserved for depressed women. Henry Maudsley, in *The Physiology and Pathology of the Mind* (1867), for example, typified mid-nineteenth-century medical opinion by describing male melancholia as a disorder signalled by symptoms of emasculation – weakness, both physical and mental; a sense of helplessness; inactivity; even incipient madness.

Novelists, in particular, viewed the pervasive unmanliness of the middle-class melancholic with alarm. Many of Charles Dickens's protagonists from this period – Arthur Clennam in *Little Dorrit* (1857), Pip in *Great Expectations* (1861), Eugene Wrayburn and John Harmon in *Our Mutual Friend* (1865) – struggle to overcome their oppressively commonplace, emasculating melancholia. Similarly critical portraits of male melancholia include the eponymous hero of George Meredith's *Evan Harrington* (1861), Robert Audley of Mary Elizabeth Braddon's *Lady Audley's Secret* (1862), Margaret Oliphant's Arthur Vincent in *Salem Chapel* (1863), and a long succession of Anthony Trollope's protagonists, including Sir John Ball of *Miss Mackenzie* (1865), Louis Trevelyan of *He Knew He Was Right* (1869), and Squire Gilmore of *The Vicar of Bullhampton* (1870). There have been many explanations for the proliferation of mid-Victorian male melancholia, and for its association with mediocrity and impotence. Some have seen middle-class male melancholia as a demoralised response to the growing social power of both middle-class women and lower-class men.[6] Others have attributed it to the deindividuating effects of commodity culture; the growing sense of middle-class irrelevance in the face of continued political dominance by the upper class; and the increasing gulf between the Victorian worlds of respectability and trade, a gap that could sometimes make middle-class men nostalgic for their social origins in productive labour.[7] Victorian diatribes against male melancholia have also been understood as one effect of the cult of the 'stiff upper lip', which, fuelled by public school athleticism and 'muscular Christianity', stigmatised all displays of male vulnerability.[8] Whatever the causes of this general shift in the history of British affect – and all these factors no doubt played a role – male melancholia came to be viewed in the mid-Victorian years as dangerously effeminate, debilitating and banal, even though its traditional association with male genius persisted to some extent, and conflicted with this newer, critical perspective.

Collins's *Basil* (1852) is the earliest Victorian novel to portray the dangerous feminisation of male identity that occurs when melancholia is divorced from narcissistic power. The second of Collins's published novels – but the first to display the characteristic themes and styles of his signature 'sensation fiction' – *Basil* dramatises this psychological splitting through a method of characterisation that would become standard in his great works of the 1860s. In all these novels Collins ranged his male characters on one side or the other of a pathological axis, in which melancholia and grandiosity defined opposing but equally problematic personality types. In effect, Collins fragmented the heroic male ego of the pre-Victorian past around an unsatisfactory opposition between melancholic and self-aggrandising men. In the process he represented both fragmented versions of traditional male genius as effeminate. That a disarticulated heroic male psyche lies behind Collins's array of inadequate men is underscored by his tendency to oppose melancholic and grandiose men of the same family to one another. His novels pit cousin against cousin, brother against brother, and father against son in familial contests that suggest the intimate yet conflicted affinity of polarised melancholic and narcissistic types.

Basil himself is one of the most antiheroic, debilitated male melancholics in Victorian fiction. Presenting the pages of his narrative as an expiation – the confession of 'an error' that he hopes will be read after his death 'as relics solemnized by the atoning shadows of the grave' (p. 1) – Basils finds that his demoralisation is regarded as extraordinary by everyone who knows him. His brother Ralph tells Basil he will 'take good care that you don't ruin yourself gratuitously' (p. 262), and even Basil's 'simple' Cornish neighbors 'could not reconcile my worn, melancholy face with my youthful years' (p. 312). Tellingly, Basil identifies with his sister Clara, a conventionally self-effacing woman whose eyes have a 'slight tinge of melancholy in their tenderness' (p. 18), rather than with the self-aggrandising Ralph, who is described by a minor character as 'the pleasantest, liveliest gentleman I ever saw' (p. 335).

Basil's melancholia follows an increasingly precipitous downward spiral. At the beginning of the narrative proper, he still enjoys his 'earliest and best ambition' (p. 267), which is to become a novelist – a vocation that defines his manly independence, since it flouts his father's wish that he pursue a political career. But Basil quickly abandons novel writing, along with every other pleasure in his life (including Clara's company), for the sake of a morbid marriage to a linen-draper's daughter, the morally unworthy Margaret Sherwin. Margaret enjoys materialistic and sexual lusts that Basil does not at first detect, and her conniving father preposterously makes Basil promise not to consummate the marriage for a year. By the end of the narrative, the shock of Basil's discovery that Margaret has taken a lover (Basil masochistically listens to them making love through the walls of a cheap hotel), coupled with the shock of being disowned by his genteel father for having married into a shopkeeper's family, deepens his melancholia to the point that he cannot rejoice even in the fortunate accidents that free him from his troubles. The deaths of both Margaret and her lover, Basil's nemesis Robert Mannion, do not bring him the 'release and salvation' he expects;

instead, they only strengthen his conviction that his life is blighted by a secret 'fatality' (p. 327), the same kind of gloomy foreboding that robs many Collins protagonists of their power of will and action. He nearly descends into madness before resigning himself, finally, to enervated withdrawal: 'I have suffered too much; I have been wounded too sadly, to range myself with the heroes of Ambition, and fight my way upward from the ranks. [. . .] The mountain-path of Action is no longer a path for *me*' (p. 342).

Basil's melancholia signals his unmanliness in a variety of ways. He frequently describes himself as 'irresolute' (p. 33) and lacking 'self-possession' (p. 32), and his 'error' is first precipitated by the contaminating 'touch' of a woman (a fate that also nearly befalls Walter Hartright in *The Woman in White* (1860)). Even Basil's sexual transgressions gender him female. Ralph may have committed a man's sexual sins – 'vices of the reckless hour, or the idle day! – vices whose stain, in the world's eye, was not a stain for life! – convenient, reclaimable vices, that men were mercifully unwilling to associate with grinning infamy and irreparable disgrace!' (pp. 189–90) – but Basil's marriage to Margaret causes his father to banish him with as much horror and contempt as if Basil had been a fallen woman. Even when, in a fit of passion, Basil violently assaults Mannion, the repercussions of his attack feminise him: he wanders in a daze that bystanders mistake for madness, and then passes out, awakening later to hear his father declare, '"It deeply concerns my interest as a father, and my honour as the head of our family, to know what heavy misfortune it was . . . that stretched my son senseless in the open street, and afflicted him afterwards with an illness which threatened his reason"' (p. 189). Most of all, though, Basil's bizarre marriage unmans him. He tries to defend his sexual timidity by claiming, 'Men may not understand this; women, I believe will' (p. 99). But even his wife mocks him: '"Ha! Ha! He calls himself a man, doesn't he? A husband who waits a year!"' (p. 294). The sexual humiliation to which Basil submits parallels an even more serious emasculation, since his marriage is viewed by his father as a threat to patriarchal continuity. Endangering the chief pride of his father's life – the family's noble lineage – Basil's class transgression is presented symbolically as a gender transgression, an abdication of patriarchal responsibility, a lapse that obliges him 'to abandon my father's name' (p. 3). Appropriately, Basil's social disgrace nearly kills his father, reducing him to his sickbed with grief and shame.

If Basil embodies melancholia taken to extremes and stripped of any narcissistic compensation, Ralph and Mannion are driven, in contrast, by excesses of narcissistic grandiosity. Ralph's high-spirited selfishness maintains 'a charm about him that subdued everybody' (pp. 11–12). The darling of young English ladies, who 'fell in love with him by dozens' (p. 11), Ralph conquers the most preeminent female intellectuals, beauties, and celebrities on the Continent, and returns home laden with 'love-tokens' (p. 15). He is 'his own master' in all things, his amorous success accompanied early in the novel by other emblems of male prowess, including his athletic feats while at university and his victory in a duel.

Mannion, whose name defines him as a standard bearer for his gender, claims the 'self-possession of a gentleman' (p. 111) and 'unusual firmness of character' (p. 181). But what most enables him to subjugate others is his masculine self-control – what Basil describes in sexualised terms as 'the impossibility of penetrating beneath the unassailable surface which this man presented' (p. 114) – together with Mannion's uncanny ability to penetrate the secret wishes and anxieties of others. 'A character that ruled', Mannion nominally serves as Mr Sherwin's clerk and household assistant, but Basil has no doubt that Mannion 'was master there' (pp. 111–12). He displays his narcissistic power most gratuitously in his sexual command over Margaret, proudly declaring that he cares very little for her. Taunting Basil that Margaret had married him only for his rank, Mannion brags that her submission to him is personal and absolute: ' "I had that practical ability, that firmness of will, that obvious personal ascendancy over most of those with whom I came in contact, which extorts the respect and admiration of women of all characters, and even of women of no character at all" ' (p. 244).

Yet Ralph and Mannion prove to be ambivalent models of self-regarding male strength. Embodiments, respectively, of benign and malevolent forms of unchecked egotism – the power to charm, in Ralph's case; the power to dominate, in Mannion's – these two men both fall short of the patriarchal ideal embodied, however precariously, in Basil's father. After a long career of dissipation, Ralph reforms by submitting to a mistress older than himself, a woman who 'broke me of gaming' (p. 257) and who jealously controls his movements in London, making him the prisoner of the sexual sphere he had once mastered. More disturbingly, Ralph proves an ineffective champion for Basil because his narcissism renders him permanently immature. ' "Nothing in the world ever was serious to *me*, and nothing ever will be" ' (p. 257), he declares, despite the evident gravity of Basil's situation. This heartless and superficial jocularity – what Basil calls his 'boyish folly' (p. 263) – convinces Basil that Ralph would be no match for Mannion, were the two ever to clash directly. The novel thus links Ralph's charming version of narcissism to boyhood, as opposed to the mature, sadistic egotism of Mannion, who is, in fact, old enough to have deceived Basil by acting as his 'second father' (p. 170).

But Mannion's formidable self-control, like Ralph's sexual power, turns out to be evanescent. When he finally reveals his closely guarded secrets to Basil, Mannion turns out to be a 'madman', consumed by his quest for revenge against Basil's family. This quest, motivated by Basil's father's having long ago testified against Mannion's father for forging his name on a bond – testimony that hangs Mannion's father – symbolises the crippling exclusion from patriarchal power, authority, wealth and love that torments all the novel's male characters. Described clinically by Dr Bernard as 'a dangerous monomaniac', Mannion had only fraudulently maintained what the doctor calls 'the appearance of perfect self-possession' (p. 281). Although they offer opposed images of how unregulated male narcissism might degenerate, both of Basil's narcissistic alter egos are thus emasculated – Ralph by a woman and Mannion by mental derangement.

Similarly, the glaring opposition between Basil's melancholia and Mannion's grandiosity obscures the striking similarities that define these two characters as split halves of a single male ego. Both characters try and fail at authorship; both are dismissed from respectable households because of their social disgrace; both are 'morbidly sensitive' (p. 230) about social and personal liabilities; and both suffer at the hands of the same excommunicating patriarch. These similarities of circumstance and temperament are aggravated by the events of the novel, particularly by the two men's frustrated desire for the same woman. Appropriately, Mannion declares that he will persecute Basil by remaking his life yet more closely in the image of his own: ' "Remember what my career has been; and know that I will make your career like it" ' (p. 250). Even after Mannion's death, the doubling of the two characters persists: Basil refuses to divulge his name, his relations or his troubles to the doctor treating him at the Cornish inn, a stoicism reminiscent of Mannion's at the London charity hospital where he recovers from Basil's attack.

These doublings sometimes result in strange psychological collaborations. During the year of Basil's unconsummated marriage, for example, Mannion acts as his executive will, supplementing Basil's deficient manliness with his own uncanny power. Exercising his influence over the Sherwin household so as to gratify Basil's wishes, Mannion allows Basil 'to regulate Mr. Sherwin's incomings and outgoings, just as I chose, when Margaret and I were together in the evening' (p. 138). Such collaborations sometimes assume a perverse, mutually destructive symmetry in the context of the novel's psychological allegory. Basil, the melancholic self-hater, violently deforms Mannion's face, thus transforming 'one of the handsomest men [Basil] ever beheld' (p. 110) into someone who repulses others; Mannion, the malevolent narcissist, vows to keep the despairing Basil from committing suicide solely in order to 'make your whole life [. . .] one long expiation' (p. 304). This mutually destructive symmetry suggests the fatal consequences of divorcing male melancholia from male narcissism. Nevertheless, the novel does not reconcile the morbid but admirable moral sensitivity of its hero with either the unflappable (but shallow) self-confidence of Ralph or the passionate resolution and 'glaring triumph' of Mannion (p. 323).

In his major works of the 1860s, Collins sought to heal this rupture in the male psyche through two important psychosocial strategies. First, he revived the traditional linkage between melancholia and male grandiosity, but only by displacing it from the exclusive social elites with which it had been affiliated, and identifying it instead with an emergent nineteenth-century social niche very much like his own. Collins's melancholy narcissists of the 1860s all practise humanistic professions. His favoured journalists, writers and artists pursue vocations that fuse aesthetic sensibilities with rigorous expertise – the very fusion that Basil fatally abandons when he gives up novel writing. Distanced from the world of gentility, on the one hand, and from scientific or technocratic professionals (particularly those in medicine and law), on the other, Collins's heroes define a new social and occupational location that resuscitates the connection between melancholia and male genius. Second, Collins began to dramatise productive collaborations between male melancholics and male narcissists – rather than simply opposing these personality types, as he had done in *Basil*. Such collaborations, besides figuratively healing masculine psychic conflicts, helped to reinforce the hybrid social qualities that defined the humanistic professional, a figure who was both amateur and expert, gentlemanly aesthete and middle-class intellectual worker.

Collins's relocation of melancholic genius among this new vocational type had a number of cultural functions. While most Victorian novelists tried to strengthen middle-class cultural authority by celebrating the moral power of the domestic female – Coventry Patmore's 'angel in the house' – Collins used humanistic professionals to affirm instead a model of middle-class power that he associated with traditional male gentility.[9] This strategy enabled him to resist the moral conventions of bourgeois culture, and to bolster the virility of the intellectual, often stigmatised in Victorian England as effeminate in relation to his scientific or technocratic brethren.[10] In broader ideological terms, Collins used humanistic professionals to dramatise a 'marriage' of upper-class cultural and social authority with middle-class economic vitality – precisely the kind of marriage that literally fails to come off in *Basil*, both because of the moral corruption that Collins locates behind Margaret's façade of middle-class female purity, and because of the social rigidity of Basil's father (and the decadence of Ralph, his heir). This idealised social synthesis betrays Collins's refusal to identify entirely with either middle-class or upper-class ideology, and his wish to affirm an idealised masculinity not bound by the standards of either class. Collins's humanistic professionals thus synthesise melancholia with male power for reasons that complexly intertwine issues of gender and class.

In *The Woman in White*, to cite Collins's first positive renovation of masculine ideals, Walter Hartright's manly synthesis of melancholia and narcissism corresponds closely with his initiation into a humanistic profession. Over the course of the novel, Hartright gradually absorbs Marian Halcombe's advice that he act 'like a man' (p. 71). His experience on an expedition in Central America, in particular, teaches him to master his susceptibility to sensation and to act independently, lessons that prove critical in his quest to restore his beloved Laura Fairlie to her rightful name and inheritance: 'my will had learnt to be strong, my heart to be resolute, my mind to rely on itself' (p. 415). But Hartright's manliness crucially incorporates both grandiosity and melancholia, a combination that forges together both his personal and his professional heroism.

On the one hand, Hartright acquires an air of bravado that seems only appropriate to a hero who single-handedly confronts the novel's complementary narcissistic villains – the charmingly vain Count Fosco, and the ruthlessly domineering Sir Percival Glyde. He declares, 'Those two men shall answer for their crime to ME, though the justice that sits in tribunals is powerless to pursue them' (p. 454). Yet despite Hartright's triumph over Fosco and Glyde, he never resigns his melancholic tone. He speaks of this period of his life as 'the days of doubt and dread, when the spirit within me struggled hard for its life, in the icy stillness of perpetual suspense' (p. 490). Glyde's death leaves him 'weakened and depressed by all that I had gone through' (p. 537), and when he sees Fosco's body in the Paris morgue, he 'shuddered as I recalled' that 'struggle in my own heart, when he and I stood face to face' (p. 639). Most importantly, Hartright never loses his belief in the 'fatality' seemingly haunting him, which 'it was hopeless to avoid' (p. 73). This superstitious determinism eventually unites Hartright's melancholic and self-aggrandising tendencies – a process repeated in many of Collins's later heroes. In other words, while his sense of fatality sometimes leaves Hartright dejected, it also begins to invigorate him, as the novel progresses, with a belief in his special election. His crusade against the novel's villains, he declares, is what 'set my life apart to be the instrument of a Design that is yet unseen' (p. 278). He grandiosely attributes what he sees as his charmed life – in Central America he survives disease, Indian attack and shipwreck – to this melancholic favouring: 'Death takes the good, the beautiful, and the young – and spares *me*' (p. 279).

Hartright's synthesis of melancholia and grandiosity corresponds to the transformation in his social identity. As a drawing master, a gentleman dependant on the patronage of the wealthy, he begins the novel pursuing an archaic, marginally upper-class career model, one that had worked well for Collins's father, a painter and Royal Academician. But Hartright – like Collins himself – eschews this genteel career trajectory by adopting professional vocations: he accepts the post of draftsman on the Central American expedition, then becomes an illustrator for cheap periodicals, and finally graduates to work for an illustrated magazine. Poised as it is on the boundary between the world of art and the world of commerce, Hartright's career as an artist expresses in vocational terms a synthesis of melancholic sensibilities with practical action – a synthesis the novel repeatedly defines by opposing it to the attitudes of nonhumanistic professionals. The novel's lawyers, for example, are unable to comprehend what they regard as Hartright's morbid fancies – Mr Gilmore rebukes him for taking 'the romantic view' rather than 'the practical view' of Anne Catherick (p. 119); Mr Kyrle, who suggests to Hartright that 'my delusion had got the better of my reason' (p. 454), tells him that in the eyes of the law he has 'no prospect' of vindicating Laura. Unlike these men, Hartright is capable of melancholy choices – professionally, he accepts obscurity and relative poverty; personally, he resigns himself to censure, suffering and risk of death. Again unlike the novel's lawyers, though, he is capable of defiantly independent action, a capacity for manly resolution that unites both personal and professional choices when it compels him to leave Laura for the Central American expedition. That the fulfilment of Hartright's quest depends on the income that his newfound work provides cements the parallel between the stalwart fortitude of the determined professional and that of the heroic man of action.

Deliberately opposed to the ineffectiveness or obstructionism of the novel's lawyers, doctors and spies, Hartright's humanistic professionalism is also opposed to the gentility of his alter ego, Fosco, a man whose genius derives from some of the same paradoxes of sensibility and intellect that characterise Hartright. Fosco's spectacular vanity, for example, his 'cherished purpose of self-display', makes him a virile match for Hartright, who claims that Fosco 'mastered my astonishment by main force' (p. 608). But this vanity, like Hartright's, is not inconsistent with melancholia: Marian is surprised to discover that Fosco has mournful 'moments of sentiment' (p. 292), which she believes are 'really felt, not assumed' (p. 291). Like Hartright, too, Fosco claims to 'combine in myself the opposite characteristics of a Man of Sentiment and a Man of Business' (p. 623). But Fosco represents precisely the archaic, genteel model of male genius that Collins sought to displace with humanistic professionalism. As Fosco's wife avows, in her biography of her husband, 'His life was one long assertion of the rights of the aristocracy' (p. 641). No wonder Collins offsets Fosco's manliness by making him 'as nervously sensitive' (p. 222) as a woman, and by the 'childish' nature of his vanity and self-indulgence – traits that link him to the novel's other effeminate figure of upper-class decadence, Frederick Fairlie.

All of Collins's mature novels reserve a special place for the melancholic hero whose genius leads him to humanistic professions. In *Armadale* (1866) Ozias Midwinter is intractably melancholic, but also the most capable of the novel's male protagonists. His prophetic theory of dreams – which serves as the idiosyncratic vehicle for his characteristically Collinsesque sense of fatality – turns out to be extraordinarily accurate, in contrast to the rational theory of dreams that Dr Hawbury calls 'the theory accepted by the great mass of my profession' (Book 1, ch. 5). Like Dr Hawbury, the novel's lawyers – who fail to save Allan Armadale from catastrophe – are also disadvantaged by their ignorance of melancholia. Mr Pedgift, Sr., for all his worldly wisdom, cannot comprehend Armadale's perverse desire to martyr himself rather than compromise a lady, nor can he understand another of the novel's self-defeating men, Mr Bashwood: 'In spite of his practised acuteness and knowledge of the world, the lawyer was more puzzled than ever. The case of Mr. Bashwood presented the one human riddle of all others, which he was least qualified to solve' (Book 3, ch. 13). Midwinter's scepticism about doctors and lawyers is complemented and validated by Lydia Gwilt's charming ability to outwit them. But although Lydia's power stems, in part, from her own mixture of captivating vanity with melancholic self-hatred, she typifies Collins's tendency to compromise the melancholic female genius by associating her with crime – as is the case, too, with the evocatively named Magdalen Vanstone of *No Name* (1862).

Like Hartright, Midwinter's manly resolution is proved, in part, by his renunciation of genteel station for a humanistic profession. Allowing his inheritance and landed estates to pass to Armadale, then resigning his post as his steward, Midwinter adopts a career in journalism, before deciding to 'take to Literature' (Epilogue, ch. 2). Significantly, his turn to professional writing parallels his extraordinary faith in narrative, which he displays by fetishising Armadale's written account of his dream – a gloomy narrative that Midwinter carries about with him everywhere, as if it were a talisman. Like Hartright's sense of fatality, Midwinter's faith in this particular narrative alternates curiously between a melancholy conviction that it is an omen of doom and a dawning hope that it might be a special, providential warning. Narrative fatality thus defines both the psychological and the aesthetic principles synthesised by Midwinter's affiliation with literature.

In *The Moonstone* (1868) the psychosocial power of humanistic profes-sionalism is asserted through a collaboration between two men, bringing together Collins's characteristically opposed male personality types. Like many of Collins's male protagonists, Franklin Blake and Ezra Jennings share some striking resemblances: both have been falsely accused, and both are parted from the woman they love in consequence. While their shared experience with opium points even more strongly to the psychic connection between them, the two men also plainly represent a polarisation of melan-cholia and narcissism: Jennings's powers of empathy derive from his 'mel-ancholy view of life' (p. 367), while Blake has a 'lively, easy way' (p. 15) that makes him charmingly self-absorbed, so much so that he is fatally obtuse about Roseanna Spearman's love for him. In addition to their emotional complementarity, Jennings and Blake also figure a social alliance between the scientific professional and the humanist: Jennings is a medical assistant, while Blake is what Gabriel Betteredge calls 'a sort of universal genius': 'he wrote a little; he painted a little; he sang and played and composed a little' (p. 15). Their collaboration in solving the riddle of the Moonstone thus yokes two oppositional male personality types, while also hybridising their disciplinary skills and values. Jennings claims that 'science sanctions my proposal, fanciful as it may seem' (p. 385), but his decoding of Dr Candy's delirium relies on strikingly literary techniques. In particular, he rewrites the doctor's incoherent and fragmented words by inventing a narrative to contextualise them. His quasi-theatrical recovery of Blake's actions under the influence of opium is also described as an 'exhibition' (p. 408). Blake's amateurism, as well as the contempt for medicine, law and police work that he expresses early in the novel, are thus tempered by his enthusiasm for Jennings's expertise, while Jennings remains a maverick experimentalist, someone whose unconventional, 'fanciful' procedures result in 'a serious difference of opinion' between himself and 'physicians of established local repute' (p. 367).

This kind of alliance – between melancholics and narcissists, humanistic amateurs and experts – is repeated in a number of Collins's mature novels, notably in the friendship of Midwinter and Armadale. The fragility of such alliances is betrayed, however, by Collins's grudging, ambivalent admiration throughout his career for imposing, nonhumanistic professionals, as well as by as his persistent tendency to undermine these figures. In *The Moonstone*, for example, Sergeant Cuff, whose blend of 'melancholy rapture' (p. 152) with unassailable self-confidence threatens for a time to align melancholic genius with the alluring figure of the detective, is undercut, finally, by his failure to solve the crime. Although he does not share Cuff's melancholy genius, Mr Bruff, the lawyer – who does come close to playing a heroic role as protector of the Verinder family – must also be put in his place: Collins uses Bruff's fierce scepticism about Jennings's experiment to reveal his limitations. As Blake tells the lawyer, 'You have no more imagination than a cow!' (p. 415). Fosco, in *The Woman in White*, is perhaps the most striking instance of a male genius whose professional expertise – in his case, espionage – must be vilified.

Mainstream Victorian culture increasingly regarded middle-class male emotionalism of any kind as unproductive and effeminate. But Collins was not alone in countering this bias by resuscitating the tradition of melancholic genius through the humanistic professional. Dickens carried out a similar project when he made the overly sensitive, extravagantly nostalgic hero of *David Copperfield* (1850) a novelist; William Thackeray did much the same in *Pendennis* (1850). Collins's own later novels tend to lapse away from the psychological and social resolutions he maintained throughout the 1860s. Many of these novels abandon the collaborative relationships between melancholics and narcissists, and between dilettantes and professionals, reverting to an intractable opposition between these forces, as dramatised by figures such as Arnold Brinkworth and Geoffrey Delamayn of *Man and Wife* (1870), Oscar and Nugent Dubourg in *Poor Miss Finch* (1872), and, more complexly, Eustace Woodville and Miserrimus Dexter in *The Law and the Lady* (1875), and the narrator and the Lodger in *The Guilty River* (1886). But the synthetic personalities and collaborations typical of his 1860s novels, which helped Collins and others to shape the social and affective history of mid-Victorian culture, had a lasting impact on later nineteenth-century and early twentieth-century fiction. They resonate with George Gissing's struggling professional writers, with many of Thomas Hardy's wistful young architects and scholars, and even with the jaded but sentimental journalist-narrator of Rudyard Kipling's early stories. The social function of the humanistic professional certainly shifts for these later writers, but the general ideal of melancholic male greatness, as embodied by such figures, lived on in their work.

NOTES

1. D. A. Miller, '*Cage aux folles*: Sensation and Gender in Wilkie Collins's *The Woman in White*', in Miller, *The Novel and the Police* (Berkeley: University of California Press, 1988), pp. 146–91.
2. See Juliana Schiesari, *The Gendering of Melancholia: Feminism, Psychoanalysis, and the Symbolics of Loss in Renaissance Literature* (Ithaca: Cornell University Press, 1992), pp. 1–32.
3. Guinn Batten, *The Orphaned Imagination: Melancholy and Commodity Culture in English Romanticism* (Durham: Duke University Press, 1998), pp. 7–8.

4. Julia Kristeva, *Black Sun: Depression and Melancholia*, trans. Leon Roudiez (New York: Columbia University Press, 1989), p. 7.
5. Sigmund Freud, 'Mourning and Melancholia' (1917), *The Standard Edition of the Complete Psychological Works of Sigmund Freud*, 24 vols., trans. and ed. James Strachey (London: Hogarth, 1953–73), XIV, p. 244.
6. Donald E. Hall, *Fixing Patriarchy: Feminism and Mid-Victorian Male Novelists* (New York: New York University Press, 1996), pp. 177–8.
7. See, respectively, Batten, pp. 1–20; Wolf Lepenies, *Melancholy and Society*, trans. Jeremy Gaines and Doris Jones (Cambridge, MA: Harvard University Press, 1992), pp. 55–86; and Janice Carlisle, *Common Scents: Comparative Encounters in High-Victorian Fiction* (Oxford: Oxford University Press, 2004), pp. 51–4.
8. See David Newsome, *Godliness and Good Learning: Four Studies on a Victorian Ideal* (London: John Murray, 1961).
9. Tamara S. Wagner, '"Overpowering Vitality": Nostalgia and Men of Sensibility in the Fiction of Wilkie Collins', *Modern Language Quarterly* 63 (2002), 471–500.
10. See G. M. Young, *Portrait of an Age* (Oxford: Oxford University Press, 1936), p. 187, and Deirdre David, *Intellectual Women and Victorian Patriarchy* (London: Macmillan, 1987), p. 11.

IO

LILLIAN NAYDER

Collins and empire

Reviewing *The Moonstone* for the *Athenaeum* in July 1868, Geraldine Jewsbury noted that Wilkie Collins brought his readers to tears as the novel ended – not by uniting the English hero and heroine but by dividing three South Asian men. These men are Hindu priests who have together travelled to England and back, violating caste restrictions to restore a sacred Hindu diamond to its shrine in remote Kattiawar:

> Few will read of the final destiny of *The Moonstone* without feeling the tears rise in their eyes as they catch the last glimpse of the three men, who have sacrificed their cast[e] in the service of their God, when the vast crowd of worshippers opens for them, as they embrace each other and separate to begin their lonely and never-ending pilgrimage of expiation. The deepest emotion is certainly reserved to the last.[1]

Although critics often identify sentimentality as politically evasive, the sympathy that Collins evokes for the Hindus here is politically charged. In a novel published on the tenth anniversary of the rebellion that Victorians termed the 'Indian Mutiny' – an uprising that generated racial hatred towards South Asians among the British – Collins humanises figures commonly represented as bestial by his contemporaries and identifies as their rightful property a valuable diamond looted by British forces in Seringapatam fifty years before the main action of his story is set.[2] Depicting the 1799 Siege of Seringapatam in his Prologue, Collins prefaces *The Moonstone* with an instance of British violence against Indians and suggests that their later acts of violence against Britons are marks of retribution triggered by an original, imperial crime.

In a career spanning nearly fifty years, Collins bore witness to many of the events that made 'Rule, Britannia' a catchphrase of the Victorian era; but he also perceived how so-called 'subject races' and rival European powers threatened British hegemony. During Collins's lifetime the British abolished slavery in their possessions (1834); they defeated the Chinese in the Opium

Wars (1840–2, 1860) and annexed the Punjab (1848–9); they brutally suppressed the Indian Mutiny (1857–8) and the Jamaica Insurrection (1865); they designated Victoria 'Empress of India' (1876); and they saw General Charles Gordon 'martyred' in the Sudan (1884). Some of these events enabled the British to justify imperialism morally and cast themselves as self-sacrificing liberators. But others called into question their moral mission: the Opium Wars, for instance, which ensured their 'right' to import opium from India to China against the laws of that land, resolving their trade imbalance.

Both directly and obliquely, Collins responds to such imperial endeavours in his fiction, journalism and melodramas, considering their moral and political meaning and addressing various issues raised by empire building: the grounds and significance of racial identity and difference, for example, and the relation between the civilised and the primitive. In the process, Collins often calls attention to imperial crime – lawless acts committed in the name of empire. While the Prologue of *The Moonstone* (1868) depicts British looting and murder in Seringapatam, *Antonina, or the Fall of Rome* (1850) describes Roman abuses, for which the invasion of the Goths provides an apt punishment and foreshadows the possible decline of an oppressive British empire. In *Armadale* (1866) Collins examines the criminal legacy of British slave ownership in the West Indies, and in *The Frozen Deep* (1856) he dramatises the class exploitation on which imperialism depends. Collins often links imperial crime to patriarchal oppression, combining a critique of empire and British domination with one of male privilege and enforced powerlessness among women. Thus in *The Moonstone* Rachel Verinder, the English heroine, comes to resemble the Hindus in her angry sense of violation, while the rebellious Lydia Gwilt is horsewhipped like a slave by her husband in *Armadale*.

However, Collins also qualifies his political critiques, reinscribing the beliefs that his works question or otherwise muting their subversive implications. In *The Moonstone* he pointedly elides the story of Ezra Jennings, an injured, half-caste figure whose writings are literally buried in his own grave.[3] Moreover, he uses as a primary narrator an English steward whose fondness for *Robinson Crusoe* and its celebration of empire building counters the treatment of the subject in the frame narrative.[4] In *Antonina*, too, Collins associates the Goth invasion with a menacing, feminist insurrection led by an enraged mother, highlighting the dangers posed to civilisation by mother nature, which threatens cultures from within. Such elements of Collins's writing suggest his own ambivalence about imperialism and patriarchy, and his willingness to defend as well as criticise them. But they also indicate the pressures placed on him by publishers and readers anxious to defend the British empire and the social status quo, and reticent to acknowledge imperial wrongdoing.

From the start of his career, the subject of empire and the presumed differences between savage and civilised societies attracted Collins. *Ioláni, or Tahiti as it was*, his first novel, was written in 1844 and centres on life in Tahiti when the island 'was yet undiscovered' (Book 1, ch. 1).[5] Recalling *Ioláni* in 1870, Collins disparaged it as a tale in which his 'youthful imagination ran riot among the noble savages, in scenes which caused the respectable British publisher to declare that it was impossible to put his name on the title page'.[6] But the novel anticipates Collins's later, successful stories about savagery and empire, despite its focus on an aboriginal culture *before* the arrival of Europeans – a subject unique among Collins's works.

As a source for his novel, Collins used William Ellis's *Polynesian Researches* (1831). An Evangelical missionary, Ellis envisaged a time when the 'cruel, indolent and idolatrous' barbarians of the South Seas would become 'a comparatively civilised, humane, industrious, and Christian people'.[7] In portraying Tahitian savagery Ellis emphasised the 'revolting and unnatural' practice of infanticide, which originated among the religious Areoi society and was then adopted by the islanders at large, and which Christian missionaries would eradicate by converting the heathen.[8]

Like Ellis, Collins contrasts the savage with the civilised in representing Tahiti and looks to family dynamics among the islanders to do so – citing their disregard for marriage, for example, which most see 'as a tie to be broken . . . at will'. As he notes in describing the 'unhallowed love' between his heroine, Idía, and Ioláni, a fanatical Areoi priest, their connection would be 'considered as a serious moral infraction . . . in civilised countries' but 'excited, among the luxurious people of the Pacific Islands, neither indignation, nor contempt' (Book 1, ch. 1). Yet as Collins develops his story, the terms of this opposition shift: rather than opposing savage Tahitians to civilised Europeans, he ascribes savagery to Tahitian fathers eager to sacrifice their children to the gods and civilised feeling to Tahitian mothers who risk their lives to protect their infants. Although Ellis found that Tahitian men and women alike practised infanticide and never 'met with a female . . . who had not imbrued her hands in the blood of her offspring', Collins identifies it as a solely patriarchal rite.[9] Pitting the 'remonstrance and resistance of the mother, against the savage intentions of the father' (Book 1, ch. 3), Collins structures his plotline around the flight and 'glorious courage' (Book 3, ch. 6) of Idía, who saves her infant son by taking refuge in the forest with him and Aimáta, her foster daughter.

In the 1830s and 1840s, Tahiti provided English writers with a site on which to imagine a Christian triumph over barbarism or to preach the civilising gospel of free trade.[10] But in *Ioláni* Collins uses Tahiti to define as primitive a society dedicated to gratifying men, one in which women are considered 'inferior creature[s]', with little or no claim to their children (Book 1, ch. 3). As Collins knew, this definition suited much of the ostensibly civilised world, including England itself, where the Infant Custody Act (1839), passed only five years before Collins wrote *Ioláni*, had granted mothers highly circumscribed rights to their young children. Inverting the sexual status quo in *Ioláni* by representing women whose 'duty' is 'to govern and not obey' (Book 1, ch. 3), Collins envisions a cultural advance among Tahitians that is made possible not by religious conversion but by the feminising influence of 'the gentle Aimáta' over the 'bloodthirsty' warrior chief Mahíné, who learns from her the value of mercy, a virtue Collins associates with maternal feeling rather than Christian belief (Book 2, ch. 10). Refusing to exterminate his vanquished enemies, Mahíné abandons his martial ethos and the barbarism of his patriarchal culture, joining a peace-abiding colony on an outlying island with Aimáta and Idía's son.

In *Ioláni* Collins equates the primitivism of Tahiti with a patriarchal ethos that devalues and disempowers women, linking the savage society to his own and subverting the usual polarities of missionary writing. Yet Collins is left uneasy by the conception of women converting manly warriors to their own more civilised, maternal ways. Under Aimáta's influence Mahíné rises above his bloodthirsty counsellors but also appears an emasculated figure whose newfound 'indifference' to matters of war and state imperils him. Conversely, the heroic Idía appears 'horribly unfeminine' in her animosity towards Ioláni and her fierce determination to save her infant son (Book 2, ch. 5). For Collins, Idía and Aimáta incarnate the womanly and civilised virtues of mercy and peace but also embody the force of nature, which aligns the maternal with the barbarous and threatens to usurp the power of men.

Collins proves even more apprehensive about the barbarism of women in *Antonina*, his first published novel, which again links imperial themes to gender politics. Charting Rome's decline, Collins attributes the fall of the empire to the ruthless oppression of Roman masters, who bring the forces of retribution to their gates and foster unrest at home. Conquering foreign lands, the Romans slaughter and enslave their subject peoples in Africa, Europe and the Middle East. At home, Roman aristocrats treat their social inferiors unjustly and thus members of the lower classes welcome the invading Goths, asking them to 'level our palaces to the ground' (ch. 3). Collins interconnects the oppression of the subject races and the lower social orders with that of Roman women, seen merely as domestic slaves by husbands and fathers. Hence Collins represents his Roman heroine,

Antonina, as 'Oriental' in appearance and allies her with the savage Goths, to whose camp she flees after being sexually assaulted by a powerful Roman senator and banished from her home by her tyrannical father Numerian, who falsely accuses her of being a harlot.

Like Aimáta, Antonina helps to civilise the barbarians by feminising them. Already more humane than the Romans at the novel's outset, the Goths grant their women the privileges that women are denied in Rome. But Antonina promotes the civilising process. Offered protection by the Gothic warrior Hermanric, Antonina influences him as Aimáta does Mahíné: 'She had wound her way into his mind, brightening its dark places, enlarging its narrow recesses, beautifying its unpolished treasures'; converted from a martial to a merciful ethos, Hermanric abandons 'the warlike instincts of his sex and nation' (ch. 13). For Collins, the 'dark places' of the earth are not barbarous lands to be brightened by Christian missionaries but savage male psyches to be enlightened by the civilising powers of womankind.

In *Antonina* Collins reworks the imperial motif of Christian conversion to a feminist end as his heroine enlightens the warrior's dark consciousness. But he also reinscribes the conservative values of much imperial writing, positing the savage Gothic mother, Goisvintha, as Antonina's foil. Dedicated to avenging the murder of her children by Romans and outraged by her brother Hermanric's willingness to protect the Roman Antonina, Goisvintha cuts the tendons in his wrists to mark what she perceives as his cowardice, making possible his murder by the Huns. Ostensibly a victim of Roman brutality, Goisvintha becomes the victimiser, undermining Collins's own critique of imperial oppression. Transformed into a 'wild beast' by her thwarted maternal instincts (ch. 8) – her ferocity directed against Goths and Romans alike – Goisvintha amplifies the social threat posed by the 'horribly unfeminine' mother in *Ioláni* and justifies the restoration of patriarchal rule in the empire and the home. As Numerian atones for the wrongs he has done his daughter, Antonina willingly submits to his kindly control after Hermanric's death. Too 'effeminate' to wear the armour of their heroic ancestors and too corrupt for reform, the Romans will be replaced as rulers by the 'manly' Alaric, king of the Goths, whom Collins envisions as the rightful heir of Rome's imperial power.

Collins continued to interconnect forms of domination in his more topical representations of empire in the 1850s, when public attention focused on the loss of the Franklin expedition and the Indian Mutiny, and he began to collaborate with Charles Dickens in response. In October 1854 *The Times* published a report by Dr John Rae, who had discovered, in Repulse Bay, traces of Sir John Franklin and his men, who had left England nine years before to find a Northwest Passage but who had perished after their ships were destroyed by ice. Disturbed by Rae's allegation that the explorers had become cannibals – a charge that undermined their status as civilised Britons – Dickens defended their heroism and refuted these charges, first in a series of articles he wrote for *Household Words* and then in a melodrama he recruited Collins to draft.

As he and Dickens agreed he would, Collins ultimately vindicates the explorers in his draft of *The Frozen Deep* by dramatising the self-control of Richard Wardour, who saves rather than murders his rival Frank Aldersley, for whose life he hungers. But Collins explores the possibility that working-class Britons, exploited by their superiors in what was presumably a common cause, were themselves being cannibalised – a familiar metaphor for class oppression – and, in turn, desired to cannibalise their masters. Hence Collins focuses on the expedition's English cook, a starving worker aptly named Want, who eagerly anticipates his officers' deaths even as his humour partly defuses the social threat he poses.

At the same time, Collins aligns Want with another exploited and resentful worker – a former wet nurse and Highlander, Nurse Esther – whose disenfranchisement is threefold: that of a 'barbarous' Scot in England, a maternal provider in a patriarchal culture, and a servant in a society in which the leisure class feeds off working-class labour. A working-class provider like Want, Esther hungers for the privileges her superiors enjoy and wishfully envisions, through second sight, their deaths in the Arctic. Rather than simply celebrating the explorers' heroism, Collins's draft of the melodrama examines the class tensions underlying imperial enterprises and compares those tensions to the conflict between colonisers and colonised in the Empire, and to the strife between fathers and mothers in patriarchy. More conservative than his subordinate, Dickens heavily revised Collins's draft before producing the play in 1857, emphasising Esther's menacing racial otherness, separating her from Want, and obscuring what Collins foregrounds: class divisions and working-class resentment among the explorers.[11]

When Collins and Dickens turned to the Indian Mutiny, their collaborations again revealed conflicting visions of empire. Like many Victorians, Dickens promoted accounts of the rebellion that ignored oppressive colonial policies and blamed it, instead, on the innate treachery of what he termed 'that Oriental race'.[12] Imagining himself 'Commander in Chief in India', Dickens wrote of doing his 'utmost to exterminate the Race upon whom the stain of the late cruelties rested', alluding to widespread allegations that the sepoys not only murdered British officers and soldiers but tortured and raped British women.[13] Much more circumspect than Dickens in reacting to events in India, Collins occasionally mocked the racist language used to vilify treacherous Orientals and rather than simply blaming the sepoys for the rebellion, he suggested that colonial abuses were largely responsible for it.

In 1857 Collins and Dickens collaborated on 'The Perils of Certain English Prisoners' for *Household Words*, a story that Dickens intended to 'commemorat[e] . . . the best qualities of the English character . . . shewn in India'.[14] Its striking discrepancies in characterisation and tone mark the diverging aims of the two writers. In his two chapters Dickens unifies the British against their common 'Sambo' enemy, enabling a heroic but angry English private in a besieged colony to overcome his class resentment; and he treats with high seriousness the sexual threat posed to virtuous British women by lascivious rebels, a stock theme of Mutiny literature.[15] But in his chapter of 'The Perils', Collins sharply alters Dickens's tone; he emphasises the comic foppishness of the rebel captain, whom he models on dandified British officers in India rather than on mutinous sepoys, and he depicts the dehumanisation of the natives under the captain's control, allying them with British privates forced to labor for the benefit of their social superiors, not their own.

When it suited his purposes, Collins, like Dickens, suggested that empire building dissolved class divisions and transformed common men into masters. In *The Woman in White* (1860), he sends the struggling artist Walter Hartright to 'a wild primeval forest' in Central America to elevate him to the level of his romantic rival, the baronet Sir Percival Glyde (p. 200). But Collins dispelled imperial myths of the common man's ascendancy when collaborating with Dickens, his radicalism piqued by his more conservative co-author and by his sense that Dickens sought to curb what he wrote on volatile issues. At the same time, Collins felt compelled to express his radical ideas indirectly when working with and for Dickens. The contradictions that inform his writings on empire are due, in part, to the pressures placed on him as a contributor to middle-class periodicals and presses and the necessity of challenging mainstream opinions covertly to have his work published there.

In 'A Sermon for Sepoys', his 1858 article on the Indian Mutiny for *Household Words*, Collins echoes Dickens's inflammatory rhetoric about the rebels, calling them 'human tigers' in his opening sentence and 'Betrayers and Assassins' in his last.[16] Yet this language conflicts with the central point of Collins's article. At a time when Dickens spoke of 'exterminat[ing]' Orientals and the British generally abandoned their ethnocentric hope of civilising Indians,[17] Collins argues that the Indians can and should be reformed – not through Christian sermonising but by studying 'their own Oriental literature' and its 'excellent moral lessons', a Muslim equivalent of Christ's parable of the talents.[18] While the rhetoric framing his article represents sepoys as members of a treacherous race, Collins depicts their ancestors as benevolent and suggests that Oriental parables can benefit 'the Human Race', Indians and British alike.[19]

Collins again defends the sepoys, albeit in historically displaced fashion, in *The Moonstone*, his most extended treatment of British India. In 'A Sermon for Sepoys' he countered public opinion about the Mutiny by representing benevolent Muslims and acknowledging the moral worth of Oriental literature. In *The Moonstone* he does so by contrasting the faith and self-sacrifice of Hindus with the hypocrisy of Christians who use their religion to benefit themselves. To the popular preacher and philanthropist Godfrey Ablewhite, the Moonstone is not sacred but a 'marketable commodity' (p. 454) and it comes into his extended family's possession when it is stolen by his uncle, the English officer John Herncastle, in Seringapatam in 1799. Referring to Herncastle ironically as 'the Honourable John' (p. 30) – which was also the nickname for the East India Company – Collins ties the thievery of a seeming renegade to the official policies of those governing India in the years leading up to the Mutiny. Herncastle brings the Moonstone to England, bequeathing it to his niece Rachel Verinder. She receives it on 21 June 1848, her eighteenth birthday. That night, it is stolen again by two of her cousins: first by Franklin Blake, whom she loves and hopes to marry, and then by Ablewhite, who plans to have the diamond cut up and sold before his embezzlement of a ward's trust fund can be discovered.

Identifying Herncastle as the murderer of the three Hindus who guard the Moonstone and depicting the lawlessness through which a sacred Hindu diamond becomes English property, Collins casts the Indians as victims of imperial greed and violence and equates colonisation with theft.[20] Aligning the next generation of Hindu priests with Rachel, from whom the diamond is stolen again, and the gem itself with her chastity, Collins equates colonisation with rape. He bases his detective plot on a complex sexual subtext in which Blake, influenced by an opiate that he has unwittingly ingested and thus unconscious of his actions, removes the diamond from an Oriental cabinet in Rachel's bedroom late at night, staining his nightshirt. Returning to his room, still in an opium trance, he gives Ablewhite the gem to take to the bank for safekeeping. Ablewhite then keeps the diamond for himself. Rachel's shame and outrage after her loss of the Moonstone, which she sees Blake remove, the importance of a stained nightshirt to the thief's identification, the diamond's connection to the moon, and the familiar association between a woman's virginity and a priceless gem, all point to the sexual symbolism of the Moonstone and its second theft.[21] Rachel's striking resemblance to the Hindus and the importance of opium to Blake's actions connect her symbolic violation to India's. Like the Hindus – 'swarthy', 'lithe', 'supple' and 'cat-like' (pp. 275–6) – Rachel is described as 'dark' and 'lithe and supple . . . as a young cat' after the Moonstone is stolen from her (p. 150). Exploited by male relatives, she exhibits an angry desire for independence that parallels that of the Indians resisting British exploitation and control. So, too, does the working-class resentment and the call for revolution expressed by Lucy Yolland, who 'flam[es] out' against Blake (p. 183), blaming him for the suicide of her lovelorn friend, the housemaid Rosanna Spearman. As in earlier works, Collins again ties class resentment to a desire for revenge among the colonised. '"The Moonstone will have its vengeance yet on you and yours!"' a dying Brahmin warns Herncastle (p. 4). '"The day is not far off when the poor will rise against the rich,"' Lucy warns Gabriel Betteredge, referring to Herncastle's nephew. '"I pray Heaven they may begin with *him*"' (p. 184).

The unconscious nature of Blake's theft and his stated purpose in taking the diamond – to safeguard it – appear to exonerate him from wrongdoing and Rachel ultimately forgives and marries him. Yet Collins links protection with violation, providing a critique of guardianship in English homes and in the colonies. 'Here was the man . . . plainly revealing the mercenary object of the marriage, on his side!' the lawyer Bruff notes of Ablewhite, one of Rachel's suitors. 'And what of that? – you may reply – the thing is done every day' (p. 268). Just as English wives are daily exploited by men who presumably protect them and denied property rights as the alleged beneficiaries of coverture, so the colonised are robbed by those claiming to guide them. Having 'planted the English flag' in Seringapatam, the British plunder it, with '"Who's got the Moonstone?"' their 'rallying cry' (p. 4). '"A Hindoo diamond is sometimes part of a Hindoo religion,"' the celebrated English traveller, Mr Murthwaite, tells those at the Verinder estate once the Moonstone is brought there, identifying it as Indian property, not their own (pp. 66, 73).

While Herncastle's actions are plainly condemned, Blake's are not. Indeed, Collins appears an apologist for empire when he supplies Blake with an alibi for his theft of the diamond. Yet the use of opium to acquit Blake also renders him suspect, since this commodity was widely associated with the imperial wrongdoing of the British and discredited their high claims to moral guardianship of benighted peoples. The largest cash crop produced in British India and one that the Indian peasantry was forced to grow, opium was smuggled into China in exchange for tea imported to Britain. When the Chinese began to enforce their laws in the 1830s, the British fought to protect their illicit trade, easily defeating their enemy and ultimately forcing them to legalise the importation of opium in the Treaty of

Tientsen (1860). 'The [East India] Company claimed to itself the high prerogative of being the guardian of the laws, and the preservers of the morals of the people over whom they ruled,' one MP complained in 1833; yet the Company was 'poisoning the health, and destroying the morals of the people of that country', a point reiterated by Victorian critics of empire.[22] Acting for his uncle, 'the Honourable John', in bringing the Moonstone to Yorkshire, Blake is associated with the East India Company and its suspect practices from the outset and his involuntary consumption of opium turns the tables on the colonisers just as their home country is 'invaded' (p. 33) by Hindus in an instance of reverse colonisation. When Blake expresses scepticism about the benefits of medicine, the local doctor surreptitiously adds an opiate to his drink to prove him wrong; like those subject to British rule and forced into economic and physical dependence on opium, Blake experiences, under its influence, a loss of selfhood and autonomy that mirrors the condition of the colonised.

In *The Moonstone* Collins uses his plotline to dramatise the power of psychological and political denial as well as the importance of confession and exposure. Although the British seek to obscure their imperial crimes and vilify the Hindus, Collins reveals Blake's complicity in his uncle's crimes as the hero reenacts his theft of the Moonstone towards the close of the novel and finally becomes conscious of his trespass.[23] Nonetheless, Blake's guilt is acknowledged only partially, since he is simultaneously convicted and exonerated by the novel's logic and its displaced representation of his imperial crime.

Collins's portrait of Murthwaite, the English expert on India, proves equally equivocal and implicitly supports British hegemony even as Murthwaite acknowledges the claims of the Hindus. Murthwaite defends the Indians who travel to England to retrieve the Moonstone, acknowledging it as theirs, recognising its religious significance, and countering Betteredge's claim that they are 'murdering thieves' by describing them as 'a wonderful people' (p. 73). With a knowledge gained from extensive travel in Asia, Murthwaite distinguishes among Hindus, identifying those at the Verinder estate as high-caste Brahmins despite their disguise as Indian jugglers. Yet Murthwaite's celebrated knowledge of Indians is a tool of surveillance and control, not simply a sign of understanding. Testing his theory about the men's identity, Murthwaite charges them with disguising themselves – with an effect that Betteredge likens to their being 'pricked . . . with a bayonet' (p. 70) – and he ultimately infiltrates Hindu society disguised as a pilgrim, witnessing the Moonstone's restoration to a Kattiawar shrine.[24] 'I know the language as well as I know my own, and . . . am lean enough and brown enough to make it no easy matter to detect my European origin,' he reports, and 'passed muster with the people readily' (p. 464).

Murthwaite's ability to pass as a South Asian Hindu suggests his affinity for Indian culture, which he prefers to 'humdrum' English life (p. 65). But it also illustrates his superiority over those who mistake him for one of their own, since the ability to cross racial boundaries is a privilege only the Englishman enjoys. When the Hindus try to disguise themselves in England, first as Indian jugglers of low caste and then as Europeans, they are caught in the act. 'The moment my mysterious client was shown in,' Bruff recalls, 'I felt . . . that I was in the presence of one of the three Indians – probably the chief. He was carefully dressed in European costume. But his swarthy complexion, his long lithe figure, and his grave and graceful politeness of manner were enough to betray his Oriental origin' (p. 275). Whereas Murthwaite successfully disguises his European origin, the Indian cannot hide his Oriental one; his skin colour, body type and manner give him away. In showing that Murthwaite's Englishness is not indelibly written on his figure in the way that the Orient is inscribed on the Indian's, Collins voices a common Victorian assumption about racial difference, one that subtly justifies imperial rule – the idea that the Indians rather than the English possess a racial identity, an inescapable essence that defines them and fixes them in their place.

Unlike the Indians in *The Moonstone*, Murthwaite easily crosses racial boundaries, making his own whiteness invisible and transcending categorisation. Yet his ability to transcend racial identity and pass as Indian is not shared by other Englishmen. In the novel's climactic scene, Sergeant Cuff exposes Ablewhite's masquerade as a dark-skinned sailor, just as Bruff sees through the Indian's European disguise. Pulling off his black wig and beard and 'washing off' his dark colour, Cuff reveals the 'livid white' beneath 'the swarthy complexion', a whiteness echoed by the dead man's name (p. 464). Calling attention to the Englishman's whiteness, Collins makes visible his racial identity, denying him the power exercised by Murthwaite and thwarting his scheme to destroy the integrity and sacred character of the Moonstone. Ablewhite's unmasking underscores Collins's concern with imperial greed even as Murthwaite's ability to avoid a similar exposure reveals Collins's investment in empire.

Collins returned to the subject of racial identity in the melodrama *Black and White* (1869), a collaboration with Charles Fechter, and the novel *Poor Miss Finch* (1872). In both, Collins extends his analysis of racial identity by considering its very origins. Suggesting that racial identities are socially constructed rather than inborn – invented and reinvented, not revealed or disguised – Collins appears at his most radical, challenging assumptions on which Victorians based their imperial ideals. Written and performed in the wake of the Jamaica Insurrection and the trial of Governor Eyre, criticised for his repressive measures in suppressing the 1865 revolt, *Black and White* is set on Trinidad in 1830 but questions ideas of racial difference prevalent throughout the Victorian period. Midway through the plot, the hero, a French count, learns that he is the son of a slave woman raped by a colonist and thus himself the property of his father's heir. Sold to an English plantation owner, the count is saved only when a long-lost paper of manumission granting his freedom is discovered. Collins uses his enslavement and liberation to subvert the racial categories of 'black' and 'white' and to demonstrate that the grounds of racial difference are arbitrary and shifting.

In *Poor Miss Finch* Collins again challenges racial categories – not by dramatising the legal redefinition of his hero's racial identity but by having his skin colour literally and permanently darken: because of his treatment for epilepsy, Oscar Dubourg turns dark blue and Collins represents his change in pigmentation as if it were a racial transformation. Ultimately, Collins unites his dark blue hero with Lucilla Finch, a blind Caucasian woman who overcomes her irrational aversion to dark-skinned peoples, South Asians particularly, to marry the man she loves. Set in 1858, the second year of the Mutiny, the novel persistently refers to British India without naming the rebellion itself. Lucilla's hysterical response to a 'Hindoo gentleman' at her aunt's London home and her embarrassed sense of her irrationality critique the virulent British response to the uprising:

> My mind drew a dreadful picture of the Hindoo, as a kind of monster in human form . . . The instant I felt him approaching, my darkness was peopled with brown demons. He took my hand. I tried hard to control myself – but I really could not help shuddering and starting back when he touched me. To make matters worse, he sat next to me at dinner. In five minutes I had long, lean, black-eyed beings all round me; perpetually growing in numbers, and pressing closer and closer on me as they grew. It ended in my being obliged to leave the table. When the guests were all gone, my aunt was furious. I admitted my conduct was unreasonable in the last degree.   (ch. 20)

Describing Lucilla's aversion to dark-skinned people as one common among the blind, Collins points to the blindness of racial prejudice, which he counters by imagining the happy 'interracial' marriage of the white Lucilla and the dark blue Oscar. Although Victorians generally stigmatised such unions, Collins dispels the anxieties they provoked: those felt by Lucilla's parents for her younger sister, for example, who lives with them in a 'distant colon[y]' and may 'end in marrying "a chief"' (Epilogue).

In *The Moonstone* Collins exposes Ablewhite's whiteness, washing off his blackface and thus dissociating crime from racial otherness. In *Poor Miss Finch* Collins achieves a similar end by showing how Lucilla constructs a 'brown demon' out of a friendly Hindu and by questioning the idea of whiteness itself. Anticipating E. M. Forster's *A Passage to India* (1924) and the observation 'that the so-called white races are really pinko-grey',[25] Collins demonstrates that Caucasians are not really 'white'; their colour, far from neutral, is naturally subject to variation. Without undergoing treatment for epilepsy, Oscar's twin brother 'change[s] colour' (ch. 43) with his changing emotions, as does Lucilla, 'her colour chang[ing] from pale to red – from red to pale' (ch. 28). But while questioning the idea of whiteness, Collins also describes Oscar's darkened hue as a 'disfigurement' and 'discolouration', treating whiteness as the healthy norm (ch. 19). Collins intends Oscar's change in pigmentation and Lucilla's ability to 'see' beyond it to challenge polarised racial categories. Yet the displacement through which he imagines Oscar's otherness – as the unfortunate consequence of medical treatment – not only disguises but compromises his aim, pathologising racial difference. Such displacements often recur in Collins's representations of race and empire, dividing text from subtext. In so doing, they enable such novels as *The Moonstone* and *Poor Miss Finch* to pass as conventional rather than subversive – as 'sensation novel[s] for Sunday reading', as a reviewer in the *Athenaeum* put it – while also revealing Collins's desire to assimilate and conform.[26]

NOTES

1. Geraldine Jewsbury, unsigned review, *Athenaeum* 25 July, 1868; *CH*, pp. 170–1.
2. Patrick Brantlinger, *Rule of Darkness: British Literature and Imperialism, 1830–1914* (Ithaca: Cornell University Press, 1988), pp. 199–224.
3. Tamar Heller, *Dead Secrets: Wilkie Collins and the Female Gothic* (New Haven: Yale University Press, 1992), pp. 142–63.
4. See Lillian Nayder, 'Robinson Crusoe and Friday in Victorian Britain: "Discipline", "Dialogue", and Collins's Critique of Empire in *The Moonstone*', *Dickens Studies Annual* 21 (1992), 213–31.
5. *Ioláni, or Tahiti as it was* was first published in 1999 by Princeton University Press, edited by Ira B. Nadel.
6. Quoted in 'Wilkie Collins', *Appleton's Journal of Popular Literature, Science, and Art* (3 September 1870), 279.
7. William Ellis, *Polynesian Researches during a Residence of Nearly Eight Years in the Society and Sandwich Islands*, 4 vols. (1831) (London: Henry G. Bohn, 1853), I, p. viii.
8. Ibid., p. 248.
9. Ibid., p. 252.
10. See Brantlinger, *Rule of Darkness*, pp. 30–2.

11. See Lillian Nayder, *Unequal Partners: Charles Dickens, Wilkie Collins and Victorian Authorship* (Ithaca: Cornell University Press, 2002), pp. 60–99.
12. Charles Dickens to Angela Burdett-Coutts, 4 October 1857, in Madeline House, Graham Storey and Kathleen Tillotson (eds.), *The Letters of Charles Dickens*, 12 vols. (Oxford: Clarendon Press, 1965–2001), VIII, p. 459.
13. Dickens, *Letters* VIII, p. 459; see also Dickens to Emile de la Rue, 23 October 1857, *Letters*, VIII, p. 473.
14. Dickens, *Letters*, VIII, pp. 482–3.
15. See Brantlinger, *Rule of Darkness*, p. 206, and Nancy L. Paxton, 'Mobilizing Chivalry: Rape in British Novels about the Indian Uprising of 1857', *Victorian Studies* 36 (Autumn 1992), 5–30.
16. Wilkie Collins, 'A Sermon for Sepoys', *Household Words* 17 (27 February 1858), 244, 247.
17. Brantlinger, *Rule of Darkness*, p. 200.
18. Collins, 'A Sermon for Sepoys', 244.
19. Ibid., 247.
20. John R. Reed, 'English Imperialism and the Unacknowledged Crime of *The Moonstone*', *Clio* 2 (June 1973), 281–90. See also my 'Collins and Empire' in Lillian Nayder, 'Wilkie Collins Studies: 1983–1999', *Dickens Studies Annual* 28 (1999), 257–329.
21. See Albert D. Hutter, 'Dreams, Transformations, and Literature: The Implications of Detective Fiction', *Victorian Studies* 19 (December 1975), 181–209.
22. Hansard's Parliamentary Debates, 3rd Series (London: Wyman, 1830–91), XVIII, p. 770. See Bruce Johnson, 'Righteousness Before Revenue: The Forgotten Moral Crusade Against the Indo-Chinese Opium Trade', *Journal of Drug Issues* 5 (Autumn 1975), 304–26.
23. See Ronald R. Thomas, *Dreams of Authority: Freud and the Fictions of the Unconscious* (Ithaca: Cornell University Press, 1990), pp. 203–19.
24. See Jaya Mehta, 'English Romance; Indian Violence', *Centennial Review* 39 (Autumn 1995), 611–57.
25. E. M. Forster, *A Passage to India* (New York: Harcourt Brace Jovanovich, 1984), p. 65.
26. Unsigned review, *Athenaeum*, 17 February 1872; *CH*, p. 191.

11

KATE FLINT

Disability and difference

Writing in Henry Mayhew's encyclopaedic *London Labour and the London Poor* (1861–2), Andrew Halliday gives a vivid impression of the numerous types of physical disability which could be encountered on the capital's streets in the mid-century. Although the Mendicity Society had recently cleared the streets of many imposters, a number of beggars continued to use their bodies as a source of income, and, in the spirit of this work's incessant drive to impose order on the disorderly, Halliday proceeds to list them:

> The bodily afflicted beggars of London exhibit seven varieties. 1. Those having real or pretended sores . . . 2. Having swollen legs. 3. Being crippled, deformed, maimed, or paralyzed [some of these fall into the further category of 'Disaster Beggars'] 4. Being blind. 5. Being subject to fits [and hoping, for the most part, to be offered brandy to revive them]. 6. Being in a decline. 7. 'Shallow Coves', or those who exhibit themselves in the streets, half-clad, especially in cold weather.[1]

When their conditions are genuine, Halliday considers these individuals as 'certainly deserving of sympathy and aid; for they are utterly incapacitated from any kind of labour'.[2] Those who exhibit their deformed, maimed or impaired bodies simultaneously provoke revulsion and compassion, and seem to inhabit a quite different sphere from those who encounter them in the street.

Wilkie Collins's fiction repeatedly foregrounds a number of individuals who are challenged in their relationship to the material world. His interest in obstacles to full physical functioning – in those who, as the influential psychologist Alexander Bain would put it, lack one or more of their 'intellectual' senses (those that provide what was thought of as objective information) may well stem in part from his own problems with his eyesight – he complained of chronic 'eye gout', and consulted the ophthalmic surgeon George Critchett about this (Peters, p. 336). But it must also be placed within a broader Victorian concern with the operation of the senses. This concern was not just demonstrated in those popular texts, often with a theological bias, which sought to stress the spiritual consolation that could come from physical deprivation. It was also found within scientific works which explored developments in physiology and psychology, and which, in their turn, paid as much attention to variation and aberration within human perceptual systems as they tried to generalise about what constituted the 'normal' functioning of the senses. And while many of Collins's figures might seem to differ conspicuously from assumed social norms, he employs them not just to add attention-grabbing elements to his characterisation and his plots, but also to make his readers reflect on the broad operations of phenomenological knowledge, and the simultaneous reliability and in-stability of what, in *The Moonstone* (1868), Collins terms 'the evidence of [the] senses' (p. 351).

Moreover, if most of these characters are presented in terms of lack, or deformation, or other kinds of deviance from the average (like the alarming blue colour which Oscar Dubourg, in *Poor Miss Finch* (1872), turns as a result of taking silver nitrate to control his epilepsy), so there can be some-thing aberrant about the norm carried to extremes, as we see through the figure of Geoffrey Delamayn, the physical fitness fanatic in *Man and Wife* (1870). Even outside the realm of the recognisably freakish, Collins uses certain individuals in order to collapse boundaries between the able-bodied and the impaired. The hypersensitive Frederick Fairlie, in *The Woman in White* (1860), is another case in point. He affects to be able to detect a smell of 'horrid dealers' and brokers' fingers' on the drawings which he shows to Walter Hartwright, who rightly, in his turn, senses not an 'odour of plebeian fingers' but the far less palatable stench of class prejudice behind this remark (p. 42).

While Collins is primarily, of course, setting up Mr Fairlie as an unsym-pathetic, self-absorbed and, by contrast with Hartwright, feminised figure, one might also pursue another line, that the novelist is underscoring the generalisation made by the influential physiological psychologist William Carpenter, that the senses 'vary considerably, as regards general acuteness, amongst different individuals'.[3] For overall, Collins seems fascinated not so much by the *difference* of the disabled, but by their similarity to the able-bodied. For a start, few are distanced from the readership in class terms, unlike the London beggars – though there are exceptions: Rosanna Spearman, in *The Moonstone*, is a housemaid with a badly deformed shoulder, and her friend, the fisherman's daughter Limping Lucy, has a misshapen foot. Even though 'Madonna', the deaf-mute heroine of *Hide and Seek* (1854), is illegitimate, and is discovered working as a juvenile circus-performer, one may fairly argue that her disability combines with the purity of her features and the sweetness and generosity of her disposition to turn her, as is signalled by the very epithet by which she is known, into an exaggerated epitome of an ideal. Her infirmity is translated, to quote Elizabeth Gitter, into 'the speechlessness of the angelic type of mid-century heroine'.[4]

Disabled figures are not unusual within Victorian fiction. Women who face physical challenges include the diminutive persons of The Marchioness in Dickens's *The Old Curiosity Shop* (1841) and Jenny Wren in *Our Mutual Friend* (1864); the crooked-postured artist of Dinah Craik's *Olive* (1850); Geraldine Underwood in Charlotte Yonge's *The Pillars of the House* (1873) and Ermine Williams in her *The Clever Woman of the Family* (1865). As Martha Stoddard Holmes has written, these tend to occupy very similar roles:

> [as adults] consigned to eternal childhood, a celibate version of the 'fallen' woman, or some other kind of 'odd' and superfluous female. Her chief importance in the plot is to generate emotion and moral development in others by being innocent and saintly, surprisingly cheerful, justifiably melancholy, tragically frustrated from achieving her goals as woman, suicidal or dead – *or simply by being disabled,* without any of these other conditions.[5]

Those women who do achieve the 'reward' of marriage and financial stability are, in turn, very rarely sexualised, and become mothers through adoption. Nor are disabilities confined to women: consider the hunchbacked Philip Wakem in *The Mill on the Floss* (1860), or Colin, in Francis Hodgson Burnett's *The Secret Garden* (1911). Both experience deformities which often have a feminising effect, making them especially sensitive, attuned to the affective aspects of culture, imaginatively sympathetic towards women – and yet also, at times, peevish; adopting a selfish whine when they feel that they are somehow frustrated in occupying what ought, by gender, to have been their 'natural' role. Only the rare, symbolic male character – such as the preternaturally cheerful, and preadolescent, Tiny Tim in Charles Dickens's *A Christmas Carol* (1843) – seems to escape this fate.

Collins both draws on this tradition, and mutates it when he creates the figure of Miserrimus Dexter in *The Law and the Lady* (1875). Lacking his lower limbs, his upper half is that of 'an unusually handsome, and an unusually well-made man . . . he would have looked effeminate, but for the manly proportions of his throat and chest: aided in their effect by his flowing beard and long moustache' (ch. 20). But despite Dexter's dandy-like propensities in dress; his love of colourful fabrics, of velvets and ruffles, he is a completely different kind of man from the frustrated and emasculated Wakem. In his capacity for sudden bursts of anger and physical passion, followed by extreme inertia when his heightened energy burns itself out, and above all in his exceptional powers of imaginative projection – even in his excesses of melancholia, Dexter presents an instance of someone whose physical limitations are to an extent compensated for by extraordinary mental capacities. Despite the ways in which he hops around on his hands, he is no freak-show exhibit, but rather claims the talents of a serious performer: "'I play the parts of all the heroes that ever lived. I feel their characters. I merge myself in their individualities. For the time, I *am* the man I fancy myself to be. I can't help it. I am obliged to do it"' (ch. 25).

With his aptitude for uncontrolled imaginative projection, Dexter is more than the detective genius necessary to supplement Valeria Woodville's admirably tenacious persistence in getting to the bottom of the mystery of how her husband's first wife met her death. He is the monstrous figure who may be seen to represent the popularly conceived tendencies of the reader of sensation fiction run riot: he is given over to identification, to concentrating on the matter at hand to the exclusion of the 'real world', to obsessive involvement with following a plot, and he collapses with eventual enervation. Or, to put it slightly differently, and in Valeria's words: "'It seems to me that he openly expresses – I admit in a very reckless and boisterous way – thoughts and feelings which most of us are ashamed of as weaknesses, and which we keep to ourselves accordingly"' (ch. 26). Here, as elsewhere, Collins sets out to show that there is no clear dividing line between the disabled and the normally-bodied, however much appearances may suggest – sometimes startlingly – the contrary. This is not to say, however, that he ignored the prejudice – or the condescension – which the disabled could face; nor the ways in which they might attempt to compensate for their relative powerlessness – witness Dexter's sadistic, erotic games with his 'slave' and cousin, the sexually ambiguous Ariel.

But Miserrimus Dexter is unusual among Collins's major disabled characters in that his challenges stem from a visibly deficient bodily frame. For what particularly stands out in the remainder of these protagonists is their relationship to sensory perception. Collins is notably interested in those who suffer from problems with one of the major sensory organs – sight or hearing – and with the compensatory mechanisms which they develop as a result. In part, his stance reflects the bias in charitable activity, in mid-nineteenth-century Britain, towards disablement. As Anne Borsay writes:

> Blind and deaf people, denied access to the word of God, appealed to Christian sympathies, particularly since new methods of teaching them to communicate offered a justification for schools. Employment facilities often followed, as ex-pupils struggled to find work in the open labour market. Provision for

physical, as opposed to sensory, impairments, on the other hand, was slower to materialize.[6]

But as well as tapping into these sources of sympathy, something more experimental is, I believe, at stake. Collins is offering, through these exceptional characters, a commentary on the role played by the senses in perception in general – something which was very much a live issue for many commentators in the mid-nineteenth century in the rapidly consolidating field of psychophysiology.[7]

The scope for reflection which Collins's treatment of disabled characters offers his readers about the role of the senses in everyday perception is reinforced by the attention he pays to the vocabulary of sensory cognition – both literal and metaphorical – throughout his prose. Indeed, it often appears as though contact with those whose physical senses are in some ways deficient infects the prose of individual narrators, making them hyper-conscious of their own sensory powers. Thus, for example, in *Poor Miss Finch* Madame Pratolungo explicitly startles the reader's imagination into seeing her when she speeds up her narrative on the occasion of the oculists' arrival at the rectory, saying that she will take 'a jump, like a sheep, over some six hours of precious time, and present my solitary self to your eye, posted alone in the sitting room to receive the council of surgeons on its arrival at the house' (ch. 30). In *The Guilty River* (1886) Gerard Roylake establishes the stagnation of both natural environment and aristocratic society on the very first page of his narrative, calling attention to the oppressive effects caused by the absence of clear visible markers of distinction, and of sound that should be audible, even before an actual deaf man is introduced: 'A time passed, dull and dreary. The mysterious assemblage of trees was blacker than the blackening sky. Of millions of leaves over my head, none pleased my ear, in the airless calm, with their rustling summer song' (ch. 1). In turn, this foregrounding of a narrator's alertness to the part played by their senses reinforces the degree to which connections are made between the reader's imagination and the sensory information which is stored in their own memory, and on which they will draw when responding to the text. In other words, Collins consistently makes us acknowledge and reflect on the part which our own bodies play in our interpretative strategies.

Three sense-impaired figures stand out for the sustained attention which Collins pays to their disabilities: the deaf and dumb Mary – 'Madonna' – in *Hide and Seek*, the blind Lucilla Finch in *Poor Miss Finch*, and the far less sympathetically portrayed deaf Lodger of the novella *The Guilty River*. An additional blind man, Leonard Franklin, in *The Dead Secret* (1857), seems less of interest in his own right than as an enabling device: as Lillian Nayder comments in her book on Collins: 'In effect, Collins uses Leonard's invalid condition to invert the traditional relation between husband and wife. His blindness makes possible Rosamond's gender transgressions, by placing the husband in a subordinate and wifely position of dependence'.[8] Rosamond is thus a very different kind of woman from Madonna, who, as we have already seen, is presented as an exaggerated type of feminine virtue. She is also a type in another sense: a case study of the deaf-mute. Collins's own footnote to Chapter 7 explains how he based her history on that of John Kitto, who lost his hearing as the result of a fall when he was just thirteen, and whose speech rapidly deteriorated thereafter. Gitter surmises that the story of the famous American deaf-mute Laura Bridgman, too, underpins that of Madonna; this would have been familiar to Collins not just from a chapter in Kitto's *The Lost Senses* (1845), but also, for him, and for many of his readers, from the attention which Dickens paid to her in *American Notes* (1842).

'There is no recovery, no adequate compensation', Kitto wrote of the effects of his accident, 'for such a loss as was on that day sustained.'[9] In *Hide and Seek* Collins determinedly draws out the full sentimental potential of Madonna's plight. 'Shall she never hear kindly human voices, the song of birds, the pleasant murmur of the trees again? Are all the sweet sounds that sing of happiness to childhood, silent for ever to *her*?' (Book 1, ch. 3), he muses, from Valentine Blyth's perspective, before the artist takes her into his home to be surrogate child and revivifying presence in the life of his invalid wife. Yet Collins is especially interested in the compensatory mechanisms which an individual develops in order to cope with 'incurable misfortune' (Book 1, ch. 2). Madonna's 'affliction had tended, indeed, to sharpen her faculties of observation and her powers of analysis to such a remarkable degree' that not only can she follow the gist of a conversation well without hearing the actual words, but she also becomes a preternaturally gifted judge of character, reading 'a stranger's manner, expression, and play of features at a first interview' (Book 1, ch. 7). Such a facility – though Collins does not elaborate on this – is implicitly predicated upon the soundness of physiognomy as a tool for uncovering what lies beyond vision: even if Madonna is not mistaken in her judgements, other novelists (and one might instance George Eliot) would be quick to point to the dangers of such credulous readings of surfaces. Nonetheless, Madonna's 'seeing sense' gives her delights of a less potentially hazardous kind:

> All beautiful sights, and particularly the exquisite combinations that Nature presents, filled her with an artless rapture . . . She would sit for hours, on fresh

summer evenings, watching the mere waving of the leaves; her face flushed, her whole nervous organization trembling with the sensations of deep and perfect happiness which that simple sight imparted to her.   (Book 1, ch. 7)

Madonna's quivering alertness to natural beauty – 'artless', despite what proves to be her facility in drawing – is presented as a Ruskin-inflected attribute, making up – it would seem – for what she had lost. Although Collins does not place this response within a religious framework, it is highly similar to mid-century Christian glosses on the importance of the senses. 'Is not the earth full of riches? Has not the Creator adapted it to our pleasures, as well as our necessities, and endowed us with every sense requisite for enjoyment?' gushes the writer of *The Senses and the Mind*, published by the Religious Tract Society in the year before *Hide and Seek*.[10]

Yet Madonna's responsiveness to aesthetic beauty also makes her particularly susceptible to the charms of the nineteen-year-old, exuberant, irresponsible and designedly irresistible Zack Thorpe. Near the beginning of the novel, a putative romance narrative is established around the couple, which is, of course, to be squelched by the discovery that they are half-brother and sister. Critics have, understandably, taken this as Collins diving away from what, according to the fictional conventions of the time, would have been something of a radical possibility: the fulfilment, and affirmation, of the affective and physical desire of someone with impaired senses. But there is a more positive way of understanding the mechanics of the novel. Half-brothers and sisters are another version of one of Collins's favourite structural devices: the double, or twin. Such formulations contribute substantially to the dance and exploration of confused and intertwined identities upon which his compelling, if convoluted, plots so consistently depend. They also, necessarily, raise more thematic concerns of similarities and difference. The revelation of Madonna's and Zack's consanguinity is not so much an act of protoeugenics, a keeping apart of the healthy-bodied and the disabled (a feature of certain fictions that appeared after Galton had proposed his theory of eugenics later in the century), as it is a means of emphasising the continuum between the fully able and the impaired.[11] The fact that this is a novel which emphasises connectivity – the language of brotherhood is frequently invoked as Zack and his friend Mat Grice affirm and reaffirm their homosocial closeness in the novel's closing chapters – underscores this point.

The enhanced role which the visual holds in Madonna's life finds its counterpart in the ways in which the blind Lucilla, in *Poor Miss Finch*, uses her senses of hearing and of touch to locate herself in her environment. Her 'delicate ear' (ch. 3) readily picks up the sound of a strange footstep; she can tell when a medicine spoon is full by the sound of the liquid falling into it (ch. 16). As G. H. Lewes remarked in the chapter of *The Physiology of Common Life* (1859) which deals with 'our senses and sensations':

> How delicate is the susceptibility to shades of difference, may best be illustrated by the wonderful accuracy with which blind men thread their way along crowded streets: not only do they learn to recognise the different kind of persons – policeman, porter, or gentleman – by the sound of the tread, but they learn, it is said, to recognise the difference between a man standing still, and a lamp-post at a short distance, simply by means of the reverberations of their own footsteps.[12]

Moreover, Lucilla has a finely developed sense of touch – '"eyes in the tips of her fingers"', to quote her beloved Oscar (ch. 24). Touch is the most intimate of the senses, and the emphasis on her possession of this ability is highly appropriate to Collins's portrayal of this highly sexualised individual. As Diana Fuss has put it in *The Sense of an Interior*, the prime instrument of touch, the hand, 'can be the subject or object of touch; it can be agent or receiver, and often both at once. Unlike vision, which depends upon the spatial distancing of the object from the perceiving subject, touch immediately brings subjects and objects into closer conversation.'[13] Lucilla reads faces by passing her fingertips lightly over them; she identifies the tooled pattern on a vase as owls sitting in ivy nests, using her tactile memory of other shapes; and, when she temporarily regains some degree of sight, she has – just like the very well-known example of the eighteenth-century surgeon William Cheseldon's patient – to revert to touch, rather than sight, in order to learn to distinguish between a dog and a cat, and in order to understand the phenomenon of perspective.[14]

Somewhat less reliable is her ability – on which she nonetheless prides herself – to be able to tell the difference between light and dark coloured surfaces by feeling them: an exercise which allows her to voice her determined (if apparently irrational) abhorrence of dark colours. This is something on which the plot, of course, turns: when Oscar turns that unappetising shade of blue, this is something which his twin brother Nugent believes he can exploit to his advantage if Lucilla can see them both. But as Lillian Nayder points out in her chapter in this volume on Collins and empire, this antipathy towards dark coloration also allows Collins to make a point about how racism functions: he goes to some lengths to explain that while at first a different skin colour from one's own may be a cause of revulsion, the shock of this difference soon wears off (and this is a response which Nugent had not foreseen). Yet as well as showing the powers which Lucilla has developed in order to counter her visual handicap, Collins also explores, in a much more sustained fashion than he did with Madonna, the frustrations of disability. She knows that people can tease and trick her; that she may be placed deliberately at a disadvantage. '"It is sometimes *so* hard to be blind!"' she exclaims, in an uncharacteristic outburst that reveals her habitual suppression of negative emotion, when she fails to distinguish accurately between the twin brothers (ch. 24). While applicable to any blind person, such a comment can necessarily take on a metaphoric resonance as well. If to be deprived of sensory information is to be barred from full access to knowledge, someone in Lucilla's position may well be read as feminised: not by reason of weakness so much as by drawing an analogy between physical and cultural circumstances.

Yet Lucilla's infirmity does not turn her into a victim, whether in the eyes of others, or in her own self-assessment. She boasts of having advantages not possessed by her companion, Madame Pratolungo – *she* can 'see' in the dark. '"Just tell me which knows best in the dark – my touch or your eyes?"' she demands. '"Who has got a sense that she can always trust to serve her equally well through the whole four-and-twenty hours? You or me?"' (ch. 23). As we have seen, she prides herself on her touch, falling in line with the widely diffused belief in the development of compensatory mechanisms, becoming one of what George Sexton, writing in 1880, termed 'the numerous instances of persons in whom the power of touch has been made to supply, with great perfection, the deficiency arising from the loss of one of the other senses, particularly that of sight'.[15] However, it is not made clear whether her means of distinguishing Oscar from his twin brother Nugent – the 'delicious *tingle*' that she feels when he touches her (ch. 43) – is the product of this finely developed sense of touch, or is something much more common, and potentially available to all of us: a frisson of sexual attraction. While this might nowadays be thought of as a response to bodily pheremones – and hence as closely tied in with the sense of smell as Lucilla's initial 'little irrepressible shudder of disgust' at the tobacco-reeking Herr Grosse (ch. 30) – it may be seen, in context, less as a comment on blindness as such, as an important counter-suggestion to the theory which Charles Darwin was to go on to develop in *The Descent of Man* (1871), that sexual attraction is based primarily upon visual appeal.

In relation to her responses to Nugent, the apparent ease with which Lucilla resigns herself to her permanent blindness – after the brief interval of time during which she can see – becomes significant. Not only is Collins acknowledging medical plausibility, but he is refusing the reader a conventional happy ending in which true love is accompanied by full, or returning, vision. In an inversion of the protofeminist ending of *Jane Eyre* (1847), where Rochester's blindness makes him dependent on the heroine, Lucilla seems content to resume her womanly position of dependency. That the narration does not wholly endorse this position, or at least wishes the reader to examine it critically, is clear from the way in which the feisty, outspoken Madame Pratolungo is used to frame the entire novel. Whatever her biases – or ideological partial-sightedness – she is, in her independent-mindedness, presented as a far more compelling character than Lucilla, whose blindness, ultimately, becomes an inseparable part of her near-caricatured role as a type of female dependency. The effect is somewhat double-edged. While *Poor Miss Finch* presents a highly sympathetic view of blindness as such, its metaphorical extension, when it is used to amplify a circumspect world-view, reinforces the equation of physical condition with social limitations in a broader sense.

However, Collins is, I think, also drawing our attention to the tendency of the differently-abled to practise an understandable form of self-protection. For despite the emphasis he places on the compensatory aspects of sensory deprivation, he is also very alert to its power to isolate the individual concerned, or to produce particular sources of panic or terror. In *Hide and Seek* Zack's friend Mat enters Valentine's studio at night, determined on stealing the hair bracelet which will lead to proving that Madonna is, indeed, the child of his sister and Zack's father (the fact that Mat himself is follically challenged, having been scalped in America, is something which, when taken together with the composition of this bracelet, reveals Collins to have been unusually concerned with bodily margins of all kinds when composing the novel). In order to accomplish his mission, he is forced to blow out Madonna's candle, so that she cannot see him. He rightly reasons that she will not be able to use her hearing to detect his presence:

> He had not calculated, however, on the serious effect which the success of his stratagem would have upon her nerves, for he knew nothing of the horror which the loss of her sense of hearing caused her always to feel when she was left in darkness; and he had not stopped to consider that by depriving her of her light, he was depriving her of that all-important guiding sense of sight, the loss of which she could not supply in the dark, as others could, by the exercise of the ear. (Book 2, ch. 12)

But Madonna, like Lucilla during those moments when others deliberately disorient her, is only temporarily disconcerted. Collins's most sustained treatment of the mental anguish which may be caused by disability can be found in his portrayal of the Lodger in *The Guilty River*: never named, he is rendered less of an individual by this refusal to grant him an identity, suggesting the problems he has in reaching out to others. He exemplifies what G. H. Bosanquet had, earlier in the century, identified as one of 'the sorrows of deafness': 'a mind preying upon itself; which, the more highly it has been cultivated, the more certainly it will do'.[16] Collins renders him a type of 'the horrible isolation among humanity of the deaf" (ch. 5), 'living the death-in-life of deafness, apart from creatures – no longer my fellow-creatures – who could hear' (ch. 5). This recently deafened man finds his character changing, becoming morose, vindictive, scheming and resentful – causing him to ask rhetorically, 'Is there a moral sense that suffers when a bodily sense is lost?' (ch. 5) In this respect, he enacts the tendency within disability representation noted by David Hevey when he remarks how, often, 'it is the impaired body of the disabled person on to which is projected the negative manifestations of that impairment in society . . . the anti-hero's limited and semi-human consciousness glimpses their tragic existence through the cracked mirror of their hatred for themselves'.[17]

But Collins's portrayal of the Lodger is far more subtle than a characterisation of him as a tortured individual – even one who makes some mixed claims on our fellow feeling. For, as one might by now expect, his condition appears to feminise him, and this becomes the means through which the narrator, Gerard Roylake, expresses the degree to which he is inescapably fascinated by him. While Roylake explicitly states that it would be impossible to mistake the stranger renting a room at the mill for a woman, he nonetheless possesses 'the most beautiful face that I had ever seen'; he has 'long finely-shaped hands' (ch. 3). His eyes at first appear as those of a *femme fatale* – 'Dark, large, and finely set in his head, there was a sinister passion in them' (ch. 4) – and Collins overdetermines the Lodger's outsider status by making him a half-caste, son of a freed slave. Later, the gender ambiguity is even more emphasised when Roylake, at some length, perceives that:

> his eyes were of that deeply dark blue, which is commonly and falsely described as resembling the colour of the violet. To my thinking, they were so entirely beautiful that they had no right to be in a man's face. I might have felt the same objection to the pale delicacy of his complexion, to the soft profusion of his reddish-brown hair, to his finely shaped sensitive lips, but for two marked peculiarities in him which would have shown me to be wrong – that is to say: the expression of power about his head, and the signs of masculine resolution presented by his mouth and chin. (ch. 6)

He is far more sexually compelling than the more conventionally described (if endearingly companionate and resourceful) Cristel, the ostensible object of both their desires – compelling, at least, until he breaks from communicating by letter and note, and speaks – usually in an unvarying monotone, but on one memorable occasion: 'his voice broke suddenly into a screech, prolonged in its own discord until it became perfectly unendurable to hear' (ch. 13). He had forgotten, the Lodger confessed miserably, that he was deaf. Cristel sits unmoved by any womanly compassion; Roylake rises and puts his hand on his shoulder: 'It was the best way I could devise of assuring him of my sympathy' (ch. 13).

To be sure, the tense and complex relationship between Roylake and the Lodger, taken together with the tale's preternaturally gloomy setting, provides a classic instance of what Eve Kosofsky Sedgwick has termed the 'paranoid Gothic tradition'. From the erotic rivalry between the two men proceeds those 'male homosocial bonds [in which] are concentrated the fantasy energies of compulsion, prohibition, and explosive violence; all . . . fully structured by the logic of paranoia'. And just as with the texts on which Sedgwick dwells, 'the revelation of intrapsychic structures' is 'inextricable from the revelation of the mechanics of class domination' in *The Guilty River*.[18] But I think that the feeling between Roylake and the Lodger, triangulated as it is by Cristel, is also of central importance to understanding Collins's representation of the sensorily disabled. In *The King of Inventors* Catherine Peters writes of him as an author 'haunted by a second self', both attracted to and repelled by rebellious female figures (Peters, p. 1), but the second selves that count in Collins's fictions of disability are all, significantly, male. Rylake and the Lodger have a strong, uneasy, affective bond in their competition for the same woman, the disabled man feeling at a distinct disadvantage. In *Poor Miss Finch* Oscar's selfish and manipulative brother Nugent competes against his twin for possession of the blind Lucilla, while *Hide and Seek* concludes with Zack and Mat melded into an unorthodox family unit through their unfulfillable loves for Madonna and her late mother. These connections, tying in ablebodied and disabled alike, allow us to see the differently-abled not so much as Others, but as placed on a human continuum of affective relationships: this is why it is important that we see them as capable of love and desire.

Near the beginning of her study of representations of disability, *Extraordinary Bodies*, Rosemarie Garland Thomson writes that she is setting out 'to challenge entrenched assumptions that 'able-bodiedness' and its conceptual opposite, 'disability', are self-evident physical conditions. Her intention, she says:

> is to defamiliarise these identity categories by showing how the 'physically disabled' are produced by way of legal, medical, political, cultural, and literary narratives that comprise an exclusionary discourse . . . In other words, I want to move disability from the realm of medicine into that of political minorities, to recast it from a form of pathology to a form of ethnicity. By

asserting that disability is a reading of bodily particularities in the context of social power relations, I intend to counter the accepted notions of physical disability as an absolute, inferior state and a personal misfortune. Instead, I show that disability is a representation, a cultural interpretation of physical transformation or configuration, and a comparison of bodies that structures social relations and institutions.[19]

While Thomson explicitly invokes ethnicity here, the same generalisations about representation and categorisation are palpably true when it comes to how gender is presented and understood. In this respect, Collins's stress on sexualised and emotionally charged relationships can be seen to have anticipated Thomson's work, since it starts to interrogate the terms in which disabilities are interpreted. Although he employs external observations concerning the constitution of physical difference – and he clearly researched the topic in outside sources – his true interest lies not in bodily impairment as such, but in its psychological effects. In turn, these impact on, and are influenced by, emotions which are experienced by able-bodied and disabled alike.

'Normalcy and disability are part of the same system,' Lennard J. Davis has written.[20] However, what he has in mind is the frequency with which one category is used to define the other, later explaining that the structures on which the nineteenth-century novel is based 'tend to be normative':

Thus the middleness of life, the middleness of the material world, the middleness of the normal body, the middleness of a sexually gendered, ethnically middle world is created in symbolic form and then reproduced symbolically. This normativity in narrative will by definition create the abnormal, the Other, the disabled, the native, the colonized subject, and so on.[21]

Yet in Collins's fiction the 'abnormal' and the 'normal' are not made clearly distinct from one another. Strong affective plots are used to hook in the readers, and to make them care about both the emotions of the disabled, and the emotions of those who care passionately – rather than compassionately – for them. The conditions of disablement are evoked in ways which make able-bodied readers reflect on the workings of their own senses, and their deficiencies, as well as their powers. Above all, in entering into the world of the differently-abled, Collins rejects the kind of distancing and categorisation which Andrew Halliday employed in his taxonomy of the 'bodily afflicted'. The implications of this, of course, stretch beyond our understanding of the blind, the deaf, the mute and the physically disabled themselves, and this is why it is so important to recognise the fact that Collins complicates their representation with markers of sexual and, to a lesser extent, racial ambiguity. What Collins ultimately conveys to his readers is the need to maintain a wary suspicion of the grounds on which assumptions concerning differences, in general, may be used to structure social thinking.

NOTES

1. Henry Mayhew, *London Labour and the London Poor. A Cyclopædia of the Condition and Earnings of those that* will *work, those that* cannot *work, and those that* will not *work* (reprint of enlarged edition of 1861–2), 4 vols. (London: Frank Cass, 1967), IV, p. 431.
2. Ibid. , p. 433.
3. William Carpenter, *Principles of Human Physiology* (Philadelphia: Blanchard and Lea, 1843), p. 261.
4. Elizabeth Gitter, 'Deaf-Mutes and Heroines in the Victorian Era', *Victorian Literature and Culture* 20 (1992), pp. 179–96 (p. 189).
5. Martha Stoddard Holmes, '"Bolder with Her Lover in the Dark": Collins and Disabled Women's Sexuality', in Maria K. Bachman and Don Richard Cox (eds.), *Reality's Dark Light: The Sensational Wilkie Collins* (Knoxville: University of Tennessee Press, 2003), pp. 59–93 (pp. 60–1).
6. Anne Borsay, 'History, Power and Identity', in Colin Barnes, Mike Oliver and Len Barton (eds.) *Disability Studies Today* (Cambridge: Polity, 2002), pp. 98–119 (pp. 105–6).
7. See Edwin G. Boring, *A History of Experimental Psychology* (New York: Appleton-Century-Crofts, 1957), pp. 211–45; Lorraine J. Daston, 'British Responses to Psycho-Physiology, 1860–1900', *Isis* 69 (1978), 192–208 and Kurt Danziger, 'Mid-Nineteenth-Century British Psycho-Physiology: A Neglected Chapter in the History of Psychology', in W. R. Woodward and M. G. Ash (eds.), *The Problematic Science: Psychology in Nineteenth-Century Thought* (New York: Praeger, 1982), pp 119–46.
8. Lillian Nayder, *Wilkie Collins* (New York: Twayne, 1997), p. 57.
9. John Kitto, *The Lost Senses: Series I – Deafness* (London: Charles Knight, 1845), p. 8.
10. Religious Tract Society, *The Senses and the Mind* (London: Religious Tract Society, 1853), p. 191.
11. See Angelique Richardson, *Love and Eugenics in the Late Nineteenth Century: Rational Reproduction and the New Woman* (Oxford and New York : Oxford University Press, 2003).
12. George Henry Lewes, *The Physiology of Common Life*, 2 vols. (1859) (Leipzig: Bernhard Tauchnitz, 1860), II, p. 227.
13. Diana Fuss, *The Sense of an Interior: Four Writers and the Rooms that Shaped Them* (New York and London: Routledge, 2004), p. 117.
14. For this, and for further information relating to Collins's use of the literature of blindness, see the excellent Introduction by Catherine Peters to the World's Classics edition of *Poor Miss Finch* (Oxford: Oxford University Press, 1995).
15. George Sexton, *The Physiology of the Five Senses* (London: Austin & Co., 1880), p. 6.

16. G. H. Bosanquet, *The Sorrows of Deafness* (London: Saunders and Otley, 1839), p. 15.
17. David Hevey, *The Creatures Time Forgot: Photography and Disability Imagery* (London: Routledge, 1992), p. 12.
18. Eve Kosofsky Sedgwick, *Between Men: English Literature and Male Homosocial Desire* (New York: Columbia University Press, 1985), p. 162.
19. Rosemarie Garland Thompson, *Extraordinary Bodies: Figuring Disability in American Literature and Culture* (New York: Columbia University Press, 1997), p. 6.
20. Lennard J. Davis, *Enforcing Normalcy: Disability, Deafness, and the Body* (London and New York: Verso, 1995), p. 2.
21. *Ibid.*, p. 41.

12

JIM DAVIS

Collins and the theatre

'But if I know anything of my own faculty it is a dramatic one.'
– Wilkie Collins (1862)[1]

Victorian theatre 1850–1880

Wilkie Collins liked the theatre, wrote plays and published highly theatrical novels, many of which he adapted for the stage, and his engagement with the theatre spanned the whole of his writing life. During the late 1840s he had been involved in private performances with John Everett Millais, William Holman Hunt, W. P. Frith and Edward Ward in the Collins family household in Blandford Square, and he first met Charles Dickens through amateur theatricals when Augustus Egg persuaded Collins to undertake the part of the valet in Edward Bulwer-Lytton's *Not So Bad As We Seem*, to be performed by the Guild of Literature and Art. Dickens's amateur performances were fuelled by his own enthusiasm for acting, while ostensibly aimed at raising funds for charitable or benevolent causes. His reputation (and often the reputations of his fellow-actors) ensured maximum exposure, turning the performances into significant public and private events rather than replicating amateur theatricals in the more homely sense of that activity. Through his involvement in Dickens's company Collins laid the ground for future theatrical collaboration with the novelist.

Collins also immersed himself in visits to the professional theatre, and had been a keen theatregoer since visiting the Paris theatres with Charles Ward in the mid-1840s. While much theatrical activity centred on the West End of London, there were also neighbourhood theatres scattered throughout the rest of the metropolis, concentrating more often than not on popular melodrama. Professional theatre was also strong in the provinces, with new theatres opening in such industrial centres as Liverpool and Manchester. This period also saw the rapid development of the music hall, in the West End and the suburbs of London as well as in the provinces. In the West End itself, theatres and managements often had specific specialisations, which included burlesque at the Strand, the Shakespearean productions of Charles Kean at the Princess's in the 1850s and of Irving at the Lyceum later in the century, and melodrama at the Adelphi. Among those theatres which looked to attract the upper end of the market were the Olympic and, from 1865, the Prince of Wales's; Collins chose to be associated with both. By 1860, according to G. A. Sala, the Olympic had become one of the favourite resorts of the aristocracy and the entertainments had a reputation for elegance and brilliance.[2] The Prince of Wales's theatre under the Bancroft management also cornered this market in the late 1860s and 1870s.

Melodrama dominated the nineteenth-century stage. At its crudest it could be excessive, bombastic and fair prey for the burlesque authors who regularly satirised its language and conventions. In the hands of Dion Boucicault, whose 'sensation' dramas were popular from the 1850s on-wards, Tom Taylor and Charles Reade, it could also provide a focus for the exploration of more serious issues and for the presentation of less conventionalised characterisation and dialogue. However, the drama rarely dealt quite as immediately or as complexly with the contemporary world as did the novel, and the 'sensation' dramas of Boucicault lacked the depth and subtlety that could be found in the better sensation novels of the period. Despite the lower status of the drama in relation to the novel (Shakespeare and a few other established dramatists excepted), the theatre thrived. Pantomime was also a popular genre, performed at most theatres in London and the provinces from Boxing Day onwards – Collins himself often organised visits to the pantomime with family friends. Comedy and farce were other popular genres. Comedy was to be refined during this period through the work of such dramatists as Tom Robertson and H. J. Byron, while farce was a frequent addition to the playbills at a time when two or even three pieces might be performed at any given theatre in the course of an evening.

The actor rather than the playwright dominated the Victorian stage. As a theatregoer, Collins admired actors with a penchant for naturalism and for the representation of repression. Like Dickens, he greatly admired the French actor Charles Fechter, with whom he later collaborated and about whom he wrote a short memoir. He also admired the comic actor William Farren, credited with introducing a more natural approach to comic roles in the mid-nineteenth century. He concurred with the view that French acting was generally superior to English acting – he and Dickens agreed that Frédérick Lemaître was responsible for one of the greatest performances they had ever seen, in Paris in 1856. But he was unimpressed with the Italian actress Adelaide Ristori, whom he saw in Paris, writing to Edward Ward that he found her exaggerated, stagy and commonplace (8 March 1856, B&C I, 149).[3] He was often scathing about the state of the English stage, complaining to Frederick Lehmann that a troupe of monkeys he was about to see perform could not be any worse than human actors if they attempted Shakespeare (25 October 1869, B&C II, 327). '[T]he less said about it (with one or two exceptions) the better', he commented to William Winter on the English theatre in 1878 (5 August, *B&C* II, 414).

The theatre during Collins's lifetime was a vibrant presence throughout both Europe and the English-speaking world. As Collins became an established novelist, the dramatisations of his novels had as much of a global impact as the novels themselves. North Americans were frequently regaled with dramatisations of the novels – invariably unauthorised – and versions of the novels were often performed in Australia and other colonies. Collins himself collaborated on French adaptations of his novels, but there were also versions in many other languages including German and Italian.

Collins's early plays, 1855–1858

The first drama by Collins to be performed, in June 1855, was *The Lighthouse*, loosely based on the short story 'Gabriel's Marriage'. He showed it to Dickens, who appropriated it for his amateur performances, referring to it as 'a regular old-style melodrama'.[4] Dickens himself played the old lighthouse keeper who, under duress caused by starvation, confesses his complicity in a murder to his son, but then denies it. Like Richard Wardour in *The Frozen Deep*, a highly successful amateur production written jointly by Collins and Dickens and performed two years later, the role offered Dickens the opportunity to represent the outer man repressing inner turmoil, leading a double life and being stretched to the limits.

The Lighthouse itself is a compact, intense, claustrophobic drama, reliant on too much exposition and a number of improbable coincidences. Nonetheless, the play subsequently enjoyed a successful professional production at the Olympic theatre with the comic actor Frederick Robson in Dickens's role. 'The Play has been a great success,' Collins wrote to his mother, 'the audience so enthralled by the story that they would not even bear the applause at the first entrance of *Robson*. Everybody breathless' (10 August 1858, *BGL&L* I, 149). Robson was famed for veering towards the edge of tragedy and for the performance of grotesque roles, both characteristics of his embodiment of the malign title character in *The Yellow Dwarf*, J. R. Planché's 1854 Christmas extravaganza for the Olympic. For Sala, 'this little stunted creature, with his hoarse voice and nervous gestures, and his grotesque delivery, his snarls, his leers, his hunchings of the shoulders, and his grindings of the teeth, was a genius'.[5] Collins capitalised on these qualities by writing the role of zany misfit Hans Grimm for Robson in *The Red Vial* (Olympic, 1858), a rather heavy, convoluted drama concluding in a morgue where the dead are placed to rest with a rope and bell tied to their right hands in case they should suddenly revive. Audiences found it all too intense and unrelieved and greeted it with laughter. 'Nothing', said John Hollingshead, who attended the first night, 'could have saved the *Red Vial*', while Henry Morley criticised its poor dialogue and one-dimensional characterisation.[6] More favourably, E. L. Blanchard called it 'a very strong melodrama', and claimed that Robson was 'great' in the role of Hans Grimm.[7] Nevertheless, the failure of *The Red Vial* seems to have dissuaded Collins from writing again for the theatre for almost a decade.

1867–1869: working with Fechter

The Frozen Deep, the Dickens/Collins collaboration that had been so successful in 1857, was also less than effective when professionally revived at the Olympic theatre in 1867. Dickens's extraordinary performance as Richard Wardour had been highly praised, but devoid of his brooding presence the play failed to come alive.[8] As he told Nina Lehmann, Collins received a letter from the Olympic's manager announcing 'the total failure (in respect of attracting audiences) of "The Frozen Deep"! Not a sixpence made for me by the play (after all the success of the first night!) . . . no alternative that I can see, or the manager either, but to put "The Frozen Deep" on the shelf by, or before, Christmas.' In Collins's view, however, it was the audience, not the play, that was at fault – he is scathing in his critique of the poor taste of British audiences:

> The play is . . . beautifully got up, and very well acted. But the enlightened British Public declares it to be '*slow*'. There isn't an atom of slang or vulgarity in the whole piece from beginning to end – no female legs are shown in it – Richard Wardour does'nt [*sic*] get up after dying and sing a comic song – sailors are represented in the Arctic regions, and there is no hornpipe danced, and no sudden arrival of 'the pets of the ballet' to join the dance in the costume of Esquimaux maidens – finally, all the men on the stage *don't* marry all the women on the stage, at the end – and nobody addresses the audience, and says:- 'If our kind friends here to-night will only encourage us by their applause, there are brave hearts among us which will dare the perils for many a night yet, of – The Frozen Deep!' (9 December 1866, *BGL&L* II, 53–4)

This is a significant statement, despite its levity, for it clearly aligns Collins with those who wished to reform or improve the calibre of current provision for the stage. He evidently wished to offer the theatregoing public something more substantial than the popular burlesques and melodramas they appeared to favour. 'I will take John Bull by the scruff of the neck, and force him into the theatre to see it – before or after it has been played in French, I don't know which – but into the theatre John Bull shall go,' his letter to Nina Lehmann continued. Collins's attitude suggests a new confidence in his powers as a dramatist, perhaps emboldened by his growing reputation as a novelist, and a reaffirmation of his commitment to the theatre.

In the same year that *The Frozen Deep* failed professionally, *No Thoroughfare*, a dramatisation of a Christmas story on which Collins and Dickens had collaborated that hangs on the effects of the substitution of two children in the London Foundling Hospital and culminates in a dramatic struggle in the Alps, was performed at the Adelphi theatre. Fechter, who also played the role of the villainous Obenreizer, assisted Collins with the stage adaptation. The play does not read well – it seems muddled and confused – but it worked well on stage, largely because of Fechter's performance. 'In delineating Obenreizer', Collins noted in his memoir of the actor,

> Fechter gave one more proof of his great versatility. His easy colloquial acting in the beginning was delightful . . . His quick transitions from repose to action . . . were phases as marvellous in combination as the changes of the kaleidoscope . . . The . . . last tableau showed Fechter at his best in the exquisite pathos of action and expression, as Obenreizer, dying of despair and nervous exhaustion, looked upon by the woman he loved.[9]

Fechter, observed Collins, lived and breathed the role and remained in character off stage as well as on during rehearsals. The play was an immense success, much to Collins's delight: 'Every night the Theatre is crammed', he wrote to his mother. 'This speculation on the public taste is paying, and promises long to pay me, from fifty to fifty-five pounds a week' (17 January 1868, *BGL&L* II, 105).

Perhaps inspired by the success of *No Thoroughfare*, Collins and Fechter next developed *Black and White* (Adelphi 1869), set on a West Indian slave plantation. Fechter played the adopted son of a French nobleman, who discovers that he is the natural son of a quadroon and therefore a slave himself. Despite the quality of Fechter's acting and the tumultuous applause with which the first night audience responded to the performance ('There is no doubt that it ought to run, for it has real merit and is most completely and delicately presented,' Dickens wrote to W. H. Wills) the play did not draw and lost money.[10] Collins attributed this to a surfeit of 'Oncle Tommerie' (too many adaptations of *Uncle Tom's Cabin*), but it may also be the case that the relative failure of Boucicault's English production of *The Octoroon* in 1861 had already indicated a limited taste for plays on this theme. Nevertheless, it was a relief to the critic Dutton Cook to witness a drama 'with an intelligible plot, legitimately stirring the audience by the unstrained development of its incidents, and affording good opportunities for dramatic effect'. While not a play of 'a high order', it was also not indebted to the machinist and scene painter for its effects, Cook claimed.[11]

Major novel adaptations, 1871–1876

In many ways there had been something hit and miss about Collins's success as a dramatist prior to the 1870s, but from 1871 to 1876 he achieved four major successes, all dramatisations of his own novels.[12] The adaptation of novels for the nineteenth-century stage had become frequent ever since the novels of Sir Walter Scott in the second and third decades of the century had been omnivorously transformed into romantic operatic melodramas for consumption at a range of theatres. Subsequently, the novels of Dickens and Harrison Ainsworth had been adapted for the stage, often without the consent of the authors, who also failed to benefit financially. Learning from the experiences of such authors as Dickens, multiple adaptations of whose novels at home and abroad secured him little monetary advantage, Collins sought to protect his copyright and income by adapting his own novels (as Graham Law's chapter in this volume discusses).

In 1871 his adaptation of *The Woman in White* for the Olympic theatre won considerable acclaim, largely because he focused on radically reworking the novel for the stage. The relationship between Anne Catherick and Laura Fairlie was made much more obvious from the start, for example. Care was also taken with staging the play: the sets were as realistic as possible and unencumbered with flats; the final scene consisted of a lawn set in front of the house, inside which characters were seen to move on two levels, in study, dining room and bedrooms. Ada Dyas in the double role of Anne and Laura was highly praised, though the critics were divided over George Vining's representation of Count Fosco. Collins himself saw Vining's performance as crucial to the play's success, refusing a request by an American management to stage the play until Vining was available to play there:

> I am more and more convinced that there would be a very poor chance of success with a 'Fosco', who had *not* rehearsed the character with me. It is a character outside all theatrical conventions . . . The play is *all Fosco*. If he does not take the audience by storm, failure is certain. Mr Vining is privately rehearsing with me – every line in the dialogue is a matter of consultation between us. If this hard work is repaid by a great triumph *here* – Mr Vining is almost certain to repeat the success with you. If he fails – there is an end of the play, on both sides of the Atlantic. ([7] August 1871, *BGL&L* II, 267)

Yet despite Collins's public support for his performance as Fosco, Vining did not take the play to America. The role was later played on tour and with more success by Wybert Reeve, who was also permitted by Collins to condense the final scenes of the play during its American run to create a more powerful conclusion.[13]

One reason for the play's success may have been a deliberate choice by Collins not to emphasise the more sensational moments in the novel for dramatic effect, but to present a more restrained version. Fred Walker's poster for the play – the first theatrical poster to be designed by a well-known artist – both implied and announced the production's intention to focus on the dramatic situation rather than on sensational effects. Indeed, according to Janice Norwood, contemporary illustrations of scenes from the play placed an emphasis on domestic rather than sensational moments. Norwood also suggests that Collins's dramatisation, along with Leopold Lewis's *The Bells* (Lyceum, 1871), was seminal in pointing towards greater restraint and realism in melodrama, towards a contemplative rather than sensational focus on situation, and towards more psychologically complex characterisation.[14] Like Henry Irving's character of Mathias in *The Bells*, Fosco was too complex to be a conventional villain. Given these factors, it may be correct to assume not only that Collins was attuned to the theatrical developments of the time, but also that he was deliberately breaking away from the excesses of the sensation drama. Perhaps if Fechter or Irving, rather than the less adequate Vining, had played Fosco, our current perception of Collins's theatrical significance would be quite different.

The theatre most associated with progressive and more restrained dramas at this time was the Prince of Wales's. Under the management of Marie Wilton and Squire Bancroft, this theatre had pioneered a detailed, restrained and seemingly more realistic style of play and performance, especially through the presentation of a series of comedies by Tom Robertson. It is not altogether surprising therefore that Collins should seek an association with this theatre. In 1873 *Man and Wife*, which attacks the Scottish marriage laws and the cult of athleticism, was staged there.[15] John Hare, who had achieved a reputation playing elderly gentlemen, apparently brought the play to the attention of the Bancroft management, who had accepted it in 1871, the year in which Collins informed Augustin Daly, 'This is the favourite theatre here – as you no doubt know. It has the best company and the most intelligent audience, (2 December 1871, *BGL&L* II, 306). Cook claimed that *Man and Wife* was too melodramatic to be a typical Prince of Wales's play, but it fared well when finally performed, with Hare in the part of Sir Patrick Lundie, 'a shrewd, sarcastic and yet kindly elderly gentleman'.[16] Blanchard, who noted the wonderful gallery of celebrities present on the first night, considered it wonderfully mounted and acted, but did not think it destined for a long run.[17] Collins told Reeve that the pit took to its legs and cheered when he took his curtain call, adding, 'It remains to be seen whether I can fill the theatre with a new audience.'[18] Given that the Prince of Wales's theatre had been credited with drawing a new audience for a number of years before *Man and Wife* was performed, however, the comment seems rather ambiguous. Cook felt that the adaptation was 'no confused transfer to the stage . . . but a complete and coherent work, endowed with an independent vitality of its own, and perfectly intelligible to those among the audience unsupplied with previous information upon the subject'.[19] Yet the final scene, in which the caddish villain, Geoffrey Delamayn, suffers a debilitating stroke or heart attack in his early twenties, brought on by too much athleticism, comes across as rather improbable and far too convenient, despite Collins's view that he had adapted the story 'to the exigencies of stage representation' (22 August 1870, *BGL&L* II, 207). The novel's original conclusion was arguably far more powerful.

In *The New Magdalen* (Olympic, 1873), Collins genuinely felt that he had achieved something innovative. In this drama about identity theft, he broke though the censor's taboo on presenting clergymen on the stage and, what is more, the clergyman actually married a prostitute, Mercy Merrick, the 'new magdalen' of the title. The play was a success, principally on account of the performances of Ada Cavendish and Frank Archer in the leading roles. Matthew Arnold was said to have thought highly of the play but it offended a number of critics, and *The Times* believed that the previous generation would not have tolerated it. Archer was recommended by the Bancrofts for the part of the Reverend Julian Gray, which he stated 'was an excellent and most effective part', while 'the drama had a grip that was irresistible'.[20] (Gray's final speeches, in which his passionate exhortations of repentance to Mercy have an almost erotic edge, were slightly toned down in the manuscript submitted to the Lord Chamberlain's Office for approval). In 1884 Collins told Archer, on seeing him in a revival, that his acting 'was the acting of a true artist, throughout – admirable in its quiet dignity and reticence, in its complete freedom from stage artifice, and in its easy, subtle and faithful presentation of the character'.[21]

The New Magdalen had a successful run at the Broadway theatre in New York in 1873, despite the disapproval of some American critics – 'The author . . . has opened a recruiting office for prostitutes', the *Daily Graphic* complained.[22] Oscar Wilde also much admired Clara Morris's Mercy Merrick in the 1882 New York production, but by the time the play was revived in the 1890s George Bernard Shaw found it an antiquated melodrama, with little of consequence to say about the social issues that lay behind its subject matter.[23] Shaw, of course, revisited the themes of *The New Magdalen* in *Mrs Warren's Profession*, a play that experienced inordinately more difficulty with censorship, precisely because he moved the debate away from Collins's focus on personal morality to the socioeconomic causes of prostitution. Yet Collins told Archer in 1884 that 'they had set an example in the art of the stage, which has produced a strong impression, and which was very much wanted at this time', a comment that suggests that he saw himself at the forefront of theatrical innovation and reform.[24]

The New Magdalen was followed by *Miss Gwilt*, Collin's somewhat ruthless adaptation of *Armadale*, first staged under his direction at the Alexandra theatre, Liverpool, in 1875, and at the Globe theatre in London a year later. He had published an earlier version in 1866 to protect copyright, and had subsequently collaborated with the French actor Régnier to improve its potential for performance – though it is doubtful whether it was ever performed.[25] The focus of the new adaptation is the almost unredeemable Miss Gwilt and her villainy, and while the play treats her more sympathetically than does the novel, she is still very much the adventuress in the Lady Audley mould. (Stage adaptations of Mary Elizabeth Braddon's *Lady Audley's Secret* (1862), with a strong emphasis on Lady Audley's adultery and madness, had been popular since the early 1860s). A complex novel has become a conventional melodrama, only partially drawing on the more complicated psychology of characterisation evident in the original. Nevertheless, despite some misgivings by critics and Collins's problems with drunken stage carpenters on the night of the London opening, the play was a success.

Thus from 1871 to 1876 Collins was responsible for four dramatisations of his novels that were technically skilful, attracted actors of high calibre to play in them and drew audiences. In these four plays he achieved a certainty of touch which he was never to regain and had only hinted at before. Careful plotting, characterisation with some psychological basis, excellent staging and thematic interest beyond pure narrative exposition all contributed to their impact. With the important exception of Charles Reade, who effortlessly moved between both forms, Collins showed that almost alone among his peers, he could, at best, be as competent a dramatist as he was a novelist.

Later plays and adaptations 1877–1885

When Collins turned his attention to *The Moonstone* (1868), staged at the Olympic theatre (now under Henry Neville's management) in 1877, his burgeoning dramatic skills seem to have abandoned him. While he may have been inspired by the wish to write a more subdued and naturalistic version of the original, his exclusion of the Indians and the theme of imperial expropriation, of all reference to the taking of opium and laud-anum, and of characters such as Rosanna Spearman and Ezra Jennings, diminished the play's impact and interest. Collins himself was initially satisfied with both the reception and the adaptation, writing to Augustin Daly, 'We have had a great success in London – financially speaking (so far), as well as artistically. I hear of people turned away for want of room as early as the third – and fourth nights of representation. This is rare in London' (22 September 1877, *BGL&L* III, 171). However, this was a tedious adaptation of the novel, top-heavy with detail and information and totally lacking in the suspense and tension associated with the original. Its run lasted for only nine weeks. Cook thought that the subject was better suited to narration than representation and that Collins left nothing to the imagination, a complaint he had also made in his review of *The New Magdalen*.[26]

Collins's subsequent play, *Rank and Riches*, is a workable but undistin-guished piece about money and class, the staple themes of West End drama at the time. Its first night at the Adelphi theatre in 1883 was a disaster and the play was subsequently withdrawn. The audience started to snigger at some awkwardly phrased expressions and then began to laugh unrestrain-edly. A remonstrance from a cast member only made matters worse and led to cat-calls. Collins believed that the fault lay with the Adelphi audience – more familiar with robust melodramas at this point in time – and that they were not ready for a drama that he considered to be quite innovative. As he wrote to E. A. Buck:

> (T)he withdrawal of this piece was *my* act. It was so admirably played . . . that I would have made my own arrangements to keep it before the public, if I could have trusted the Adelphi pit and gallery to back me. But that pit and gallery did undoubtedly help my enemies among the 'first-night clique' – here and there, perhaps, out of mere mischief – but, in the vast majority of cases, out of absolute incapacity to understand a story and to sympathize with characters, which had never done duty on the stage before. The riot reached its climax in the third act – where the great situation of the piece is also a situation entirely new. (1 July 1883, *BGL&L* III, 418)

The Times defended the audience's reaction, however, referring to 'the outrageous improbability of the characters and the story'. It considered that '(t)he want of dramatic purpose in the play – as the result of which the characters seemed to flounder aimlessly about – combined with action bordering at times upon burlesque, and a prevalence of unlucky lines, was more than the public could be expected to endure'.[27]

After this, Collins's long connection with the theatre more or less ended, though in 1885 his adaptation of *The Evil Genius* was performed once for copyright reasons. Throughout his working life Collins regularly attempted to dramatise his novels, as or immediately after he wrote then, so that he could claim copyright on the dramatisations and defeat piracy. Collins had learned to be cautious through the example of others; not only Dickens but also Mrs Henry Wood, to whom the many adaptations of *East Lynne* had brought little financial benefit. The relatively low status of the dramatist as compared with the novelist and the comparatively poor financial returns no doubt impacted on Collins's choice of genre. He himself lamented the situation, claiming that in France there was much more incentive to write for the stage. He objected when 'some obscure idiot' dramatised *Poor Miss Finch* (1872), a book he considered unfit for the stage: 'What I refuse to do with my own work, another man (unknown in literature) is perfectly free to do against my will and (if he can get his rubbish played) to the prejudice of my novel and my reputation.'[28]

Collins as dramatist

Dramatisations of Collins's novels were performed throughout the world. Often, whether or not Collins had assented, stage versions of his novels were performed overseas before they were staged in Britain. Yet, despite his long experience in reshaping his novels for the stage and his openness to new trends and developments in the theatre, Collins's plays and adaptations constitute a rather uneven body of work. There are points where they attempt to move beyond the conventions of melodrama and explore serious issues. Yet ideas about masculinity, repression, the social situation of women and insanity, which are seriously examined in the novels, are continually subsumed into plot devices or simplified in characterisation in the plays. Despite his desire to breathe new life into the theatre of his time, Collins could not break free of some of the limitations imposed by melodramatic conventions. A sensation novelist who eschewed sensation on the stage, he produced stage dialogue that is often rhetorical at a time when other dramatists, including Boucicault, were moving towards more natural dialogue. He also fails to address social issues and problems with the force or focus of, say, Charles Reade in *It is Never Too Late to Mend* (1856) or Tom Taylor in *The Ticket of Leave Man* (1863).

So Wilkie Collins contributed less than might be expected to the theatre of his time. His novels, despite reliance on melodramatic conventions, break through these restrictions and achieve considerable depth. His plays and dramatisations, on the other hand, are more limited: they retain the melodramatic conventions but often jettison the depth. Nevertheless, Collins was aware of the different demands posed by the novel and the drama. As Archer noted, 'In speaking of the novelist's and the dramatist's art, he held that they were absolutely distinct, and approached from different sides entirely.'[29] Dutton Cook believed that Collins 'had done much to disprove an opinion too generally entertained, that a novelist is of necessity disqualified as a candidate for theatrical honours'.[30] He was also able to offer fellow-authors such as Reade advice on their own dramatisations of their novels (*B&C* II, 339–40). We know that Collins had a good understanding of the theatre, not only as an amateur actor, but also as an author who contributed effective advice to professional actors on the staging of his plays. He regularly acted out his adaptations for himself at home and spoke the speeches to try to judge their effect. (In 1873–4 he even emulated Dickens by embarking on a reading tour of America, albeit with less success.) However, despite his dramaturgical skills and strong interest in the theatre, Collins's reputation is more likely to endure on account of his novels rather than his plays and adaptations.

NOTES

1. Wilkie Collins, 'Memorandum relating to the Life and Writings of Wilkie Collins 1862', in a letter to an unknown recipient, 21 March 1862 (*B&C* I, 208).
2. G. A. Sala, *Robson, A Sketch* (London: John Camden Hotten, 1864) p. 32.
3. Collins's dramatic tastes were quite wide-ranging. His writings on performers include an account of the music hall performer J. H. Stead, 'The Perfect Cure', for *Household Words*. See John Hollingshead, *My Lifetime*, 2 vols. (London: Sampson Low, Marston & Co., 1895), I, p. 127.
4. Quoted in William Clarke, *The Secret Life of Wilkie Collins* (Stroud: Sutton Publishing, 2004), p. 72.
5. Sala, *Robson, A Sketch*, p. 39
6. Hollingshead, *My Lifetime*, I, p. 127; Henry Morley, *The Journal of a London Playgoer* (1866) (Leicester: Leicester University Press, 1974), pp. 189–90.
7. Clement Scott and Cecil Howard (eds.), *The Life and Reminiscences of E. L. Blanchard*, 2 vols. (London: Hutchinson & Co., 1891), I, p. 205.
8. See *Saturday Review*, 1 August 1857, 106–7.
9. Kate Field, *Charles Albert Fechter* (Boston: James R. Osgood and Co., 1882), p. 7.
10. Letter to W. H. Wills, quoted in Peters, p. 312.
11. Dutton Cook, *Nights at the Play: A View of the Stage*, 2 vols. (London: Chatto & Windus, 1883), I, p. 106.
12. See also Peters, pp. 333–54.
13. See Wybert Reeve, *From Life (Recollections and Jottings)* (London: F. V. White & Co., 1892), p. 117.
14. See Janice Norwood, 'Sensation Drama? Wilkie Collins's Stage Adaptation of *The Woman in White*', in Andrew Mangham (ed.), *The Topical Wilkie Collins:*

Interdisciplinary and Historical Essays on a Victorian Writer (Newcastle: Cambridge Scholar Press, 2006).

15. An unauthorised version had run at Daly's theatre in New York in 1870.
16. Cook, *Nights at the Play*, I, pp. 253–4.
17. Scott and Howard, *E. L. Blanchard*, I, p. 422.
18. Reeve, *From Life*, p. 112.
19. Cook, *Nights at the Play*, I, p. 250.
20. William Archer, *An Actor's Notebooks* (London: Stanley Paul & Co., 1912), p. 147.
21. Letter, 8 February 1884, quoted in Archer, *An Actor's Notebooks*, p. 251.
22. See Robert Ashley, 'Wilkie Collins and the American Theatre', *Nineteenth-Century Fiction* 8 (March 1954), 250.
23. G. B. Shaw, *Our Theatres in the Nineties*, 3 vols. (London: Constable, 1932), I, pp. 230–7.
24. Letter, 6 March 1884, quoted in Archer, *An Actor's Notebooks*, p. 253.
25. On the four adaptations of the novel, see John Sutherland's Appendix to his edition of *Armadale* (New York and London: Penguin, 1996).
26. Cook, *Nights at the Play*, II, p. 154.
27. *The Times*, 11 June 1883.
28. Quoted in Hollingshead, *My Lifetime*, II, p. 152.
29. Archer, *An Actor's Notebooks*, p. 301.
30. Cook, *Nights at the Play*, I, p. 169.

13

RACHEL MALIK

The afterlife of Wilkie Collins

Andrew Lloyd Webber's musical spectacular *The Woman in White* opened in London in September 2004. Posters featuring a back-lit, white-clad woman had appeared on buses and Tube trains for months before, and the casting of Michael Crawford (the most famous star in Lloyd Webber's *The Phantom of the Opera*) as the first Count Fosco seemed to lodge Collins's novel firmly in Lloyd Webber world. The official publicity paid its dues to Collins but acknowledged that the story had been appropriated to a familiar repertoire – 'a love story to which a layer of unrequited love [Marian for Walter] has been added for the musical' – and the evening clearly offers a branded 'Lloyd Webber' experience, complete with souvenir tapestry kits and pill-boxes. Nonetheless, the modern musical *Woman in White* was strongly shaped by the contexts and forms of Collins's writing, sensation fiction and the mid-Victorian practices of writing and publishing popular fiction. Far from being a travesty of the 'original' novel or a postmodern rerendering of Victorian Gothic, this new musical version can be viewed as a natural offspring of Collins's novel and its first set of contexts. My emphasis in this chapter will be on the *continuities* between Collins's novels in their first intertextual setting and in their many and varied versions in film, radio and television, with a focus on the British Broadcasting Corporation, and in novels. In addition to the publishing history of the texts themselves, the history of Wilkie Collins in the twentieth century encompasses some of the earliest silent films, the changing traditions and conventions of British radio and television drama, and the historical fiction of Sarah Waters, James Wilson and other 'contemporary Victorian' writers. It forms a crucial part of the continuities and shifts in the significance of the 'Victorian' across the twentieth century and into the twenty-first.

The 'afterlife' of Wilkie Collins suggests many histories, and in a chapter such as this it is not possible even simply to sketch them all. My aim is to consider the versions and revisions of Collins's writing as a set of processes of production and reception which in turn reflect back on the publishing and reading cultures that shaped Collins's own work and to which he was highly responsive. This emphasis makes it possible to explore continuities as well as differences across media and time, opening up an idea of 'adaptation' that is neither transhistorical (accurately reproducing the original) nor narrowly bound within its own time. For example, the BBC television family serial slot for which *The Moonstone* (1868) and *The Woman in White* (1860) were serialised several times from the late 1950s to the 1990s, predominantly imagines a mixed audience in a flow of other texts in ways directly comparable with Victorian periodical fiction.[1] In contrast, *The Dark Clue* (2001), James Wilson's sequel to *The Woman in White*, offers a decisively modern experience of novel reading as retreat, quite alien from the reading contexts and practices of much Victorian fiction, despite its sometimes startling echo of Collins's writing.

Adaptation almost always implies a media translation that *succeeds* the original and a focus on the *differences* between media practices and institutions, especially where literary 'classics' are concerned. But unauthorised adaptations (both printed and performed) often preceded the completion of the original in the mid-nineteenth century, and there were important continuities across drama, painting and the novel.[2] And while some of the specifics of contemporary publishing – such as the current force of copyright – would look very alien to Victorian eyes, many would not. The mid-Victorian and the contemporary moments of book publishing share many features: fiercely competitive, international in both ambition and practice, dependent on and significantly constituted by the possibilities and limitations of other media, with marketing and promotion as central processes.[3] *The Woman in White* was a bestseller in America as well as Britain and was rapidly translated into most European languages. Collins's writing cuts across a range of media and explicitly addresses different types of reader in ways that facilitate its subsequent translation into film, radio and television. The practices and institutions of these new media were in turn shaped by mid- and late Victorian periodical publishing.

Collins's novels are also intensely dramatic and highly visual. Like that of many of his contemporaries, his work was written to be read aloud as well as to be adapted for the stage and the modes of both speech and drama are already inscribed within his writing. Collins did not share Dickens's talent for gripping public readings (his reading tour of America in 1873–4 was not entirely successful), and he does not adopt the kind of idiolectal and dialectical variation so characteristic of Dickens; but there are many compositional traits that anticipate a spoken and quasi-dramatic context of reading and performance. The use of multiple character narrators, some with highly distinctive speech and thought patterns is, in part, the effect of an imagined context of reading aloud: Pesca's benign hyperbole and out-of-context English colloquialisms in *The Woman in White* and the honest no-nonsense of Gabriel Betteredge in *The Moonstone*, for example. And Collins's writing acutely engages with the drama of speech: witness the deathbed confession that opens *Armadale* (1866).

It is also saturated in the culture of the image. Collins's own biography (discussed by Tim Dolin in this volume) and his keen interest in the illustration of his novels are only a particular twist on a general culture where the sheer quantity and range of new and/or improved technologies, forms and contexts of seeing – including illustration in books and periodicals, photography, prints for middle-class domestic spaces and the spectacle of the diorama – charged the relation between observing subject and observed object in distinctive ways. The professional artist as paternal figure in *Hide and Seek* (1854) and as hero in *The Woman in White*; Franklin Blake's and Rachel Verinder's decorative painting as flirtation in *The Moonstone*; the disturbing paintings and photographs that haunt Miserrimus Dexter's walls in *The Law and the Lady* (1875), and the John Everett Millais frontispiece to the 1864 edition of *No Name* (see fig. 2) are vivid examples of this interrelation of image and text.[4] And time and time again the viewer, observer or voyeur is a central figure, calling for modes of description which foreground the spatial placing of objects and persons. These dramatic and visual elements have been taken up in various ways in film, radio and television.

Early cinema

Between 1909 and 1916 at least eleven Collins 'adaptations' were produced: four based on *The New Magdalen* (1873), one on *The Dead Secret* (1857), one on *Armadale*, three on *The Moonstone* and two on *The Woman in White*.[5] During roughly the same period, there were seven Braddon adaptations (four of *Lady Audley's Secret*, 1862, and three of *Aurora Floyd*, 1863), and while this cannot compete with Dickens – between 1898 and 1915 there were at least sixty films based on Dickens texts – Collins proved a rich resource for early film, though little still exists to view or hear and records are patchy. It is *The Woman in White* which emerges as the favourite for adaptation after 1915, with at least six productions, the best known being the 1948 American version starring Sydney Greenstreet as Count Fosco (the 1940 version, entitled *Crimes at the Dark House* is really a gory horror vehicle for Tod Slaughter, king-villain of British B-movies).[6] The familiarity of melodrama, the versatility of Gothic across media, and a shared commitment to producing 'bodily' effects must in part explain the

Figure 2. John Everett Millais's frontispiece to the Sampson Low
edition of *No Name*.

appeal of sensation fiction for early film. As Tom Gunning has argued, early
cinema aimed, above all, to shock or thrill the viewer: 'the impact derives
from a moment of crisis, prepared for and delayed, then bursting on the
audience' – the train rushing towards the audience was the most vivid
example.[7] Such tactics immediately recall sensation fiction (though without
sensation fiction's complex narrative), and Gunning also locates this strand
of cinema in a line of continuity with magic shows and other spectacles
which tested the credulity of sophisticated and sceptical *fin de siècle* audiences. Like sensation fiction, early cinema provoked in the reader the
question: but how can this be possible? And then went on to show us that
it is – usually without any recourse to 'real' magic or matters supernatural.

Recent work on the early years of silent film has also emphasised
the continuities between film and the cultural forms and institutions that

preceded it. Music hall and variety have long been acknowledged as models, but the content and reception contexts of early cinema were significantly shaped by nineteenth-century periodical publishing, with its mix of popular fiction, essays and curiosities, and, of course, the important role accorded to illustration. Ian Christie views *The Strand* magazine (founded in 1891) as a central model, and it is notable that there were twenty-six adaptations of Arthur Conan Doyle stories (mainly Sherlock Holmes) between 1903 and 1915.[8] But the idea of the literary periodical as a model for early cinema also has a more general force. In the earliest period films were just a few minutes long, and comprised a character vignette (for example, *Mr Bumble the Beadle*, 1898) or a single moment of dramatic confrontation or sheer spectacle. The film as character vignette, like the early readings of famous Dickens episodes on BBC radio in the 1920s (for example, *Barkis is Willing* in 1924), immediately recall the performances of Dickens. Many Victorian contexts of production (as today) presumed abridgement, extraction and authorial performance, and these possibilities were likewise textually inscribed.

In these early stages, too, films were packaged and consumed alongside each other: romance and revenge dramas viewed alongside 'stand-up' comedy, holiday travel narratives and self-styled anthropology.[9] They were also viewed alongside a variety of other entertainments: live variety and music hall acts, for example. This frame of consumption supplied one local and immediate intertextual context for viewers. It also suggests an audience conversant with frequent and complex genre switching, and highly capable of varying their intensity and mode of attention. Such patterns of consumption in turn recall the periodical context of much nineteenth-century novelistic production, in which Collins's writing was so strongly embedded – *The Law and the Lady*, for example, can be read in part as a celebration of popular reading practices, where reading reports of criminal trials and solving popular periodical puzzles are central to discovering the narrative's enigmas. Just as the Victorian reading experience was frequently a cross-media one that incorporated spoken sound, image and other printed text, so the early filmic experience was richly intermedial. Early film made varied use of organ and piano music; story outlines and scripts were sometimes distributed to audiences, and 'lecturers' were employed to narrate the story, improvise additional dialogue and, latterly, read the intertitles. And film studios were quick to exploit the serial potential of film. Pearl White, who played Mercy Merrick in the 1910 version of *The New Magdalen*, was dubbed the 'Serial Queen' for her roles in the adventure film serial *Perils of Pauline* (1914), where she was routinely subject to great dangers from which she equally routinely escaped.[10]

Collins's characters and narratives do not lend themselves as easily to extraction as those of Dickens. But increased running times (to between fifteen and thirty minutes) during the first half of the 1910s opened up narrative possibilities which begin to sound more like conventional adaptations in the reviews which often now supply the only surviving evidence.[11] The Gem production of *The Woman in White* in 1913 cuts Marian and centres on Count Fosco, whose arrival in London seems to instigate the narrative. He and his wife take charge of Laura Fairlie and employ Walter Hartright. Sir Percival Glyde is still the husband-to-be. Laura and Anne Catherick are swapped before Anne's death; so Anne spends some time passing as Lady Glyde. The film ends with the murder of Fosco 'by the knife of an assassin'. In the Thanhouser production of the previous year, a gory Gothic script is supplied by Anne, who writes a message in blood in her dying moments. This directs Walter and Laura to the church where Glyde confesses the truth before going up in flames. As in other early versions, the story is radically simplified. Count and Lady Fosco are cut, as are Marian Halcombe and Frederick Fairlie, so constructing a Gothic-tinged melodrama where Glyde is the evil obstacle to the true love of Walter and Laura (who escapes unaided from the asylum). As in the current Lloyd Webber musical, Anne seems more central, trying to warn Laura about her prospective husband, and present as a silent witness at the wedding. It is she who directly confronts Glyde with the words, 'I am not mad, and you are not Sir Percival.' Glyde shows no premeditation: there is no plot or conspiracy. He is simply struck by Anne's resemblance to Laura when she confronts him, and when she conveniently faints, he drags her body into a room, quickly drugs Laura and dumps her body outside the asylum gates. In contrast, the 1918 Thanhouser production is much more ambitious. All the key characters from the novel are in position (including Pesca), though it is left to Walter to rescue Laura from the asylum because Marian's attempt fails. Fosco is the mastermind of the substitution plot, though it is Glyde who sends Walter to Africa (not Central America) to get him out of the way.

However, Gothic was not the only mode, and reworkings of sensation fiction occasionally took the form of contemporary moral dramas. The 1920 Ideal Films version of *Lady Audley's Secret* makes the morality tale its narrative dominant: 'Blind yielding to callous selfishness and brooding discontent' . . . from 'first false deed' to 'new treacheries' until the 'whole edifice of evil tumbles and crashes from its own rottenness'. Yet a variety of other genres are stitched in between the moralising melodrama. There is the conventional comedy of servants and a set-piece adventure scene of George Talboys sitting by a campfire in the Australian outback. Lucy Audley pushes him down the well wearing a well-above-the-ankle pleated tartan skirt and a fur-trimmed rain jacket. She also smokes, at one point placing a cigarette in Sir Michael Audley's mouth. If this is an indictment of modern girls, the Thanhouser productions of *The Woman in White* play on the continuities with Victorian melodrama while giving Anne a more 'modern', active role. The 'Laura' of Acme Pictures's 1919 *The Twin Pawns* is feisty enough to threaten Bent (an amalgam of Fosco and Glyde) with a gun on her wedding night and devise a cunning plan to escape from the asylum, though it is finally her true love Bob (the Walter Hartright figure) who confronts Bent.[12] With the exception of the substitution plot (Violet (Laura) and Daisy (Anne) are estranged full sisters), Daisy's poor health and the asylum sequence, the film owes rather little to the novel's narrative, centring on Bent's deception of Violet and her rich father. The setting of contemporary New York, part Violet's high society, part Daisy's slum tenement world, coupled with their steel magnate father's death in a factory fire, distances the film yet further from the novel. But although it is a conventional fable of corrupting greed, there are some startling and jagged moments: Daisy's death from shock when Bent deliberately 'haunts' her, and a strange eruption of slapstick into the final fight scene where Bob picks up an oversized candelabra at exactly the same moment as Bent picks up an oversized bust. Moments later, Bent has fallen out of the window to his death.

Family audiences

It is in radio and television that the links between modern forms of serial narrative and the reading, writing and publishing cultures that Collins participated in become most strikingly visible. For many years Collins's stories occupied the BBC Sunday teatime slot (usually beginning at around 5.30pm), first on radio (there were radio adaptations of *Armadale* and *No Name* (1862) in 1948 and 1952, for example) and then on television, alongside other favourites – Dickens, Alexandre Dumas and Walter Scott – and adaptations of children's classics such as *Moonfleet* and *Treasure Island*.[13] A six-part version of *The Woman in White* in 1966 and two adaptations of *The Moonstone* in 1959 and 1972 (of seven and five parts respectively) occupied this slot. The 1982 production of *The Woman in White* shifted the mood, for it was broadcast after nine on Wednesday evenings, a time-slot continued into the 1990s. Victorian serials, of course, ran for far longer than their television counterparts, but the television serial also demands an investment from the viewer in exchange for a promised return of pleasure, a dynamic accentuated if the narrative is finite rather than ongoing.

Embedded in the schedule, many of the television serial's immediate intertexts – as with Victorian periodical fiction – were local and immediate and created by the contexts of production: the previous serial, the adjacent programming of the day, perhaps. And like Victorian family magazines, the BBC predominantly constructed a family audience, jointly and severally: the 1966 teatime serial slot was succeeded by *Captain Pugwash* and preceded by a postlunch film matinée that follows, for example, motor racing from Le Mans – a sequence that imagines a very particular kind of family day that is less marked now as television imagines and constitutes other types of individual and collective viewers. The teatime serial addressed a family collectivity, though its members did not all need to be sitting round the television. The slot was arguably as important a repository and prompt for memories as childhood reading (and latterly listening and viewing), and the history evoked by such programmes was, importantly, the viewer's own. In this sense, there is a sharp distinction between the exciting novelties of serial sensation fiction and the 'classic' teatime serial. This slot may also have done much to create a particular class of classics, to which Collins, like Dickens, belongs: the 'much-loved', the 'favourite' book, where an emotional relationship becomes the key index of the text's value.

The 1996 *The Moonstone*, broadcast in Britain in a two-part primetime Christmas season slot, belongs to the same tradition, despite its post-9pm scheduling. Packed with well-known British actors, many associated with period drama, the adaptation does not shy away from the 'dark side' of the novel but insists most strongly on all-round entertainment.[14] An image of the Shivering Sands bookends the drama and Rosanna's disturbing compulsions and suicide are richly played on. But these eerie pleasures are strongly constrained by romance, comedy (much is made of the attempted ministrations of Drusilla Clack) and the detective fever that drives the narrative. The role and effect of detective fiction is seemingly contradictory, making the adaptation simultaneously faithful and anachronistic. Fidelity is possible, even in this highly condensed form, because the audience is presumed to know the rules of the detective genre, from both classic fiction and television, and their expectations are richly confirmed. It takes only a short scene to establish the contrast between the ponderous local 'plod', Seegrave, and the eccentric, sharp-witted, metropolitan Cuff. Reconstructions, red herrings, outcasts with pivotal knowledge, disguise and amateur detection abound. But it is fidelity to the conventions and audience expectations of classic period drama and classic detective fiction, particularly as stamped by BBC traditions, which shapes the adaptation, at least as much as the text itself. Yet at the same time, the adaptation necessarily misses the instability and ingenuity of the emerging genre in the novel, and its departures from what became familiar conventions.

In contrast, the British 1997 two-part version of *The Woman in White* diverges distinctly from the conventions of teatime family viewing, despite occupying the same big-budget, period-drama Christmas slot.[15] Directed by Tim Fywell (director of television adaptations of contemporary crime writers such as Minette Walters and Barbara Vine), it is strongly modernising and reworks key sensation tropes in the light of current definitions and anxieties. Tara Fitzgerald's Marian is an all-action feminist hero who must revive a jaded Walter to help her to avenge the murder of her 'sister'; it is she, not Walter, who faces out Glyde in the church after Walter has been immobilised by a timely bump to the head. It is also very much Marian's narrative (hers is the only voiceover): Walter functions mainly as love interest and unwitting pawn of Glyde during the first half at least, and it is Marian's voice that encompasses Walter's first encounter with the woman in white. Yet this frequently transhistorical feminist reading is sometimes modulated by more specific understandings of Victorian gender relations, as, later, Walter functions to mark the highly circumscribed space in which women can move. Marian seeks him out after her attempt to discover the whereabouts of Anne by searching Fosco's (Simon Callow) London hotel ends in humiliating failure. Titled male power, even if Italian, will always triumph over an anonymous unmarried woman. This intermittent historicism also seems part of a strategy to preserve a darker version of the novel as some kind of 'family viewing'. Child sexual abuse replaces illegitimacy as the crucial secret: Glyde, who repeatedly rapes and beats Laura, has also abused Anne as a child. In this sense, the adaptation confirms expectations about the dark underside of a repressive society viewed through a late twentieth-century lens. Yet there is only one scene where violence is directly represented (and this is figured as a nightmare – though it turns out to be true); and there is no explicit sex. As a lady, Laura haltingly refers to 'the act'; Anne's letter tells of Glyde 'behaving like a husband' to her when she was a child of twelve. Such phrases meet producers, and viewers, expectations of certain kinds of Victorian speech – euphemistic and formal – but the adaptation also perfectly fits the 12 certificate on the ubiquitous video or DVD, at least in part imagined as a multigenerational, family viewing experience.

Contemporary Victorian fiction

Collins has also provided a crucial reference point in the emerging genre of 'contemporary Victorian' fiction, which started with Michael Sadleir's

Fanny by Gaslight in 1940 and which has burgeoned since the late 1980s with (for example) A. S. Byatt's *Possession* (1990) and *Angels and Insects* (1992), Margaret Atwood's *Alias Grace* (1996) and Michel Faber's *The Crimson Petal and the White* (2003). James Wilson's *The Dark Clue* and Sarah Waters's *Fingersmith* (2002) are most directly bound to Collins. In their preoccupation with the shaping drives of Victorian fiction, and the relations between narrators and knowledge, they are typical of contemporary Victorian fiction, which, as Kate Flint has argued, engages modern theorising about Victorian fiction as it reworks nineteenth-century narrative.[16] *The Dark Clue* is a direct sequel to *The Woman in White*, and begins with Laura once more out of the picture, and Walter and Marian on a quest for a secret that leads them through the double life of J. M. W. Turner, a life which indirectly echoes Collins's own. Walter is in search of a symbolic father and engaged in a quest for self; but the repressed motivations he discovers amount to a predictable set of masculine drives, as the gentle man turns sexual predator, soliciting prostitutes, even raping Marian.

Wilson's overfamiliar tale of a repressed Victorian sexuality that returns in violence against women is a disappointing resolution of a previously nuanced narration. In contrast, Waters's fiction is less concerned with reproducing a distinct authorial 'voice'. *Fingersmith* deploys the narrational strategies of sensation fiction to reveal and conceal, rewriting and meshing the tropes of the double and the orphan and turning Collins's implicitly homoerotic traces into an explicit exploration of lesbian sexuality. Two women, whose lives are both further apart and closer together than seems initially possible, are embroiled in a complex substitution plot whose author appears to keep changing. Sue and Maud can be *made* to look like each other, as the maid becomes the lady and the lady becomes the maid, but each needs the other to be (mis)taken for the other. The compelling disturbance of narrative expectations is shaped by queer desires, as the novel effects a compelling twist on the double, moving from resemblance and identification to sexual passion. The manoeuvres in the plot are thus intimately bound to the unfolding of desire – until Maud and Sue acknowledge their love, they are doomed to be substitutes, alternatives, separate narratives that do not add up.

The texts and discourses that shape Waters's work are richer in their range than Wilson's and embedded in contemporary as well as historical traditions. *Fingersmith* draws strongly on Dickens, too, but it is a Dickens who has already been reinscribed for the twentieth century, most visibly by Angela Carter. The modes of masculine authority, from the most thuggish and crude to the most chillingly perverse – the obsessive collector and curator of pornography, Christopher Lilly, for example – strongly echo

Carter's ritualised and claustrophobic patriarchy. Carter's vision inflects some key figures of the feminine too. Mrs Sucksby is a case in point: a baby farmer who has killed as many children as she has saved, as ruthless as she is sentimental in the interests of her 'own', and, finally, the mother who makes the ultimate sacrifice.

Wilson's and Waters's preoccupation with sexuality is shared with many other contemporary Victorian novels: John Fowles's *The French Lieutenant's Woman* (1968), for example, and Faber's *The Crimson Petal and the White*, which tells the story of a prostitute, Sugar. Sexuality may be canonical and oppressive or dissonant and liberating, but in nearly every case it functions as explanation and resolution. Waters's earlier *Affinity* (1999) centres on a female spiritualist and her relationship with a neurasthenic middle-class girl who visits her in prison; the whole interest in whether she is an authentic medium or a grand illusionist is negotiated through the emergence of a powerful and unexpected desire. Every other kind of knowledge seems exposed as a kind of blindness. Waters's narratives have the merit (among others) of turning conventional narratives of desire upside down, but in 'modernising' the no longer sensational secrets that underpin so much of Victorian fiction, sexuality is usually played out in a far more conventional key: the Lloyd Webber musical, like the BBC serial of *The Woman in White*, replaces the 'secret' of illegitimacy with the modern trauma of child abuse.

In *Victorian Afterlife* John Kucich and Dianne Sadoff argue that much contemporary cultural production refashions the Victorian period as its privileged other 'because the nineteenth century provides multiple eligible sites for theorising' various forms of cultural development that appeal to postmodern enquiry.[17] This is persuasive, but we also need to consider the relations between texts and readers, and the institutions and practices that have constituted this rather intimate relationship between the Victorians and 'us'. One of the reasons, surely, that the Victorians speak to 'us' is their place in childhood reading, listening and viewing (real or imaginary) as much as their formal place in school and university curricula as fiction and history. The cover of Peter Carey's reworking of *Great Expectations*, *Jack Maggs* (1997) – a sepia photograph of a 'real' Artful Dodger, staring tersely at the camera – is a clear instance of this distinctive appeal. These texts are at once compelling page-turners and familiar and reassuring: a place of childhood nostalgia for readers, sharpened with contemporary 'edge'. And in this sense they differ sharply from the experiences of shock and novelty recorded by Victorian readers.

Perhaps we must look to other media for renewed versions of these experiences of nervous shock and complexly constructed incredulity. As we have seen, early film played richly on the 'magical' properties of the medium. Nearly all the silent versions of *The Woman in White* had the same actress play Anne and Laura. The 1913 adaptation of *The Dead Secret*, considered a prototext for *The Woman in White*, also deployed the same actress, Marion Leonard, to play a double role, and has earned its footnote in film history as an early instance of double-exposure – magically allowing the actress to be present in both roles in the same scene. This same play on the technical possibilities of illusion, combined with the play on (in) credulity and doubling so typical of Collins's work, is strongly present in Lloyd Webber's musical. The stage is a circle bounded by a continuously curving screen, used to project the scenery and propel us – sometimes at disorienting speed – to the next scene. Indeed, the whole musical is structured within a dioramic conceit: the audience is drawn into a spinning dioramic narrative, whose first image, an abandoned room of discarded toys, provides a clue to the losses, literal and symbolic, that lie at the heart of the mystery. Beyond this, the musical as form exploits various established forms of repetition. Songs are often repeated to powerful effect: a euphoric country dance that Walter, Marian and Laura join becomes an ironic 'celebration' of Laura's marriage to Glyde, and a bitter-sweet marking of the marriage of Walter and Laura at the end. They and Marian all sing the same love song, a melody much repeated, sometimes just as a brief echoic sequence.

As a consequence, the past, recent as well as distant, exerts a strong if diffused force, tempering the forward drive of the plot. This gives a context to the ghostliness of Anne, which is much played upon – flesh and blood or spectral presence? – together with the disconcerting likeness of Anne and Laura. This resemblance is finally turned against Glyde when Laura haunts him as Anne's ghost and terrifies him into confession of his crimes. As in the novel, justice is not done by due process of law. But here, instead of dying in a burning church, Glyde is mown down by a train which comes out of a tunnel and rushes at the audience. Indeed, his death, which replays a mythic moment from film history, is perhaps most importantly and memorably the occasion for audience 'sensation'.

NOTES

1. *The Moonstone* was serialised by the BBC in 1959, 1972 and 1996; *The Woman in White* made a brief appearance in the UK's ITV *Hour of Mystery* series in 1957 and was serialised by the BBC in 1966, 1982 and 1997. It was also produced on French television as *La Femme en Blanc* in 1970. On film and television adaptations, see Andrew Gasson, *Wilkie Collins: An Illustrated*

Guide (Oxford: Oxford University Press, 1998), and Lyn Pykett, *Wilkie Collins* (Oxford: Oxford University Press, 2005), p. 244.

2. Martin Meisel, *Realizations: Narrative, Pictorial and Theatrical Arts in Nine-teenth-Century England* (Princeton: Princeton University Press, 1983). See also Deborah Vlock, *Dickens, Novel-Reading and the Victorian Popular Theatre* (Cambridge: Cambridge University Press, 1998), pp. 3–4.

3. N. N. Feltes, *Modes of Production in Victorian Novels* (Chicago: Chicago University Press, 1986), and Linda K. Hughes and Michael Lund, *The Victorian Serial* (Charlottesville: University of Virginia Press, 1991).

4. See Ira Nadell, 'Wilkie Collins and his Illustrators', in Nelson Smith and R. C. Terry (eds.), *Wilkie Collins to the Forefront: Some Reassessments* (New York: AMS Press, 1995).

5. *The New Magdalen* 1910, 1912, 1913, 1914; *The Dead Secret* (USA, Monopol) 1913; *Armadale* (USA, dir. Richard Garrick) 1916; *The Moonstone* (USA, Selig Polyscope) 1909; (France, Pathé) 1911; (USA, dir. Frank Hall Crane, 1915); *The Woman in White* (USA, Thanhouser) 1912, (USA Gem) 1913.

6. 1917, *Tangled Lives* (USA, Fox); 1918 (USA, Thanhouser); 1919, *Twin Pawns*, based on *The Woman in White*, and also known as *Curse of Greed* (USA, Acme Pictures, dir. Léonce Perret); 1928 (USA, dir. Herbert Wilcox); 1940 *Crimes at the Dark House* (UK, dir. George King); 1948 (USA, dir. Peter Godfrey).

7. Tom Gunning, 'An Aesthetic of Astonishment: Early Film and the (In)credulous Spectator', in Leo Braudy and Marshall Cohen (eds.), *Film Theory and Criticism* (Oxford: Oxford University Press, 2004), p. 868.

8. Ian Christie, 'Sources of Visible Delight: Towards a Typology of Early Film Adaptation', in Alan Burton and Laraine Porter (eds.), *Scene Stealing: Sources for British Cinema Before 1930* (Trowbridge: Flicks Books, 2003).

9. Reviews of *Bloomer's Mother-in-Law*, *Andegli* ('Insights into the Habits and Industries of the Natives of Somaliland') and *Holiday Resorts of Italy* in Supplement to *The Bioscope*, January 16 1913, pp. xxxiii, xxxiv.

10. Donald W. McCaffrey and Christopher P. Jacobs, *Guide to the Silent Years of American Cinema* (Westpoint: Greenwood Press, 1999), p. 295.

11. The discussion of various versions of *The Woman in White* is drawn from reviews from *The Bioscope*, one of the leading British trade papers of the period.

12. *Twin Pawns* (see note 6 above) is archived on site and can be viewed at the BFI Library, Stephen Street, London.

13. On radio adaptations, see Gasson's *Illustrated Guide*.

14. The British actors Anthony Sher, Patricia Hodge, Greg Wise and Keeley Hawes are just some of the stars.

15. Broadcast at 8.50pm on 28 December and 9.20pm on 29 December.

16. See Kate Flint, 'Plotting the Victorians: Narrative, Post-modernism and Con-temporary Fiction', in Barrie Bullen (ed.), *Writing and Victorianism* (London: Longman, 1997).

17. John Kucich and Dianne F. Sadoff (eds.), Introduction, *Victorian Afterlife: Postmodern Culture Rewrites the Nineteenth Century* (Minneapolis: University of Minnesota Press, 2000), p. xi.

FURTHER READING

There is a growing body of critical work on Wilkie Collins. What follows is a necessarily incomplete selection of primary sources and reference materials and a selected list of critical studies published over the past twenty years. For a full bibliography of recent criticism, see Lillian Nayder, 'Wilkie Collins Studies: 1983–1999', *Dickens Studies Annual* 28 (1999), 257–329.

PRIMARY SOURCES AND REFERENCE MATERIALS

Baker, William and William W. Clarke (eds.), *The Letters of Wilkie Collins*. 2 vols. Basingstoke: Macmillan, 1999.

Baker, William, *Wilkie Collins's Library: A Reconstruction*. Westwood, CT: Greenwood Press, 2002.

Baker, William, Andrew Gasson, Graham Law and Paul Lewis (eds.), *The Public Face of Wilkie Collins: The Collected Letters*. 4 vols. London: Pickering and Chatto, 2005.

Gasson, Andrew, *Wilkie Collins, An Illustrated Guide*. Oxford: Oxford University Press, 1998.

Page, Norman (ed.), *Wilkie Collins, The Critical Heritage*. London: Routledge and Kegan Paul, 1974.

BIOGRAPHY

Clarke, William M., *The Secret Life of Wilkie Collins*. Rev. edn., Stroud: Sutton Publishing, 2000.

Collins, Wilkie, 'Reminiscences of a Story-Teller'. *Universal Review* 1 (May–August 1888), 182–92.

Ellis, S. M., *Wilkie Collins, Le Fanu, and Others*. London: Constable, 1931.

Peters, Catherine, *The King of Inventors: A Life of Wilkie Collins*. Princeton: Princeton University Press, 1991.

Terry, R. C., '"Myself in the Background and the Story in Front": Wilkie Collins As Others Knew Him'. In Nelson Smith and R. C. Terry (eds.), *Wilkie Collins to the Forefront: Some Reassessments*. New York: AMS Press, 1995.

BOOKS AND EDITED COLLECTIONS ON WILKIE COLLINS

Bachman, Maria K. and Don Richard Cox (eds.), *Reality's Dark Light: The Sensational Wilkie Collins*. Knoxville: University of Tennessee Press, 2003.

Heller, Tamar, *Dead Secrets: Wilkie Collins and the Female Gothic*. New Haven: Yale University Press, 1992.

Lonoff, Sue, *Wilkie Collins and His Victorian Readers: A Study in the Rhetoric of Authorship*. New York: AMS Press, 1982.

Mangham, Andrew (ed.), *The Topical Wilkie Collins: Interdisciplinary and Historical Essays on a Victorian Writer* (Cambridge: Scholar Press, 2006).

Nayder, Lillian, *Wilkie Collins*. New York: Twayne, 1997.
  Unequal Partners: Charles Dickens, Wilkie Collins and Victorian Authorship. Ithaca: Cornell University Press, 2002.

O'Neill, Philip, *Wilkie Collins: Women, Property and Propriety*. Basingstoke: Macmillan, 1988.

Pykett, Lyn, *Wilkie Collins*. Oxford: Oxford University Press, 2005.
  (ed.), *Wilkie Collins: Contemporary Critical Essays*. Basingstoke: Macmillan, 1998.

Rance, Nicholas, *Wilkie Collins and Other Sensation Novelists: Walking the Moral Hospital*. Basingstoke: Macmillan, 1991.

Smith, Nelson, and Terry, R. C. (eds.), *Wilkie Collins to the Forefront: Some Reassessments*. New York: AMS Press, 1995.

Taylor, Jenny Bourne, *In the Secret Theatre of Home: Wilkie Collins, Sensation Narrative and Nineteenth-Century Psychology*. London: Routledge, 1988.

Thoms, Peter, *The Windings of the Labyrinth: Quest and Structure in the Major Novels of Wilkie Collins*. Athens, OH: Ohio University Press, 1992.

ESSAYS AND ARTICLES

Ashley, Robert, 'Wilkie Collins and the Detective Story', *Nineteenth-Century Fiction* 6 (1951), 47 60.

Bachman, Maria K. and Don Richard Cox, 'Wilkie Collins's Villainous Miss Gwilt, Criminality and the Unspeakable Truth'. *Dickens Studies Annual* 32 (2002), 319–37.

Balée, Susan, 'Wilkie Collins and Surplus Women: The Case of Marian Halcombe'. *Victorian Literature and Culture* 20 (1999), 197–215.

Beetz, Kirk, 'Wilkie Collins and the *Leader*'. *Victorian Periodicals Review* 15:1 (Spring 1982), 20–9.

Booth, Bradford, 'Collins and the Art of Fiction'. *Nineteenth-Century Fiction* 6 (1951), 131–43.

Brantlinger, Patrick, 'What is Sensational About the Sensation Novel?' *Nineteenth-Century Fiction* 37 (1982), 1–28.

Collins, Richard, 'Marian's Moustache: Bearded Ladies, Hermaphrodites, and Intersexual Collage in *The Woman in White*'. In Maria K. Bachman and Don Richard Cox (eds.), *Reality's Dark Light: The Sensational Wilkie Collins*. Knoxville: University of Tennessee Press, 2003.

De la Mare, Walter, 'The Early Novels of Wilkie Collins'. In John Drinkwater (ed.), *The Eighteen-Sixties*. Cambridge: Cambridge University Press, 1932.

Dolin, Tim and Lucy Dougan, 'Fatal Newness: *Basil*, Art and the Origins of Sensation Fiction'. In Maria K. Bachman and Don Richard Cox (eds.), *Reality's Dark Light: The Sensational Wilkie Collins*. Knoxville: University of Tennessee Press, 2003.

Duncan, Ian, '*The Moonstone*, the Victorian Novel and Imperialist Panic'. *Modern Language Quarterly* 55 (1994), 297–319.

Elam, Diane, 'White Narratology: Gender and Reference in Wilkie Collins's *The Woman in White*'. In Lloyd Davis (ed.), *Virginal Sexuality and Textuality in Victorian Literature*. Albany: State University of New York, 1993.

Eliot, T. S., 'Wilkie Collins and Dickens'. In Eliot, *Selected Essays 1917–1932* London: Faber and Faber, 1932.

Farmer, Steve (ed.), Introduction, *Heart and Science* by Wilkie Collins. Ontario: Broadview Press, 1996.

Frick, Patricia, 'Wilkie Collins's "Little Jewel": the Meaning of *The Moonstone*'. *Philological Quarterly* 63 (1983), 313–21.

   'The Fallen Angels of Wilkie Collins'. *International Journal of Women's Studies* 7:4 (September–October 1984), 343–51.

Gruner, Elizabeth Rose, 'Family Secrets and the Mystery of *The Moonstone*'. *Victorian Literature and Culture* 21 (1993), 127–45.

Holmes, Martha Stoddard, '"Bolder with Her Lover in the Dark": Collins and Disabled Women's Sexuality'. In Maria K. Bachman and Don Richard Cox (eds.), *Reality's Dark Light: The Sensational Wilkie Collins*. Knoxville: University of Tennessee Press, 2003.

Horne, Lewis, 'Magdalen's Peril'. *Dickens Studies Annual* 20 (1991), 281–94.

Hutter, Albert D., 'Dreams, Transformations and Literature: The Implications of Detective Fiction'. *Victorian Studies* 19 (December 1975), 181–209.

Langbauer, Laurie, 'Women in White, Men in Feminism'. *Yale Journal of Criticism* 2:2 (Spring 1989), 219–43.

Law, Graham (ed.), Introduction, *The Evil Genius* by Wilkie Collins. Ontario: Broadview Press, 1994.

   'Yesterday's Sensations: Modes of Publication and Narrative Form in Collins's Late Works'. In Maria K. Bachman and Don Richard Cox (eds.), *Reality's Dark Light: The Sensational Wilkie Collins*. Knoxville: University of Tennessee Press, 2003.

Leavy, Barbara Fass, 'Wilkie Collins's Cinderella: The History of Psychology and *The Woman in White*'. *Dickens Studies Annual* 10 (1982), 297–319.

Ledwon, Lenora, 'Veiled Women, the Law of Coverture and Wilkie Collins's *The Woman in White*'. *Victorian Literature and Culture* 22 (1994), 1–22.

Loesberg, Jonathan, 'The Ideology of Narrative Form in Sensation Fiction'. *Representations* 13 (Winter 1986), 115–38.

MacDonagh, Gwendolyn and Jonathan Smith, '"Fill Up All the Gaps": Narrative and Illegitimacy in *The Woman in White*'. *Journal of Narrative Technique* 26: 3 (Autumn 1996), 274–91.

Magnum, Teresa, 'Wilkie Collins, Detection and Deformity'. *Dickens Studies Annual* 26 (1998), 285–310.

Maynard, Jessica, 'Telling the Whole Truth: Wilkie Collins and the Lady Detective'. In Ruth Robbins and Julian Wolfreys (eds.), *Victorian Identities: Social and Cultural Formations in Nineteenth-Century Literature*. Basingstoke: Macmillan, 1996.

Mehta, Jaya, 'English Romance, Indian Violence'. *Centennial Review* 39:4 (Autumn 1995), 611–57.

Mitchie, Helena, '"There Is No Friend Like a Sister": Sisterhood as Sexual Difference'. *English Literary History* 56:2 (Summer 1989), 401–21.

Nadel, Ira B., 'Wilkie Collins and His Illustrators'. In Nelson Smith and R. C. Terry (eds.), *Wilkie Collins to the Forefront: Some Reassessments*. New York: AMS Press, 1995.

Nayder, Lillian, 'Robinson Crusoe and Friday in Victorian Britain: "Discipline", "Dialogue" and Collins's Critique of Empire in *The Moonstone*'. *Dickens Studies Annual* 21 (1991), 213–31.

Oulton, Carolyn, '"Never be Divided Again": *Armadale* and the Threat to Romantic Friendship'. *Wilkie Collins Society Journal* 7 (2004), 31–40.

Pal-Lapinski, Piya, 'Chemical Seductions: Exoticism, Toxicology, and the Female Poisoner in *Armadale* and *The Legacy of Cain*'. In Maria K. Bachman and Don Richard Cox (eds.), *Reality's Dark Light: The Sensational Wilkie Collins*. Knoxville: University of Tennessee Press, 2003.

Peters, Catherine, '"Invite No Dangerous Publicity": Some Independent Women and The Effect on Wilkie Collins's Life and Writing'. *Dickens Studies Annual* 20 (1991), 295–313.

(ed.), Introduction, *Poor Miss Finch* by Wilkie Collins. Oxford: Oxford University Press, 1995.

Pykett, Lyn, 'Sensation and the Fantastic in the Victorian Novel'. In Deidre David (ed.), *The Cambridge Companion to the Victorian Novel*. Cambridge: Cambridge University Press, 2001.

'The Newgate Novel and Sensation Fiction'. In Martin Priestman (ed.), *The Cambridge Companion to Crime Fiction*. Cambridge: Cambridge University Press, 2003.

Reed, John R., 'English Imperialism and the Unacknowledged Crime of *The Moonstone*'. *Clio* 2 (1973), 281–90.

'The Stories of *The Moonstone*'. In Nelson Smith and R. C. Terry (eds.), *Wilkie Collins to the Forefront: Some Reassessments*. New York: AMS Press, 1995.

Schmitt, Cannon, 'Alien Nation: Gender, Genre and English Nationality in Wilkie Collins's *The Woman in White*'. *Genre* 26 (1993), 283–310.

Surridge, Lisa, 'Unspeakable Histories: Hester Dethridge and the Narration of Domestic Violence in *Man and Wife*'. *Victorian Review* 22:2 (Winter 1996), 102–26.

Talairach-Vielmas, Laurence, 'Mad Scientists and Chemical Ghosts: On Collins's "Materialist Supernaturalism"'. *Wilkie Collins Society Journal* 7 (2004), 3–20.

Taylor, Jenny Bourne (ed.), Introduction, *The Law and the Lady* by Wilkie Collins. Oxford: Oxford University Press, 1992.

Thomas, Ronald R., 'Wilkie Collins and the Sensation Novel'. In John Richetti (ed.), *The Colombia History of the British Novel*. New York: Colombia University Press, 1994.

'Detection in the Victorian Novel'. In Deirdre David (ed.), *The Cambridge Companion to the Victorian Novel*. Cambridge: Cambridge University Press, 2000.

Trodd, Anthea, 'Collaborating in Open Boats: Dickens, Collins, Franklin and Bligh'. *Victorian Studies* 42:2 (Winter 1999–2000), 201–25.

Wagner, Tamara S., '"Overpowering Vitality": Nostalgia and Men of Sensibility in the Fiction of Wilkie Collins', *Modern Language Quarterly* 63 (2002), 471–500.

Wiesenthal, C. S., 'From Charcot to Plato: The History of Hysteria in *Heart and Science*'. In Nelson Smith and R. C. Terry (eds.), *Wilkie Collins to the Forefront: Some Reassessments*. New York: AMS Press, 1995.

GENERAL

Boyle, Thomas, *Black Swine in the Sewers of Hampstead: Beneath the Surface of Victorian Sensationalism*. New York: Viking, 1989.

Brantinger, Patrick, *The Reading Lesson: The Threat of Mass Literacy in Nineteenth-Century British Fiction*. Indiana: Indiana University Press, 1998.

Crosby, Christina, *The Ends of History: Victorians and the Women Question*. London: Routledge, 1991.

Cvetkovich, Ann, *Mixed Feelings: Feminism, Mass Culture and Victorian Sensationalism*. New Brunswick: Rutgers University Press, 1992.

Daly, Nicholas, 'Railway Novels: Sensation Fiction and the Modernization of the Senses', *English Literary History* 66 (1999), 461–81.

Dever, Carolyn, *Death and the Mother from Dickens to Freud: Victorian Fiction and the Anxiety of Origins*. Cambridge: Cambridge University Press, 1998.

Feltes, N. N., *Modes of Production of Victorian Novels*. Chicago: Chicago University Press, 1986.

Hall, Donald E., *Fixing Patriarchy: Feminism and Mid-Victorian Novelists*. New York: New York University Press, 1996.

Hughes, Linda K. and Michael Lund, *The Victorian Serial*. Charlottesville: University Press of Virginia, 1991.

Hughes, Winifred, *The Maniac in the Cellar: Sensation Novels of the 1860s*. Princeton: Princeton University Press, 1980.

Kucich, John, *The Power of Lies: Transgression in Victorian Fiction*. Ithaca: Cornell University Press, 1994.

Law, Graham, *Serializing Fiction in the Victorian Press*. Basingstoke: Palgrave Macmillan, 2000.

Litvak, Joseph, *Caught in the Act: Theatricality in the Nineteenth-Century English Novel*. Berkeley: University of California Press, 1992.

Meckier, Jerome, *Hidden Rivalries in Victorian Fiction: Dickens, Realism and Revaluation*. Lexington: University Press of Kentucky, 1987.

Meisel, Martin, *Realizations: Narrative, Pictorial and Theatrical Arts in Nineteenth-Century England*. Princeton: Princeton University Press, 1983.

Milbank, Alison, *Daughters of the House: Modes of Gothic in Victorian Fiction*. Basingstoke: Macmillan, 1992.

Miller, D. A., *The Novel and the Police*. Berkeley: University of California Press, 1988.

Oulton, Carolyn W. de la L. *Literature and Religion in Mid-Victorian England*. Basingstoke: Palgrave Macmillan, 2003.

Priestman, Martin, *Detective Fiction and Literature: The Figure on the Carpet*. Basingstoke: Macmillan, 1991.

Pykett, Lyn, *The Sensation Novel from 'The Woman in White' to 'The Moonstone'*. Plymouth: Northcote House, 1994.

Stephens, John Russell, *The Profession of the Playwright: British Theatre 1800–1900*. Cambridge: Cambridge University Press, 1992.

Sutherland, John, *Victorian Novelists and Publishers*. London: Athlone, 1976.

Thomas, Ronald R., *Dreams of Authority: Freud and the Fictions of the Unconscious*. Ithaca: Cornell University Press, 1990.

  Detective Fiction and the Rise of Forensic Science. Cambridge: Cambridge University Press, 1999.

Trodd, Anthea, *Domestic Crime in the Victorian Novel*. Basingstoke: Macmillan, 1989.

Tromp, Marlene, *The Private Rod: Marital Violence, Sensation and the Law in Victorian Britain*. Charlottesville: University Press of Virginia, 2000.

Welsh, Alexander, *Strong Representations: Narrative and Circumstantial Evidence in England*. Baltimore: Johns Hopkins University Press, 1992.

Wynne, Deborah, *The Sensation Novel and the Victorian Family Magazine*. Basingstoke: Palgrave Macmillan, 2001.

WEBSITES

http://www.wilkiecollins.com
http://www.deadline.demon.co.uk/wilkie/wcs/publications.htm
http://www.lang.a-u.ac.jp/~matsuoka/collins.html

INDEX

CAMBRIDGE COMPANIONS TO LITERATURE

The Cambridge Companion to Mark Twain
edited by Forrest G. Robinson

The Cambridge Companion to Edgar Allan Poe
edited by Kevin J. Hayes

The Cambridge Companion to Emily Dickinson
edited by Wendy Martin

The Cambridge Companion to William Faulkner
edited by Philip M. Weinstein

The Cambridge Companion to Ernest Hemingway
edited by Scott Donaldson

The Cambridge Companion to F. Scott Fitzgerald
edited by Ruth Prigozy

The Cambridge Companion to Robert Frost
edited by Robert Faggen

The Cambridge Companion to Sylvia Plath
edited by Jo Gill

The Cambridge Companion to Ralph Ellison
edited by Ross Posnock

The Cambridge Companion to Eugene O'Neill
edited by Michael Manheim

The Cambridge Companion to Tennessee Williams
edited by Matthew C. Roudané

The Cambridge Companion to Arthur Miller
edited by Christopher Bigsby

The Cambridge Companion to David Mamet
edited by Christopher Bigsby

The Cambridge Companion to Sam Shepard
edited by Matthew C. Roudané

The Cambridge Companion to Edward Albee
edited by Stephen J. Bottoms

CAMBRIDGE COMPANIONS TO CULTURE

The Cambridge Companion to Modern German Culture edited by Eva Kolinsky and Wilfried van der Will

The Cambridge Companion to Modern Russian Culture edited by Nicholas Rzhevsky

The Cambridge Companion to Modern Spanish Culture edited by David T. Gies

The Cambridge Companion to Modern Italian Culture edited by Zygmunt G. Barański and Rebecca J. West

The Cambridge Companion to Modern French Culture edited by Nicholas Hewitt

The Cambridge Companion to Modern Latin American Culture edited by John King

The Cambridge Companion to Modern Irish Culture edited by Joe Cleary and Claire Connolly

The Cambridge Companion to Modern American Culture edited by Christopher Bigsby